The Trolley Problem

The Trolley Problem is one of the most intensively discussed and controversial puzzles in contemporary moral philosophy. Over the last half-century, it has also become something of a cultural phenomenon, having been the subject of scientific experiments, online polls, television programs, computer games, and several popular books. This volume offers newly written chapters on a range of topics including the formulation of the Trolley Problem and its standard variations; the evaluation of different forms of moral theory; the neuroscience and social psychology of moral behavior; and the application of thought experiments to moral dilemmas in real life. The chapters are written by leading experts on moral theory, applied philosophy, neuroscience, and social psychology, and include several authors who have set the terms of the ongoing debates. The volume will be valuable for students and scholars working on any aspect of the Trolley Problem and its intellectual significance.

Hallvard Lillehammer is Professor of Philosophy in the School of Social Sciences, History and Philosophy at Birkbeck, University of London. He is the author of *Companions in Guilt: Arguments for Ethical Objectivity* (2007).

T0381648

Classic Philosophical Arguments

Over the centuries, a number of individual arguments have formed a crucial part of philosophical enquiry. The volumes in this series examine these arguments, looking at the ramifications and applications which they have come to have, the challenges which they have encountered, and the ways in which they have stood the test of time.

Titles in the series

The Trolley Problem

Edited by

Hallvard Lillehammer
Birkbeck, University of London

Shaftesbury Road, Cambridge CB2 8EA, United Kingdom

One Liberty Plaza, 20th Floor, New York, NY 10006, USA

477 Williamstown Road, Port Melbourne, VIC 3207, Australia

314–321, 3rd Floor, Plot 3, Splendor Forum, Jasola District Centre, New Delhi – 110025, India

103 Penang Road, #05–06/07, Visioncrest Commercial, Singapore 238467

Cambridge University Press is part of Cambridge University Press & Assessment,
a department of the University of Cambridge.

We share the University's mission to contribute to society through the pursuit of
education, learning and research at the highest international levels of excellence.

www.cambridge.org
Information on this title: www.cambridge.org/9781009255622

DOI: 10.1017/9781009255615

First published 2023

A catalogue record for this publication is available from the British Library.

Library of Congress Cataloging-in-Publication Data
Names: Lillehammer, Hallvard, 1970- editor.
Title: The trolley problem / edited by Hallvard Lillehammer, Birkbeck, University of London.
Description: Cambridge : Cambridge University Press, 2022. | Series: Classic philosophical arguments |
    Includes bibliographical references and index.
Identifiers: LCCN 2022041535 (print) | LCCN 2022041536 (ebook) | ISBN 9781009255622 (hardback)
    | ISBN 9781009255592 (paperback) | ISBN 9781009255615 (epub)
Subjects: LCSH: Consequentialism (Ethics) | Double effect (Ethics) | Decision making–Moral and
    ethical aspects. | Responsibility.
Classification: LCC BJ1500.C63 T76 2022 (print) | LCC BJ1500.C63 (ebook) | DDC 171/.5–dc23/eng/
    20220919
LC record available at https://lccn.loc.gov/2022041535
LC ebook record available at https://lccn.loc.gov/2022041536

ISBN 978-1-009-25562-2 Hardback
ISBN 978-1-009-25559-2 Paperback

Contents

Tables

Contributors

Ezio Di Nucci is Professor of Bioethics and Director of the Centre for Medical Science and Technology Studies at the University of Copenhagen.

Jim A. C. Everett is Senior Lecturer in Psychology at the University of Kent.

William J. FitzPatrick is the Gideon Webster Burbank Professor of Intellectual and Moral Philosophy at the University of Rochester.

Natalie Gold is Senior Director at the Behavioural Practice Kantar Public UK and Visiting Professor in Practice at the London School of Economics.

Peter A. Graham is Professor of Philosophy at the University of Massachusetts Amherst.

Joshua D. Greene is Professor of Psychology and a member of the Center for Brain Science faculty at Harvard University.

Guy Kahane is Professor of Moral Philosophy at the University of Oxford, and Fellow and Tutor in Philosophy at Pembroke College, Oxford.

F. M. Kamm is the Henry Rutgers University Professor of Philosophy and Distinguished Professor of Philosophy, Department of Philosophy, Rutgers University.

Hallvard Lillehammer is Professor of Philosophy in the School of Social Sciences, History and Philosophy at Birkbeck, University of London.

Dana Kay Nelkin is Professor of Philosophy at the University of California San Diego, and Affiliate Professor at the University of San Diego School of Law.

Sven Nyholm is Associate Professor of Philosophy at Utrecht University.

Samuel C. Rickless is Professor of Philosophy at the University of California San Diego, and Affiliate Professor at the University of San Diego School of Law.

Fiona Woollard is Professor of Philosophy at the University of Southampton.

Liezl van Zyl is Associate Professor in Philosophy at the University of Waikato.

Acknowledgments

I am grateful to Hilary Gaskin and Cambridge University Press for giving me the opportunity to work on this project. I am grateful to all the authors for the commitment and professionalism shown in writing their excellent contributions during what for many has been an unprecedentedly challenging period. I am also grateful to Alejandra Peña Lesmes for vital and ongoing support, often across large distances. Finally, I am grateful to the late Peter Lipton, with whom for seven years until his death in 2007 I spent long days at the end of Michaelmas term discussing "the trolley car" with prospective undergraduates in H6, inner right, of the Gibbs Building, King's College.

At the point of its inception, this volume was meant to start with a chapter by Judith Jarvis Thomson, who passed away in November 2020. The frequency with which Thomson's work appears during the course of this volume is a tribute to the continuing influence of her contributions to moral philosophy.

Introduction

Hallvard Lillehammer

I.1 The context

The trolley problem is one of the most notorious puzzles in contemporary moral philosophy. Over little more than fifty years, the problem has become a reference point for systematic reflection on moral theory; medical ethics; the ethics of war; the ethics of automation; neuroscience; social psychology; intercultural moral comparisons, and more. Beyond academia, the problem has been the topic of popular books; short films; TV series, and online games. In short, the trolley problem has the rare distinction in philosophy of having become something of a cultural phenomenon. This fact is itself a topic of controversy. There are those who consider the problem a conduit to discovering the nature of morality. Yet there are also those who consider it an example of academic theorizing at its most pointless. The essays in this volume critically address this dispute by discussing the main questions that have been at issue in the growing literature on this topic.

I.2 The problem

Sometimes the trolley problem is introduced by giving a single example of a tragic choice, such as that of a train driver who can save five people on one track by killing a different person on another track. Yet as standardly understood in the academic literature, the trolley problem proper arises when we compare two examples, in both of which the resulting harms are the same, yet most people judge the two cases differently. Thus, in what is normally considered its first appearance in the literature, the problem was introduced by comparing the case of the driver of a train who can save five people on a track by switching to another track and thereby killing one person to the case of a judge who can save five people by having one innocent person executed (Foot 1967/2002). Thus understood, the problem is to explain why in the one case the saving of the greater number should be thought of as permissible while in the other case it is not.

Although most contributors to the literature take as their starting point either two or more examples to which people are expected to respond in different ways, they differ importantly in how narrowly they understand the problem and the range of examples taken to instantiate it. Judith Jarvis Thomson, who gave the problem its name, gave two different specifications of what the problem is. In her first formulation, Thomson asked: "[W]hy is it that Edward [a train driver] may turn the trolley to save his five, but David [a hospital surgeon] may not cut up his healthy specimen to save his five" (Thomson 1976, 206). When returning to the issue a decade later, she defined the problem thus: "Why is it that the bystander [who, unlike the driver has had no role in previously directing the trolley] may turn his trolley, though the surgeon may not remove the young man's lungs, kidneys and heart" (Thomson 1985, 1401). Although Thomson was later to "regret having muddied the water by giving the same name to both problems," she did not think this "water-muddying" had done any real harm. After all, the explanatory challenge these two problems raised were, if not exactly the same, then very similar (Thomson 2016, 115–116).

A wider definition of the problem is provided by Frances Kamm, whose formulation abstracts away from the substance of the examples to focus on their structural features. According to Kamm, "we could see the trolley problem … as presenting a challenge to nonconsequentialists who… think there is what is called a side-constraint on harming non-threatening people to produce greater goods" (Kamm 2016, 12). The challenge is then to "explain exactly what the side-constraint on harming amounts to, and what its form is…" (13). On this definition, the problem is understood as a question about "why it is sometimes permissible to kill, even rather than let die, when we come to kill in some ways but not others" (47; 183; 195; c.f. Thomson 2016, 224). This problem also applies to cases not involving trolleys that have a similar structure, and solving the problem requires explaining the moral differences among different ways of causing death.

On a third interpretation, the label "trolley problem" picks out a way of thinking about moral questions, namely, one that invokes a set of schematic thought experiments in which a small number of actors are supposed to choose between a small number of actions the outcomes of which are normally assumed to be fixed. This is the understanding of "trolley problem" invoked by Barbara S. Fried when she complains about "the intellectual hegemony of the trolley problem" in recent moral philosophy (Fried 2012a, 2). Fried's definition includes the understanding of the trolley problem put forward by Thomson and Kamm. Yet it goes beyond their understanding to include a wider range of moral problems that either may or may not share the structural features that distinguish the problem defined by Thomson or Kamm. Although some of the chapters in this volume operate within the constraints employed by Thomson or Kamm's definition, other chapters extend their use of examples beyond those constraints to develop an argument with wider theoretical ramifications for what has come to be widely known as "trolleyology".

1.3 The chapters

This volume contains twelve original essays on the trolley problem written by some of the most influential contributors to the study of that problem; some of whom have either defined or established the research agenda in their field.

The first chapter traces the history of the problem from its initial appearance in the work of Philippa Foot, through its formal definition by Thomson, to its further elaboration by Kamm. It then confronts the problem with three skeptical responses to its claim to intellectual significance, as articulated by Fried. The historical period covered spans around five decades (from 1967 to 2012), by which time the literature on the trolley problem was experiencing an explosive growth, in ways addressed in the chapters that follow.

William J. FitzPatrick's chapter departs from Thomson's objection to Foot's original discussion. Thomson's challenge was to explain why a bystander (as opposed to a trolley driver) should be permitted to switch the trolley in spite of the fact that she would thereby be killing one as opposed to letting five die (as opposed to the driver who would be killing one as opposed to killing five). Thomson later changed her mind about this case, going on to deny that the bystander is permitted to switch. FitzPatrick argues that Thomson ought not to have changed her mind about the bystander. In doing so, he argues that there is an important challenge posed by the problem as originally defined. Moreover, this challenge can be met by giving an account of reasonable norms of shared risk to the loss of innocent life in public spaces.

Much discussion of Thomson's work has focused on whether it is *permissible* or *impermissible* for the bystander to switch. Yet it has also been argued that not only is it permissible for the bystander to switch, it is actually *required*. In his chapter, Peter A. Graham responds to a recent argument by Helen Frowe in favor of this conclusion. According to Graham, Frowe's argument depends on the premise that people have a duty to prevent harm to others when they can do so without violating anyone's rights or bearing an unreasonable personal cost. Graham argues that Frowe's premise is implausible. In addition, he presents a direct argument for the claim that it would be permissible for the bystander *not* to switch the trolley, inspired by previous work by Kamm.

Frances Kamm agrees that it is permissible for the bystander to switch. In her chapter, Kamm explains her reasons for her agreement and how those reasons derive from the non-consequentialist idea that goods brought about improperly are not morally justified. She calls this The Doctrine of Productive Purity. During the course of her chapter, Kamm explores the details of this doctrine by applying it to a range of cases discussed in the recent literature. She also discusses other conditions that need to be met in order to make the switching of the trolley permissible; the relation of those conditions to the distinction between killing and letting die; and general ideas about persons and their relations to each other that explain the significance of non-consequentialist constraints on permissible action.

In their chapter, Dana Nelkin and Samuel C. Rickless address the challenge that standard formulations of the trolley problem fail to take account of the ethical significance of risk because it considers the harms caused by the available options available as fixed. Nelkin and Rickless argue that the imposition of risk should itself be understood as a kind of harm alongside actual injury or death, and therefore something that innocent people can be considered as having a defeasible right against. By drawing on a distinction between direct and indirect harmful agency, according to which the former kind of agency is harder to justify – all other things being equal – than the latter, Nelkin and Rickless argue that insofar as a version of the Doctrine of Double Effect can be justified as one moral principle among others, so can a probabilistic version of that doctrine. It follows that the distinction between direct and indirect harm can be extended to account for other cases involving risk.

In her chapter, Fiona Woollard discusses the relationship between the trolley problem and the distinction between doing and allowing harm. According to Woollard, the distinction between killing and letting die that has been at issue in the trolley problem literature is an application of the doing/allowing harm distinction to the specific harm of death. According to Woollard, the distinction between doing and allowing should be understood as a distinction between different burdens of moral justification. In short, and other things being equal, doing harm is harder to justify than merely allowing harm. She also argues that the lesson to draw from trolley cases is not that there is something wrong with the doing/allowing distinction, but rather that there is a need for additional deontological distinctions to make sense of the full range of such cases.

Liezl van Zyl's chapter approaches the trolley problem from the perspective of virtue ethics. On the one hand, Van Zyl argues that there are reasons to be skeptical about the theoretical significance and practical relevance of the trolley problem. On the other hand, she argues that a virtue ethical approach can provide a plausible diagnosis of what distinguishes the acceptable act of a bystander saving five by turning a switch from the unacceptable act of saving five by pushing someone off a bridge. She also argues that a virtue ethical approach can account for what goes on in Thomson's infamous Loop case by noting that diverting the trolley does not necessarily involve viewing the sole workman as an object or as a means to an end, even if the death of the one is causally necessary for the saving of the five.

In their chapter, Guy Kahane and Jim Everett describe how in recent decades the trolley problem has become a central focus of empirical research in moral psychology. Much of this research has been framed in terms of a contrast between "deontological" and "utilitarian" approaches to morality. Kahane and Everett argue that this framing is misleading in two ways. First, some of the lay responses to trolley cases which psychologists have classified as "utilitarian" have only a tenuous relation to what philosophers have traditionally meant by this term. Second, even when what underlies lay responses to trolley cases echoes aspects of utilitarianism, this doesn't generalize to other aspects of moral thought. Kahane and Everett conclude that while trolley cases have a useful role to play in psychological research, the centrality of such cases in recent moral psychology is theoretically problematic.

Joshua D. Greene's chapter shows how, for more than two decades, the empirical study of trolley dilemmas has substantially improved the scientific understanding of the psychological mechanics of moral judgment. In doing so, Greene picks up on the methodological challenges raised in Kahane and Everett's chapter. By drawing on his own path-breaking work in experimental psychology and cognitive neuroscience, Greene draws attention to how the cognitive processes engaged by trolley dilemmas pose explanatory and normative challenges for traditional ways of describing and evaluating moral judgments. In particular, Greene argues that the study of trolley dilemmas has exposed the evidential or justificatory limitations of moral intuitions by bringing to light patterns in moral thought that fail to withstand critical scrutiny. During his critical survey of recent work on this topic, Greene brings out a number of potential misunderstandings that can arise from attempts to translate the results of empirical work in moral psychology into orthodox philosophical categories, such as "deontological" and "utilitarian," or vice versa.

Natalie Gold's chapter provides a critical survey of empirical studies that compare the responses to trolley cases across different cultures. Gold draws two conclusions from this survey. First, the amount of evidence available is limited. Second, with respect to statistical significance, the picture that emerges from the evidence is mixed. Gold suggests that there is some support for the claim that cross-cultural differences in moral judgments on trolley cases do exist and that those differences are shaped by the particularities of the culture in which they are embedded. Gold also considers the potential implications of these cultural differences for the epistemology and metaphysics of moral judgment. She agrees that the mere fact of cultural difference and disagreement is consistent with the claim that some cultures have a better grasp of moral facts than others. Yet all things considered, she is more inclined to consider the differences in question as evidence for a form of ethical constructivism.

The chapters by Sven Nyholm and Ezio di Nucci discuss the trolley problem in the context of applied ethics, public policy, and law. Nyholm's chapter concerns the relationship between the trolley problem and the ethics of autonomous vehicles. Nyholm argues that it can be useful to compare crashes involving self-driving cars and a range of trolley cases. It can be *directly* useful because the trolley problem brings to light ethical issues of immediate importance for the ethics of self-driving cars. It can be *indirectly* useful because by highlighting the differences between the ethics of self-driving cars and ethics of trolley cases, it is possible to clarify what really matters in the ethics of self-driving cars.

In his chapter, di Nucci considers the trolley problem in the context of healthcare, more specifically in connection with the global health crisis caused by COVID-19. The hypothesis evaluated in di Nucci's chapter is that the trolley problem can be used to distinguish between the alleged permissibility of lifting "lockdowns" and the alleged impermissibility of pursuing "herd immunity." After careful consideration, di Nucci rejects this hypothesis. In doing so, he makes a number of observations about the extent to which thinking about the trolley problem could be useful in thinking about the ethics of pandemics, on the one hand, and the extent to which thinking about the ethics of pandemics could be useful in thinking about the trolley problem, on the other hand.

1 Keeping track of your trolleys
Origins and destinations

Hallvard Lillehammer

1.1 Introduction

This chapter presents a selective overview of the emergence of the trolley problem as a theoretical concern in moral philosophy. It does so by giving a snapshot of the problem as understood by three of the most influential contributors to discussions of that problem, namely, Philippa Foot, Judith Jarvis Thomson, and Frances Kamm. The chapter ends with a review of three criticisms that have been leveled at the trolley problem when considered as an instance of a certain way of thinking about moral philosophy. It does so by considering the arguments of one vocal critic of this way of thinking about moral philosophy, namely Barbara H. Fried.

1.2 Origins

1.2.1 Foot

It all started with a thought experiment involving a tram driver, introduced by Philippa Foot in order to draw an analogy during the course of an argument about the ethics of abortion. The argument first occurred in a paper published by *The Oxford Review* in 1967 where it was responded to by her colleague and friend Elizabeth Anscombe (Anscombe 1967; Foot 1967/2002a).

Both the timing of the argument and the identity of the commentator are worthy of comment. It was the year 1967 in which abortion was legalized and regulated in the United Kingdom (UK) (with the exception of Northern Ireland) through an act of parliament. The topic of discussion was therefore one of contemporary public interest. Foot's commentator, Anscombe, was a committed practitioner of Roman Catholicism, historically associated with the endorsement of the moral distinction between intention and foresight, as embodied in the claim that an act of killing that would normally be sinful or wrong might nevertheless be permissible if committed as an act of self-defense, for example, as a side effect of saving one's own life. Some would argue that this doctrine, widely known as "the doctrine of double effect," serves to specify the conditions when an otherwise impermissible act of abortion is permissible. It was this doctrine that Foot subjected to critical scrutiny in her paper.

Although Foot did not reject outright the moral significance of the distinction between intention and foresight in her paper, she did argue that in a wide range of cases, including the case of an unfortunate tram driver who has the choice between either killing five people or killing one, the operative moral distinction is that between acting contrary to a positive duty to aid people versus acting contrary to a negative duty not to harm people, where a negative duty will normally trump a positive duty. This alternative distinction, or something very much like it, is one that has been thought to support another widely recognized moral distinction, namely, that between killing and letting die.

The case of the tram driver made only a brief appearance in Foot's paper. This is how Foot introduced it:

> Suppose that a judge or magistrate is faced with rioters demanding that a culprit be found for a certain crime and threatening otherwise to take their own bloody revenge on a particular section of the community. The real culprit being unknown, the judge sees himself as able to prevent the bloodshed only by framing some innocent person and having him executed. Beside this example is placed another in which a pilot whose aeroplane is about to crash is deciding whether to steer from a more to a less inhabited area. To make the parallel as close as possible it may rather be supposed that he is the driver of a runaway tram which he can only steer from one narrow track to another; five men are working on one track and one man on the other; anyone on the track he enters is bound to be killed. In the case of the riots the mob have five hostages, so that in both the exchange is supposed to be one man's life for the life of five. The question is why we should say, without hesitation, that the driver should steer for the less occupied track, while most of us would be appalled at the idea that the innocent man could be framed (Foot 1967/2002a, 24).[1]

---

[1] Later in the same article, Foot appeals to the example of a doctor who can either kill or let die an innocent person to save five dying patients. This example (later known as "Transplant") would soon replace the case of the judge as the standard contrast case to that of the driver, until Thomson abstracted away from such role-based complexities with her "Fat Man" example (later known as "Footbridge"), in which the five people on the track can be saved by pushing or otherwise making a very large person fall on the track in front of the five (see Thomson 1976, 207–208).

The basic elements of the puzzle that Thomson would later call "the trolley problem" are clearly visible in this passage. Some individual agent (a judge, a pilot, or a driver) is faced with a choice between a set of serious harms, the magnitude of which is quantifiably different on either side (i.e., five deaths versus one). In some cases (e.g., that of the driver), it arguably seems right to minimize the harms, whereas in other cases (e.g., that of the judge) it does not. The puzzle is to work out what, if anything, could plausibly explain the difference.[2] As already noted, Foot's proposed solution to this puzzle was to appeal to the distinction between negative and positive duties.

Foot's article is notable for its theoretical modesty. During the course of the article, she writes: "In many cases we find it very hard to know what to say, and I have not been arguing for any general conclusion" (Foot 1967/2002a, 30). Instead, she has been "trying to discern some of the currents that are pulling us back and forth" (ibid. 32). Whereas her main aim in the paper is "to show that even if we reject the doctrine of the double effect we are not forced to the conclusion that the size of the evil must always be our guide" (ibid. 31), she says that she has "not, of course, argued that there are no other principles" (ibid. 30). She describes some of her more outlandish thought experiments as having been "introduced for light relief" (ibid. 22) and apologizes for their "levity" (ibid. 32). Yet she does not think this makes them frivolous, trivial, or un-illuminating. For example, she asserts that her case of a doctor who can kill an innocent person to save five dying patients by redistributing that innocent person's organs is "not over-fanciful considering present controversies about prolonging the life of mortally ill patients whose eyes or kidneys are to be used for others" (ibid. 25). What Foot was aiming to produce by constructing her thought experiments involving the judge, the doctor, and the driver was a series of imperfect but illuminating analogies. As with all arguments by analogy, there are inevitably some respects in which the cases on either side of the analogy will differ.[3] The interesting question is whether the cases in question are sufficiently similar in morally relevant respects.

---

[2] Strict act consequentialists deny that there is a morally basic difference between these cases and so would recommend that we minimize consequent harms, all else being equal. For this reason, the trolley problem is often introduced against the background of a non-consequentialist theoretical project that consists in the articulation of so-called side-constraints on the promotion of the good (see, e.g., Kamm 2007).

[3] Foot's case of the pilot might be thought to fail the test of relevant similarity in comparison with the cases of the driver, the judge, or the doctor, given that the pilot may reasonably be assumed to end up dead themselves. Yet given the way in which the range of trolley cases expanded over the years, even that could be reasonably contested.

1.2.2 Thomson

In the United States (US), the legal counterpart of the UK Abortion Act is the Roe vs. Wade case decided by the Supreme Court in 1973. As is well known, Thomson made a seminal intervention in the philosophical debate about abortion in the run-up to that decision in her paper, "A Defense of Abortion," published in the inaugural volume of *Philosophy and Public Affairs* in 1971 (Thomson 1971). There is no tram driver in evidence in Thomson's paper on abortion. Nor is there is any reference to Foot's paper. On the other hand, there is plenty of "light relief"; most famously the example of a person who wakes up to find herself having been connected to a famous violinist by the "Society of Music Lovers" for the purpose of providing a nine month course of dialysis for said violinist. In other words, the practice of constructing imaginative thought experiments for the purposes of arguing by analogy is one in which Thomson was an expert practitioner well before she turned her attention to the trolley problem.

It was in her 1976 paper "Killing, Letting Die and the Trolley Problem" that Thomson gave the name to what she there describes as "a lovely, nasty difficulty," namely, "why is it that Edward [the driver] may turn the trolley to save his five, but David [the doctor] may not cut up his healthy specimen to save his five?" Thomson labeled this difficulty "the trolley problem, in honor of Mrs. Foot's example" (Thomson 1976, 206). As with Foot before her, the theoretical context of Thomson discussion was her interest in the moral distinction between killing and letting die. One of the main conclusions of Thomson's paper was that this distinction "cannot be used in any mechanical way in order to yield conclusions about abortion, euthanasia, and the distribution of scarce medical resources. The cases have to be looked at individually" (ibid. 217).

To show this, Thomson introduced the Passenger case, in which the driver in Foot's example is replaced by an innocent passenger whose choice is that between killing one and letting five die, given that the passenger (unlike the driver) never set the train in motion. A decade later, in Thomson (1985), the passenger was replaced with a now more famous bystander in order to avoid any ambiguity on this score. The point of the Passenger case (and later the Bystander case) is that *if* switching the trolley from one track to another is at least permissible in this case (which Thomson at this point asserts that it is), *then* there are structurally equivalent cases to that of the Driver case in which negative duties do not trump positive duties, so Foot's distinction does not after all explain the moral difference between the driver on the one hand and the doctor or the judge (or someone pushing a large person off a bridge) on the other. In other words, Foot's purported solution to the trolley problem breaks down because in a closely analogous case where the factors that Foot thought were morally relevant are the same, it wrongly classifies permissible actions as impermissible.

Thomson's critique of Foot was further elaborated a decade later in the aforementioned 1985 paper where she introduces her infamous Loop case. In the Loop case, the track on which the one person is stuck loops back towards the five, as a result of which the death of that person is causally necessary to save the five on the other track. Thomson claims that if it is permissible for the driver to switch in the original case, then surely it is permissible to switch in the Loop case as well. After all, what moral difference could be made by the addition of this further piece of track? This might seem to be another nail in the coffin for the doctrine of double effect that Foot had distanced herself from in her original paper, given that the Loop case provides an example of a permissible action in which the death of the one is naturally interpreted as an intended means to save the five.[4] With Foot's account of negative duties trumping positive duties (and so the killing versus letting die distinction) being sunk by the Bystander case and the doctrine of double effect (and so the intention versus foresight distinction) being sunk by the Loop case, we seem to be back to square one.

The alternative proposal initially offered by Thomson appeals to what she calls a "distributive exemption" (Thomson 1985, 1408). Thomson writes:

> ... it is not morally required of us that we let a burden descend out of the blue onto five when we can make it instead descend onto one *if* we can make it descend onto the one by means which do not themselves constitute infringements of rights of the one. (Thomson 1985, 1409)

The "means" on this account are meant to include the action on the part of the agent that makes the operative difference in the circumstances (such as a bystander turning a switch), and the rights in question are meant to be "stringent" (Thomson 1985, 1412). Thomson's initial suggestion was that the distinction between creating a new threat and merely redistributing a

---

[4] For doubts about that interpretation, see, e.g., Kamm 2007, who questions the assumption that the means to one's ends are necessarily intended. Foot's original case against the doctrine of double effect was partly made by appealing to a case (sometimes known as the "Gas Case") where five patients can be saved by breathing a gas, the release of which would kill an innocent patient next door. The doctrine of double effect would seem to allow this, but according to Foot it would be impermissible.

threat that already exists may hold the key to solving the trolley problem, in either of the subtly different formulations she gave of that problem in her 1976 and 1985 papers.[5]

As confident and robust as Thomson's arguments in these papers are, she is – like Foot – quite modest in what she is prepared to infer from them. "[I]t is surely a mistake to look for precision in the concepts brought to bear to solve this problem," she writes. For "[t]here isn't any to be had" (Thomson 1985, 1413). Partly for this reason, Thomson says, there will be borderline cases on which reasonable people disagree (ibid. 1412–1413; 1990, 196). It might therefore be asked if either the Bystander case or the Loop case should be so classified, and what that would show about the plausibility of Thomson's initial account. In retrospect, it is quite telling that in her 1985 paper Thomson expresses "great surprise" that there are people who seem to firmly disagree with her about certain variants of the Bystander case, for example (Thomson 1985, 1411–1412). As is now widely known, her initial surprise on this point would turn out to have been prophetic. For by the time she returned to the trolley problem at the start of the new century, Thomson had changed her mind.

In "Turning the Trolley," published in 2008, Thomson describes how the work of a PhD student at MIT, Alexander Friedman, had made her come to see the trolley problem in a new light. Or, as she quotes Friedman as saying, "we should see the (so-called) trolley problem 'for what it really is – a very intriguing, provocative and eye-opening non-problem'" (Thomson 2008, 364; c.f. Kamm 2016, 95–96). This allegedly eye-opening non-problem is the challenge of explaining why it is permissible to flip a switch to make the trolley hit the one in the Bystander case, whereas it is not permissible to have the trolley hit the one by pushing him or her off a footbridge in the Fat Man (also known as Footbridge) case. This is now said to be a non-problem because it is not, in fact, permissible to switch in the Bystander case. So there is nothing to explain. The upshot of dissolving the problem in this way is not hard to see. For in the absence of the Bystander case as an alleged counter-example, the road might still seem open to something along the lines of Foot's

---

[5] Thomson elaborates further on the theoretical assumptions about action and rights on which this proposal depends in Thomson (1977, 1986f, 1990, 2016). See also Bennett (1995). Introducing the idea of a redistributive exemption was not Thomson's only attempt to solve the trolley problem. For discussion of a solution that appeals to what the prospective victims could reasonably judge to be to their antecedent advantage, see Thomson (1990, 176–202) and Rakowski (1993, 1097–1099). I shall return to this later discussion below.

original proposal in her 1967 paper, and thereby some version of the moral distinction between killing and letting die.[6]

The reasoning that led Thomson to change her mind involves the construction of two cases that add a further element of complexity to the Driver case and the Bystander case. The further element of complexity is that the driver and bystander in question are now assumed to have a third option beyond the death of the one or the death of the five, namely, to sacrifice their own lives instead. In this case, Thomson argues, it would be wrong to sacrifice the life of another as opposed to oneself: "[I]f A wants to do a certain good deed, and can pay what doing it would cost, then – other things being equal – A may do that good deed only if A pays the cost himself" (Thomson 2008, 365). Moreover, in the Bystander case, where the choice is between killing one and letting five die (as opposed to in the Driver case, where the agent is bound to kill someone either way), "he may refrain from doing the good deed" (ibid. 365). Drawing on her judgment of the newly introduced Bystander Three Options case, Thomson argues by "consideration of an analogous case" that the bystander who has only two options of letting the five die or killing the one is not entitled to assume that the one is prepared to sacrifice their life to save the five (ibid. 368). Nor is the bystander entitled to assume the right to unilaterally volunteer the one person's life in order to save the five. From this, she concludes that the bystander is not entitled to pull the switch. In Thomson's words, because "[a]ltruism is by hypothesis not required of us," it is not permissible for other people to unilaterally decide to treat us as though it were (ibid. 367).[7]

Thomson's last published discussion of the trolley problem was her comments on Kamm's Tanner Lectures, published as *The Trolley Problem Mysteries* in 2016. There is no evidence in these comments that Thomson's approach had significantly changed. What we do see in these comments is Thomson restating her understanding of what she takes the problem to be; her impatience with a literature that has grown to include "dozens of hypothetical killings and lettings die" (Thomson 2016, 218); and her continued search for a theory "whose answers ... explain why some features of some killings and

---

[6] See Kamm (2016, 58) for a series of trolley cases that arguably puts this purported dissolution of the problem into question. See also Graham (2017).

[7] See Kamm (2007) and (2016) for a contrary argument to the effect that an impartial bystander could be morally entitled to do precisely that. It is a crucial corollary of Kamm's argument that while an impartial bystander may have the right to volunteer another to have their life sacrificed for the greater good, the person being volunteered to have their life sacrificed may also have a right to resist that sacrifice.

lettings die conduce more strongly than others to impermissibility and how strongly they do" (ibid. 218). Referring back to her previous work on the topic, she writes that her "own impression is that there is a theory that looks as if it could have been tailor-made to yield answers to those questions and their ilk, namely the theory of rights," presumably along the lines of the view developed in her 1990 book *The Realm of Rights* (Thomson 2016, 128; c.f. Thomson 1990, 176–202). By the time of her death in 2020, Thomson was still thinking about the trolley problem, writing with reference to the present volume that she thought an account was needed of where things now stand on the trolley problem in moral theory, and what its significance in moral theory now is. She was still keen to see if she could say something useful about those things. (Thomson 2019, personal communication).

1.2.3 Kamm

Whereas it was Foot who invented the problem and Thomson who named it, Kamm is the philosopher who has done by far the most to explore the many permutations of the trolley problem in depth and detail (see, e.g., Kamm 1989, 2001, 2007, 2013b, 2016).

Kamm's work is well known for the artificiality and outlandishness of the large number of trolley cases it contains. Yet on Kamm's view, if "the cases that have been the focus of attention in trolley problem discussions seem artificial and unrealistic," that is, because they have been "specifically constructed, like scientific experiments, to distinguish among and test theories and principles" (Kamm 2016, 13). Two of the best known of Kamm's trolley cases are the Lazy Susan case and the Tractor case. In the Lazy Susan case, the bystander at the switch has the choice of saving the five by triggering a revolving plate on which the five people are tied down in front of an approaching train that cannot be redirected. Unfortunately, turning the revolving plate will dislodge some large rocks nearby that will kill one bystander. According to Kamm, it would be permissible for the bystander to turn the switch and revolve the lazy Susan even if by doing so she would be creating a new threat to the innocent person who stands to be killed by the redirection of the five originally threatened people. If she is right about this, Thomson's initial diagnosis of the trolley problem in terms of redistributing versus creating new threats is inadequate (Thomson 1976, 1985).

In the Tractor case, the bystander at the switch has the choice of saving the five by turning the trolley down a sidetrack where it will gently push one person onto a tractor that is also a lethal threat to the five, with the result that the tractor will kill the one but then stop in its tracks, thereby leaving the five unharmed. According to Kamm, it would not be permissible for the bystander to turn the switch and send the trolley toward the one in this case in spite of the fact that all the bystander does is turn the trolley from the track where it will kill five down a track where it will kill only one. This is (broadly speaking) because pushing the one to their death in front of the tractor is now causally necessary in order to perform the act of saving the five. In this way, the Tractor case combines one essential element of the Bystander case (i.e., the switch element) and of the Fat Man (also known as Footbridge) case (i.e., the pushing element) in order to expose the moral relevance of how the one person sacrificed features in the causal sequence of the saving of the five. One of the central tasks of Kamm's work on the trolley problem has been to work out precisely what that moral significance is.

Starting in the 1980s, much of Kamm's work on the trolley problem has been structured around the project of formulating an acceptable version of what she calls a "principle of permissible harm" that should constrain the actions of agents who are both beneficently motivated and "impartial" (Kamm 2016, 90; c.f. Kamm 1989). Kamm gives a "rough description" of the Principle of Permissible Harm in *The Trolley Problem Mysteries* as follows:

> Actions are *permissible* if greater good or a component of it (or means having these as a noncausal flip side) leads to lesser harm even directly. Actions are *impermissible* if mere means that produce greater good . . . cause lesser harm at least directly, and actions are *impermissible* if mere means cause lesser harms . . . that are mere means to producing greater goods. (Kamm 2016, 66–67; see also Kamm 1993, 2007)[8]

When relating Kamm's project to the concerns that had previously motivated Foot and Thomson, there are two features of the Principle of Permissible Harm that are particularly worthy of note.

First, as Foot initially formulated it, the trolley problem presents us with a theoretical choice between the intention versus foresight distinction (which she goes on to criticize) and the killing versus letting die distinction (a version of which she goes on to defend). Thomson, after initially having rejected

---

[8] The language of noncausal flipsides is partly supposed to evoke the metaphor of two things being "two sides of the same coin," or two aspects of the same thing. In other words, we are not dealing with items that are merely causally or otherwise contingently related in the circumstances. For further discussion, see Kamm (2007, 2016).

Foot's solution, eventually ended up endorsing something close to Foot's distinction (Thomson 2008). In developing the Principle of Permissible Harm, Kamm effectively rejects both of these traditionally influential distinctions. In other words, in Kamm's view it is neither the doctrine of double effect nor the killing versus letting die distinction as traditionally understood that is really the key to solving the trolley problem.

Second, while the Principle of Permissible Harm lends no direct support to either the doctrine of double effect or the killing versus letting die distinction as traditionally understood, it does preserve an important element of the former, in that it substantially restricts how harms that serve the greater good can be permissibly caused. Although Kamm formulates this restriction in subtly different ways throughout her work, the basic thought is one that approximates to the historically influential idea that there is something bad, disrespectful, or wrong in thinking that human lives can be treated merely as causes, means, instruments, or tools for the promotion of otherwise good or innocent ends (c.f. Kant 1785/1994; Thomson 1985, 1401; Rakowski 1993, 1071–1084). In this way, we are morally constrained to harm innocent others in pursuit of the greater good in trolley cases only "by means that do not treat other people improperly and create improper relations between the one and the five" (Kamm 2016, 90). In some places, Kamm draws a related distinction between what she calls "harming by substitution," which is said to be permissible; and "harming by subordination," which is said not to be permissible (ibid. 69), a distinction she describes as "connected to our conception of persons and their status" (ibid. 69). To this extent, Kamm's account is arguably not a million miles away from the insight that Thomson was gesturing toward when she wrote about the agent in the Driver case having a "distributive exemption" even if, as actually formulated by Thomson, that "insight" runs up against the Lazy Susan case discussed above.

1.3 Destinations

The remarkable growth of work on the trolley problem in recent decades has given rise to a number of critical responses. Some of these responses have gone so far as to suggest that it would be better if serious academic work on this topic were to cease altogether. One representative expression of this response is found in a 2012 paper by Barbara Fried, entitled "What *Does* Matter? The Case for Killing the Trolley Problem (or Letting it Die)" (Fried 2012a). In this paper, she gives a number of arguments in favor of the view that moral and political philosophy would be better off if we were either to "kill off" the trolley problem, or just "let it die". Here I shall mention three.[9]

1.3.1 "... none can handle the problem of garden-variety risk"

One of Fried's objections to what she calls "trolleyology" is that it trades almost exclusively in the construction of cases in which "the outcomes of all available choices are known with certainty ex ante" (Fried 2012a, 5; c.f. Wood 2011). By doing so, "trolleyologists" ignore the "conduct that accounts for virtually all harm to others; conduct that is prima facie permissible ... but carries some uncertain risk of accidental harm to generally unidentified others" (Fried 2012a, 2). The downside of this tendency is that of "the various moral principles that have emerged from the now four-decades-long preoccupation with trolley problems, none can handle the problem of garden-variety risk" (ibid. 2). Yet, "if ... the appropriate epistemological point of view from which representative individuals should formulate their objections to a candidate principle is *before* they know how things will turn out *for them in particular* if that principle is adopted, then virtually the entire trolley literature becomes morally irrelevant" (ibid. 3).

The claim that the issue of risk has played a negligible role in mainstream discussions of the trolley problem hitherto is a truth with qualifications. Perhaps the most important qualification arises from Thomson's approach to the problem in *The Realm of Rights*, where she writes that the exceptions to the claim that one should not kill one person to save five others "are those in which the one who will be killed, and the five who will be saved, are members of a group such that it was to the advantage of all the members that the one (*whoever he or she would later turn out to be*) would later be killed, and the only thing that has since changed is that *now it is clear who the one was going to turn out to be*" (Thomson 1990, 195; my italics. See also Kamm 2007, 272–275; 284).[10] On this view, the permissibility of turning the trolley depends on what, from the point of view of the potential victims, would be a reasonable ex ante judgment about their risk of death. Now this is clearly a

---

[9] As the title of her paper indicates, much of Fried's argument is focused on Derek Parfit's book *On What Matters* (Parfit 2011), whose method of constructing thought experiments in which the outcomes of actions are assumed to be fixed is classified as "trolleyological" in a wider sense than what is understood as "the trolley problem" by Thomson, Kamm, and others. These wider aspects of Fried's discussion will not be at issue here.

[10] For a more detailed development of this idea along broadly "contractualist" lines, see Rakowski (1993). See also Thomson (1986f, 173–191).

different aspect of risk than that embodied in an ex ante judgment of what will happen if one either does, or does not, turn the trolley. Yet it is an aspect of risk even so. Indeed, it is one that speaks directly to Fried's question of "how things will turn out" for someone if a certain principle is adopted. Having said that, the absence of a more comprehensive treatment of risk in mainstream discussions of the trolley problem is in some ways surprising, partly in light of the existence of criticisms to the effect that insofar as the distinctions trolleyology has mainly been interested in are morally relevant, this may sometimes boil down to risk-related issues, such as the difficulty involved in bringing an optimal outcome about (see, e.g., Bennett 1995. See also Kamm 2012, 197ff and 375ff; Nelkin & Rickless [this volume]).

The underlying issue in Fried's critique is possibly more abstract than this, however. For arguably implicit in her argument is the claim that in order to deliver a plausible set of principles for deciding between alternative harms we should start with a set of conditions in which the persons involved are unable to assume what the outcome of their actions will be. In other words, it is a mistake to consider the judgments people would make about imaginary cases where the outcomes of their actions are assumed to be known and then simply add a "theory of risk" to the story afterward in order to apply those principles to the real world.

As Fried duly notes, the claim that it is somehow mistaken to treat risk-free scenarios as having explanatory priority in moral theory is controversial. The first question to ask about this claim is whether it is actually possible to make a comprehensive moral assessment of an action given some uncertainty about its outcomes independently of a prior assessment of the moral status of that action given certainty about its outcomes. This is a question that has been subject to considerable attention in the philosophical literature, sometimes under the heading of "subjective" versus "objective" theories of rightness (see, e.g., Jackson 1991). Whatever is to be made of that question, it is not one the resolution of which will depend on a prior solution to the trolley problem.

A second question that could be asked about Fried's critique is one that was already articulated by Foot in the 1967 paper, where she wrote that "in medicine there are sometimes certainties so complete that it would be a mere quibble to speak of the 'probable outcome' of this course of action or that" (Foot 1967/2002a, 25). In other words, there is a wide range of cases – whether encountered in the imagination or in the real world – where the element of risk is so limited that its presence is arguably of lesser moral significance than other features of the situation, such as the manner in which the prevention of a serious harm is brought about. While the range of such "complete certainties" undoubtedly restricts the domain of cases to which the trolley problem is directly relevant, Foot was arguably right that the domain in question is not empty.

1.3.2 "... an oddball set of cases at the margins of human activity"

A second objection raised in Fried's paper is that the attention devoted to trolley cases and similar thought experiments "has resulted in non-consequentialists devoting the bulk of their attention to an oddball set of cases at the margins of human activity," or "a moral sideshow" (Fried 2012a, 2; c.f. Edmonds 2013, 100). In making this objection, Fried is giving voice to one of the most common skeptical responses to the trolley problem, both from inside and outside philosophy.

Fried articulates this skeptical response in different ways. She writes that trolleyologists trade in "fantastical" dilemmas that bear no interesting relation to the real life (Fried 2012a, 5; c.f. Wood 2011); that trolleyology strips away from our thinking about moral dilemmas the "contextual information that in real life changes the moral complexion of tragic choices" (Fried 2012a, 5); and that the "obsession" with highly artificial thought experiments in the philosophical literature has "inadvertently led both authors and consumers of that literature to regard tragic choices *themselves* as rarely occurring and freakish in nature" (ibid. 7).

Of the three authors discussed in this chapter, it is only Kamm who can be plausibly described as having devoted anything like "the bulk of their attention" to the kind of moral theorizing objected to by Fried in her paper (Kamm 1993, 2007, 2016). The amount of attention that Foot devoted to the trolley problem and comparable thought experiments throughout her work does not merit this description (Foot 2001, 2002a, 2002b). Thomson returned to the trolley problem on various occasions throughout her career (Thomson 1976, 1985, 1990, 2008, 2016), but as her own impatience with the proliferation of trolley cases in the recent literature arguably testifies (Thomson 2016, 218), the range of her concerns cannot be described as devoting the bulk of its attention to the discussion of trolley cases or other thought experiments of a similar nature.

With respect to the relevance of the trolley problem to real life, the situation is more complicated. Once again, Foot's comparatively brief remarks on the topic put her in the clear. Thomson's work on the trolley problem is notable for some not always very encouraging remarks about the moral complexities of real life, such as her claim that "we should prescind from the possibility that the agents in the cases we are considering have special duties to the other parties... beyond those that any (private) human beings have towards any other (private) human beings"; a claim that raises thorny questions about how to interpret the relevant notion of privacy (Thomson 2008, 370). On the other hand, in her first article on the topic, Thomson does draw a direct analogy with what at the time will not have been an entirely unrealistic scenario involving a President facing the prospect of nuclear war. She writes:

> Most people ... would feel that Harry ... may deflect the Russian bomb.... But I think most people would feel that Irving may not drop an American bomb [to stop it]... [A] President simply may not launch an atomic attack on one of his own cities... [even to minimize lives lost]... Why? *I think it is the same problem.* (Thomson 1976, 208; my italics)

An explicit connection between the trolley problem and justified killing in war is also made in Kamm's work.[11] In discussing this connection, Kamm shows considerable subtlety with respect to how the trolley problem might (or might not) illuminate the ethics of killing in war. She writes:

> In my writing on war, I have often pointed to Foot's Gas Case [in which five patients can be saved by the release of a gas that will foreseeably kill a lone patient in a different room] as showing that a typical justification for collateral harm based only on the [doctrine of double effect] is inadequate .... In later work, I suggested that harming civilians collaterally in war might be permissible even when a mere causal means directly causes the harm if the civilians are citizens of an unjust aggressor. This is because they are liable to bearing risks of such harm in order to stop their country from being unjust. But I noted ... that neutrals are not liable to harm on this ground .... So neutrals seem to be more immune to such redirected threats than ordinary people in non-war contexts (such as the Trolley Cases). (Kamm 2016, 225. See also Kamm 2012)[12]

---

[11] When Fried briefly comments on the ethics of war in her paper, she actually writes: "I take no position on the usefulness of trolleyology in thinking through moral dilemmas in this area" (Fried 2012a, 2).

[12] In *The Trolley Problem Mysteries*, Kamm draws a distinction between cases in which "nonagents, such as flood waters or unmanned missiles, are out of control and need to be redirected in order to reduce deaths' and cases in which a still-responsible person ... can have his more harmful actions prevented by our intervening in ways that lead him to choose to cause less harm" (Kamm 2016, 93). She argues that although cases of the latter type "should not be used as examples of the trolley problem ... they are related to the trolley problem and are worthy of much further study because cases of their type are common in real life" (ibid. 93). See also Kamm (2012, 2020).

On this basis, Kamm concludes that her account of the trolley problem does not apply to many war contexts because those who may be harmed collaterally in war are in several ways different from "ordinary innocent people," and her account of the trolley problem is "intended to apply only to such ordinary contexts" (Kamm 2016, 225). As with Thomson's use of the word "private," there are thorny questions in this vicinity about Kamm's use of the word "ordinary." Exactly what to make of the explanatory connections between the trolley problem and the ethics of killing in war and other real-life dilemmas will partly depend on whether compelling answers can be given to these and similarly thorny questions.

1.3.3 "... confused at best, and indefensible at worst"

A third objection raised in Fried's paper is that the "hermetic" focus on trolley cases and similar thought experiments fails to illuminate even the bespoke imaginary cases that the literature on the trolley problem is designed to address. One major cause of this failure is that "once we relax the secondary features common to all trolley problems [such as context and risk]... many non-consequentialists have no clear intuitions at all" (Fried 2012, 3). The result is that trolleyology ends up "with a set of principles that is confused at best, and indefensible at worst" (ibid. 21). Moreover, so Fried argues, trolleyologists have consistently failed to "show that the decision rules they adopt... have a moral, and not merely psychological or emotional, basis" (ibid. 25). Two natural consequences to draw from this undesirable state of affairs are, first, that "trolleyology ... belongs in the domain of moral psychology rather than of non-consequentialist moral philosophy" (ibid. 3); and second, that 'the right position for consequentialists to take with respect to trolley problems is just to say no to them' (ibid. 5; c.f. Hurka 2016; Kagan 2016).

The request for philosophers to defend the moral significance of their appeal to imaginary thought experiments is perfectly fair. We have seen above that in Foot's case the trolley problem was one among a large number of imaginary examples introduced for "light relief" during the conduct of an argument primarily focused on something else. So in her case, there is arguably not much more that either can or needs to be said. In Thomson's case, there are more pressing reasons to respond to Fried's objection because her own change of mind about the Bystander case inescapably raises the question of why, if it is not permissible for the bystander to switch, so many people (including Thomson herself) have seemingly been willing to go along with the claim that it is. Thomson's answer was to suggest that we might be affected by "how drastic an assault on the one the agent has to make in order to bring about ... that the five live. The more drastic the means, the more strikingly abhorrent the agent's proceeding" (Thomson 2008, 374). This is not supposed to be an explanation of "why the bystander *may* turn the trolley" (ibid. 374). It is supposed to be an explanation of "why it seems to so many people that he may." And the answer, Thomson suggests, "may simply lie in our being overly impressed by the fact that if he proceeds, he will bring about that more live by merely turning a trolley" (ibid. 374). Regardless of the plausibility of Thomson's explanation, the fact that she offers it is of considerable interest in the present context. For by the time that Thomson wrote these words, there was a thriving literature on the causes of people's judgments on trolley cases and how a variety of morally irrelevant or otherwise questionable features of these cases may lead us astray (Unger 1996; Greene 2007, 2013). Thomson did not explicitly engage with that literature in her 2008 paper. On the contrary, she could easily be read as taking a somewhat flippant attitude toward it. Thus, after "citing" the responses to the Bystander case of ninety-three percent of "the seniors at South Regional High School in Dayton Ohio," Thomson quips: "Actually, I just invented that statistic, but it's in the right ballpark" (Thomson 2008, 373). Yet as we have seen, not only does her own change of mind about the Bystander case call out for the kind of social or psychological explanation developed in the empirical literature on the trolley problem that began to emerge around the turn of the century. At the end of her 2008 paper, Thomson was actively engaged in offering such explanations.

Of the three "trolleyologists" discussed in the previous section, Kamm is the one who has consistently been most optimistic about the potential for reliable intuitions to extend beyond a small number of simple cases, even if this potential is far from equally distributed. She writes:

> In general, the approach ... I adopt may be described as follows: consider as many case-based judgments ... as prove necessary, don't ignore some just because they conflict with simple or intuitively plausible principles ... work on the assumption that some other principle can account for the judgments ... be prepared to be surprised at what this principle is ... consider the principle on its own, to see if it expresses some plausible value or conception of the person or relations between persons. This is necessary to justify it as a correct principle, one that has normative weight, not merely one that makes all of the case judgments cohere ... this is only a working method. It remains possible that some case judgments are simply errors. (Kamm 2007, 5. Quoted in Kamm 2016, 226)

What Kamm gives expression to in this passage is a version of what has come to be known as the "method of reflective equilibrium"; in this case narrowly construed as a process by means of which particular judgments and general principles are brought into explanatory coherence by means of a process of open-ended mutual adjustment. Both the aspects of mutual adjustment and open-endedness, as well as the adoption of the label "reflective equilibrium," are explicitly on display in the following passage from *The Trolley Problem Mysteries*:

> According to the theory of reflective equilibrium . . . a deeper rationale we accept even when it conflicts with some intuitive judgments need neither prove . . . that these intuitive judgments are wrong nor provide an error theory for them. The deeper rationale need only be more plausible than the intuitive judgments about cases with which the rationale conflicts. But given that the intuitive judgments are not shown to be wrong, it is possible that we will still hope to find another deeper rationale that is as compelling and does not require that we give up these intuitive judgments. In a sense, we may not be in "equilibrium" at all but always looking out for something better . . . . My own sense is that without an explanation showing that the intuitive judgments about cases are erroneous, we should often resist "giving them up" and seek further for the rationale. (Kamm 2016, 241–242)

When considered in the broader context of contemporary moral and political philosophy, there is nothing particularly distinctive or controversial about the basic methodological commitments expressed by Kamm in this passage. If there is anything distinctive about her view, it is her optimism that there are plausible principles to be discovered that are consistent with a larger number of pre-theoretical judgments than many of her critics predict. As she herself puts it, there is room for optimism that, when conducted appropriately, moral theorizing will be able to rely on intuitions "even at great levels of complexity" (Kamm 2016, 194; c.f. Kamm 2007, 5; Hurka 2016; Kagan 2016; Thomson 2016).

As the rapidly expanding empirical literature on the trolley problem since the turn of the century shows, one potential limitation of the method of reflective equilibrium as described in the passages quoted above is that it is comparatively "narrow" as opposed to "wide"; and therefore not substantially informed by evidence from psychology and other human sciences about the various ways in which pre-theoretical intuitions and other sources of particular moral judgment both can and sometimes do lead to verdicts about cases involving humans, trolleys, and other agents that cannot, on reflection, be taken at face value (see, e.g., Haidt 2013; Greene 2013). The response to such critical discussions of moral intuitions that is most commonly associated with Kamm's work is one of intransigence, as when she writes about the many of us who fail to get our heads around one or more of the more complex trolley cases in the literature that "the fact that they did not detect the factor's presence originally may suggest that they are not as good at understanding what is going on in a case as they should be" (Kamm 2016, 236); or when she writes about some of her most influential philosophical predecessors that "the problem was that some 'greats' did not consider enough cases to begin with and therefore got the morally significant concepts and values wrong" (ibid. 201).

Yet in spite of this apparent intransigence, Kamm has on several occasions been prepared to take on empirically informed criticisms of pre-theoretical intuitions about imaginary cases, including some criticisms that have made explicit use of trolley cases (see, e.g., Kamm 2007, 190–224; c.f. 422–449). To give one example, and one that is of direct relevance to the discussion of Thomson earlier on in this section, Kamm has explicitly considered the effects on our moral judgments about trolley cases of the fact that in some such cases, including ones where we are asked to imagine pushing someone off a bridge, the harm done to the person in question would be "up close and personal," as opposed to in other cases where killing someone would only require "mechanically turning a trolley" (Kamm 2016, 237). The hypothesis to be tested here is that our pre-theoretical judgments of impermissibility track the intrinsically morally irrelevant feature of a harm being "up close and personal." The conclusion that critics have drawn from the truth of this hypothesis is that we should at the very least reduce our confidence in our non-consequentialist moral intuitions, including those to which appeal is made in developing the Principle of Permissible Harm. Kamm's response to this challenge is a clear illustration of her general approach.[13] For, so she argues, "if mechanically turning a second trolley that would have harmed no one so that it topples a fat man in front of the first trolley in order to stop it seems no more permissible, then pushing him up close and personal will not be the morally significant factor in topple cases" (ibid. 237; see also Kamm 2009, 334–346). In other words, whether causing the harm is "up close and personal" or not can consistently be regarded as a red herring from a moral point of view, also by non-consequentialists.[14]

---

[13] The literature cited in the footnote associated with this argument is Thomson's discussion of the Fat Man case (later known as "Footbridge"), "in which the fat man was pushed up close and personal." In this particular passage (Kamm 2016, 253, Note 56), Kamm does not explicitly refer to empirical work conducted on this topic by Greene and others; although she does discuss this work elsewhere (see, e.g., Kamm 2009; see also Kamm 2007, 43, 241; Greene [this volume]).

[14] I am grateful to Frances Kamm for comments that led to the improvement of this chapter.

2 Shunted trolleys and other diversions

Solving Thomson's puzzles

William J. FitzPatrick

2.1 Introduction: What is the actual trolley problem?

A half-century ago, Philippa Foot described a hypothetical example involving a "runaway tram" or trolley (Foot 1967). What is remarkable, in retrospect, is that she did so more or less in passing, viewing it – correctly, as far as her original case went – as posing neither a moral quandary nor any special problem for moral theory.

Her hypothetical case (call it "Driver") involved a trolley with brake failure racing downhill toward five innocent people who could not get out of the way but could be saved if the driver steered onto a sidetrack before reaching them, though she would then hit one similarly situated person on that track. The point of the example was not that it was hard to know what to do here: Obviously the driver should steer her trolley toward lesser harm, all else being equal, exercising damage control. And far from suggesting that the case raised deep theoretical puzzles, Foot used it simply to show how her general theory of duties – which she deployed to defend non-consequentialist intuitions about various other cases of harmful agency – could also handle cases like Driver where consequentialist verdicts seem apt. It is worth briefly reviewing the relevant background here.

Foot's general proposal was that negative duties of non-interference, such as the duty not to cause harm, are more stringent than – or take precedence over – positive duties to aid, such as the duty to save from harm, where the harms in question are comparable and all else is equal; or equivalently, formulated in terms of rights, negative rights of non-interference, such as the right not to be harmed, are more stringent than – or take precedence over – positive rights to aid, such as the right to be saved, where again all else is equal. Call this the "Precedence Thesis."[1] She argued that this explains

---

[1] I borrow this label from Warren Quinn (1993), who also puts the point (as does Foot 1994) in terms of negative rights being *less easily defeated* by other considerations than positive rights, all else being equal. Quinn goes on to offer an illuminating account of what ultimately grounds the Precedence Thesis.

the non-consequentialist intuition in cases such as "Transplant," where a surgeon is not morally permitted to harvest vital organs from one to transplant into five others who would otherwise die – even though this would bring about impartially better consequences than refraining and allowing the five to die. The surgeon's negative duty not to kill the one overrides or defeats her positive duties to aid the five, thus explaining why she may not operate and must instead forego this opportunity to bring about a better set of consequences: She may not *kill* one to save five but must instead *let the five die* if there is no other way to save them.

As Foot recognized, however, some cases involve different conflicts of duties, where the above sort of account won't apply, and she needed to have something to say about them as well. In Driver, for example, the trolley driver faces a choice between *killing* one and *killing* five, where she will accidentally kill someone no matter what she does. So whereas in Transplant the conflict was between the surgeon's negative duty to one and her positive duties to five, here the driver faces a conflict between negative duties to five and a negative duty to one. Foot therefore supplemented her Precedence Thesis with the plausible claim that in a case like Driver, where one cannot avoid accidental infringement of similar negative duties, one should minimize such infringements (all else being equal), doing the least harm. Next, consider the positive flipside, as in "Rescue," where you can save one drowning person or five other drowning people, but not everyone. Here your choice is between *letting* one *die* (to save five others) or *letting* five *die* (to save one), so the conflict is between positive duties to five and a positive duty to one. Again Foot offered a plausible addendum, roughly: In cases of conflict among similar positive duties, where you cannot fulfill them all, you should act to fulfill the most you can, all else being equal, doing the most good.[2]

Foot's original trolley case, Driver, was thus introduced along with cases like Rescue simply to deal with conflicts of duties not addressed by the Precedence Thesis: The latter explains *non*-consequentialist verdicts in cases such as Transplant, while the supplemental claims about negative/negative and positive/positive conflicts of duties explain consequentialist intuitions about cases such as Driver and Rescue. In other words, the original *trolley case* was simply an illustration to support a commonsense supplement to the Precedence Thesis.

Nothing worth calling "the Trolley Problem" emerged until Judith Jarvis Thomson introduced a simple but momentous variant of Foot's case

---

[2] The Rescue case I've used to illustrate this point is borrowed from her later article (Foot 1994).

(Thomson 1976, 1985). In Thomson's "Bystander" case, all is as before except that the agent with the power to shunt the trolley or allow it to continue is not the driver but just a bystander with access to a lever she can pull to divert the trolley onto the sidetrack. Once again, the point was not that this case posed a moral quandary: Thomson took it to be clear enough that it is at least permissible to shunt the trolley to limit the damage it does, just as in Driver (though she later famously changed her mind about this in Bystander, a point to which we will return in Section 2.5). Instead, the point was that the Bystander case posed a striking *theoretical* problem for Foot's Precedence Thesis.

The choice faced by the bystander is between doing nothing, thereby *letting the five die* when the trolley runs into them, or instead turning the trolley to save the five, thereby *killing the one* down the sidetrack. So the conflict she faces is between positive duties to save the five and a negative duty not to kill the one. But now this conflict of duties is structurally similar to that in Transplant! The Precedence Thesis thus tells us that, as with Transplant, the negative duty not to kill one overrides the positive duties to save the five. We therefore get the counterintuitive result that it is *impermissible* for the bystander to turn the trolley.

That is the original Trolley Problem: not a moral quandary, but a theoretical challenge posed by Thomson's Bystander case to a specific theory of duties developed by Foot to deal with a variety of *non*-trolley-involving cases. We might now usefully broaden the notion to refer more generally to the theoretical problem of explaining why an agent may (apparently) *kill one to save others* in cases like Bystander but not in cases like Transplant: What is it about the sort of *diversion* involved in Bystander that makes for an exception to the usual proscription against killing some to save others (assuming we accept some version of that non-consequentialist constraint in the other cases)? This is how I will understand "the Trolley Problem."

2.2 Putting the brakes on the trolley problem: Methodological issues and limitations

The above characterization of the Trolley Problem obviously contrasts with the popular use of "trolley problems" to refer simply to hypothetical moral quandaries. (The Trolley Problem we've described involves no moral quandary.) It also contrasts with the expansion of "the Trolley Problem" to encompass the broad philosophical challenge to come up with some complex normative rule or generalization that will yield intuitive verdicts for the entire range of byzantine hypothetical cases philosophers might conjure up involving causing harm to some innocents to save others.[3] This second contrast is particularly important, for two reasons.

First, as Thomson (2016) has pointed out, this broader characterization introduces a distinctive and dubious conception of the goals and methodology of this branch of normative ethics, inviting the exploration of a seemingly endless series of contrived hypothetical cases and variations in search of a general rule that will cover them all. Second, it would suggest that we can't really shed light even on the limited Trolley Problem as I've defined it until we have conducted this exhaustive (and exhausting) case-based project and arrived at the definitive general principle complex that handles all possible variants; for only then would it finally be revealed what is *really* doing the moral work in the simple cases from Foot and Thomson.

Like Thomson, I want to resist this picture. One might initially find it compelling because there is some truth in it, after all, as Foot herself demonstrated at the start. She argued for a shift away from the Doctrine of Double Effect to her Precedence Thesis precisely by showing that although we might initially seek to justify non-consequentialist intuitions in cases like Transplant by reference to the harm's being intended as a means, this doesn't ultimately seem to be satisfactory: for there are other cases where it remains impermissible to kill one in the course of saving five even where the former death would be merely a foreseen but unintended side effect. In the "Gas" case, for example, it seems impermissible to save five by manufacturing a drug that would, as a side effect, produce a toxic gas that would kill one who could not be moved in the adjoining room (Foot 1967). If that's right, then a harmful act can evidently be wrong even though it brings about better overall consequences and the harm is not itself intended as a means or as an end. And whatever that wrong-making factor turns out to be in Gas (facts about different duties, for Foot) may well be what is doing the real work, or at least much of it, in the original cases such as Transplant, rather than facts about the intention. So this was an illuminating move on Foot's part, showing that we needed to dig deeper.

The problem, however, is that as we continue down this methodological path, progressing to imaginative cases that are increasingly removed from the circumstances of actual moral practice, the intuitions cited in support of the moral significance of new and increasingly subtle factors become less and less

---

[3] This seems to be Frances Kamm's (2016) broad conception of the Trolley Problem, in line with her search for an ultimate "Principle of Permissible Harm" covering all imaginable cases of harming some to save others. Thomson (2016) criticizes this conception and approach, as explained below.

clear and widely shared. This reaches a pinnacle in the undeniably brilliant but often bewildering "trolleyology" of Frances Kamm. For large stretches of her recent Tanner Lectures, for example, we are presented with a dizzying parade of increasingly contrived examples featuring trolleys and bombs and giant lazy Susan devices and shields and tractors and rockslides and heavy weights, among other things, together with reports of her own intuitions about what is or is not permissible in each case (Kamm 2016).

It is noteworthy that even a philosopher of Thomson's caliber and renowned facility with hypothetical cases winds up struggling not only to feel the recommended intuitions but even to wrap her mind around all these examples, and her exasperation at the situation is evident in her commentary on the lectures (Thomson 2016). Not only is this methodology dubious when taken to such extremes (as noted by the other commentators as well), but it winds up transforming the activity of normative ethics into something that feels far removed from the kind of philosophical illumination we originally sought from the exploration of a handful of salient cases. Even many of us who, like Foot and Thomson, see value – and even find some philosophical enjoyment – in working through a few hypothetical cases in the course of normative theorizing may share Thomson's impatience and dissatisfaction with trolleyology taken to such extremes.

Fortunately, there is an alternative: It is possible to shed interesting, if limited, philosophical light on the actual Trolley Problem (and related puzzles in its vicinity) without becoming forever mired in the weeds of proliferating hypothetical cases. This is tricky, of course, because there is no clear point at which the addition of hypothetical variations goes too far to be helpful. Indeed, in what follows we will go on to consider a few interesting variations introduced by Thomson and Kamm in trying to make progress with the Trolley Problem, and obviously nothing guarantees that there isn't some clever new example just around the corner that would raise compelling doubts about what we say here. But I would rather just acknowledge this limitation, sticking with just a few salient cases to see what tentative moral insights we might gain, at least, with plausible points of contact with ordinary moral thought and practice.

In particular, I will focus on trying to understand what underlies the exception, in Bystander, to the usual non-consequentialist prohibition against killing some innocents to save others – that is, the actual Trolley Problem. And although I am here following Thomson's lead in how to approach this sort of work, part of my aim here is to bring out what went wrong in her own later change of mind about the Bystander case, wherein she came to think it impermissible to turn the trolley after all, thus renouncing the Trolley Problem she herself had ingeniously created and explored decades earlier (Thomson 2008). By the end I hope to have shown both why the Trolley Problem is a real challenge worth considering and how that challenge can successfully be met.

2.3 Lessons from the Driver case

Before getting into the Trolley Problem itself, it's worth looking at how the above methodological contrast applies to a complication that arises even with Foot's Driver case and what we can learn from this. I've said that this case was both morally and theoretically straightforward, as Foot took it to be. Kamm disagrees, however, finding Foot's account even of this simple case unsatisfactory, thus already starting us down the path of creating variants and looking for broader generalizations such as her own Principle of Permissible Harm (Kamm 2016). But while Kamm does show something interesting here, it does not reveal any problem with Foot's account that should set us down this path: instead, it just leads to a helpful refinement of Foot's claim when charitably interpreted.

Foot says, in effect, that faced with infringing one negative duty or five, the trolley driver should opt for infringing fewer negative duties, turning the trolley to avoid killing the five. Now as Kamm points out, this clearly won't do if interpreted as a general claim that a driver of a trolley may permissibly infringe *any* negative duty toward one person in *any* way necessary to avoid infringing her negative duties toward five she will otherwise kill. In "Driver Topple," for example, it would be impermissible for the driver to avoid killing the five by pressing a button that causes a large person to be toppled onto the tracks ahead of the trolley, slowing it to a halt as he is crushed – just as most agree it would be impermissible in Thomson's "Footbridge" case for a bystander to shove a large person off a bridge and into the trolley's path for the same end (Kamm 2016, 16). If so, then clearly the driver may not do just *anything* to one to avoid killing the five, even where this would amount to infringing only one negative duty rather than five.

Kamm is right about that, but it is not a strike against Foot's account, charitably interpreted. Foot was not attempting to provide a generalization covering everything drivers of runaway trolleys may or may not do to avoid killing five in a variety of *other* circumstances – such as those where the means would involve murderous toppling mechanisms. She was talking about the Driver case itself, along with a narrow range of others sharing its central features, and saying something entirely plausible about them. The relevant context is one in which an agent has some object under her partial control, for which she is responsible, but the causal sequence already underway will, in the circumstances, inevitably result in the object's accidentally causing harm to one or more people; and while the agent cannot avoid thus harming someone, she can at least redirect the object so that it harms fewer people in the accident.

Foot chose a trolley, but it could just as well have been a car with brake failure or even something other than a vehicle, such as a remotely controlled drone that is malfunctioning and falling but can still be steered before crashing. All of these are cases in the vicinity of actual moral life, and the claim she intended to make about such cases was just roughly this:

> **Deflective Damage Control (DDC):** When an agent faces a situation where an object under her partial control, for which she is responsible, will unavoidably cause injury through its continued motion, but she can at least direct it in such a way as to cause less harm in the accident (where "less harm" is understood to include comparable harms to a lesser number of different people), then all else being equal she should do that, exercising what control she has over the object to infringe fewer negative duties through its impact.

DDC tells us that the trolley driver should turn away from the five, even though she thereby kills one. It also tells us that in a situation where the car we're driving is either going to strike a crowd or strike one we should do our best to steer it toward lesser harm, all else being equal. Similarly with a malfunctioning drone or similar device we might be operating. Notably, however, it does *not* tell us (falsely) that a driver may push a toppling button if such an option is available. DDC is a narrow claim about resolving conflicts among negative duties *specifically in the context of unavoidable accident, where the infringements of negative duties in question would take place as a result of something already underway for which the agent is responsible* – such as the movement of the trolley, car, or drone. Driver Topple has a different structure, where the negative duty toward the one would be infringed by initiating a *new* harmful sequence against someone as a way to avoid the initial threat to the five. Nothing in DDC suggests that this would be permissible just because it would be a way of infringing only one negative duty rather than five.[4]

---

[4] Foot (1994) emphasizes the differences among initiating a new lethal sequence, refraining from intervening to stop an existing lethal sequence, and redirecting an existing lethal sequence.

The point, then, is that rather than seeing Driver Topple as raising a problem for Foot's treatment of Driver and using that as a springboard to search for more general principles covering endless further cases, as Kamm does, we can instead just stick with the intended narrow range of cases and DDC, and see what moral insight might be gained by thinking about the underlying justification for it. This in turn may provide helpful groundwork for thinking about the Trolley Problem itself (in Section 2.4).

Here we can start by thinking about reasonable social norms governing trade-offs between public risks and benefits, and the management of related harms when they arise. Roughly speaking, these will be norms that give appropriate weight to (1) the values of the social benefits made possible through tolerating certain risks, (2) the disvalues of the risked harms (taking probabilities into account), and (3) any other values in play, such as the promotion of welfare and respect for persons. For example, this package of norms is informed by a recognition that the benefits of people being able to have certain objects – such as vehicles – under their control outweigh the associated public risks, as long as reasonable measures are taken to minimize those risks. This supports norms allowing the operation of bikes, cars, and trolleys, despite the risks this poses not only to the agents but to the public, in the event of an accident, though only hand-in-hand with further norms requiring reasonably safe, responsible operation. This trade-off is meant to provide a reasonable balance, taking all values into account. And importantly, it implies that the public does not have a right against being exposed to such risks. It also acknowledges that sometimes accidents happen despite reasonable precautions. So the package of norms will also have to include consonant principles for managing such harms when they arise.

Part of this, which we can set aside here, will handle issues of liability for damages. Our concern is with the prior question of what an agent should do when she cannot avoid accidentally causing harm but can at least minimize it through redirection. And here the thought is straightforward enough: If we already recognize (as part of a reasonable scheme of risk/benefit trade-offs) legitimate public exposure to this type of risk, along with obligations to minimize that risk in certain ways, it is natural to include also a norm guiding agents to minimize this type of harm in the event that such accidental harm becomes inevitable, all else being equal, just as articulated by DDC. We are all legitimately exposed to such risk and none of us deserves the harm when things go badly, so it makes sense to include DDC in this package of norms governing risk and harm management. Whatever "inviolability" we enjoy against being killed for our organs or shoved in front of trains, it does not extend so far as to ground a right not to be harmfully impacted by a vehicle being steered toward least harm in the event of an accident.

The alternative, which would call for the trolley (or car) driver to do nothing and mow down more people than necessary, lacks any plausibility and fails to cohere with the rest of the package. It would favor the one over the five in Driver simply because the former happened, through mere chance, not to be in the path the trolley would have taken *absent human intervention following the brake failure.*[5] But that factor has no relevance in the context of norms governing social risk and harm management in connection with agents operating vehicles and other objects. The relevant aim in the event of an accident is simply minimization of harm through such operation, which obviously precludes just throwing up one's hands and ceasing agential intervention after the accidental brake failure and allowing greater than necessary harm to occur. As far as the public risk is concerned, we're all in this together and although it is *bad luck* that the one happens to be in a less populated space into which DDC prescribes steering the trolley for damage control, acceptance of exposure to such potential bad luck is simply part of this reasonable package of norms.

Interestingly, this implies that although it might seem natural to describe the one on the sidetrack as having been "perfectly safe" prior to the turning of the trolley (since it was heading toward the five and would have hit them instead, absent human intervention), this is not actually true. Given that the trolley would cause less harm on the sidetrack, and given DDC, the sidetrack constitutes what we might call a *legitimate deflection zone* in the event of this sort of situation. And this means that the one who happens to be on the sidetrack was in fact *relevantly in danger from the trolley as soon as the brake failure occurred,* by virtue of being in the trolley's legitimate deflection path – a point that will come up again later.

This therefore defuses any complaint on his part that, *unlike* the five, he was not "involved" in the threat posed by the brake failure, and was then "put newly in danger" by the driver's decision to turn the trolley. Given DDC, nothing singles out the five as somehow the more appropriate victims of the trolley just because they happen to be in its physical path absent further intervention; and the one is no less involved in the situation – in terms of

---

[5] Recall that it is not part of the case description that the one had any special expectation to be protected from harm on the sidetrack whereas the five did not: They are supposed to be equal in such respects. To avoid this distraction we could instead focus on a case involving a car that has already careened off the road, where neither the one nor the five in its potential paths had any greater or lesser claim to safety at their location (c.f. Thomson 2008, 370–372).

being at risk from the trolley following the brake failure – than the five are. By contrast, the one in Driver Topple could certainly make such a complaint: He was *not* under threat from the trolley, being neither in its natural path nor in its legitimate deflection zone, but was then put newly in danger by the distinct causal sequence involving the toppling mechanism and being thrust in front of the trolley – something in no way sanctioned by DDC. He thus has a plausible complaint of having been violated and radically disrespected in a way that the one in Driver has not been. To put it another way, the support we've given for DDC shows that it does not offend against any plausible conception of the moral significance of persons, whereas a norm permitting the toppling of someone in front of a train to stop it plausibly would.

In Foot's terms, then, we have strong negative rights not to be harmed in all sorts of ways that involve someone's initiating a harmful causal sequence against us – including shoving us in front of a train (regardless of whether or not the agent happens to be a driver of a trolley, as in Driver Topple). We have these rights even where such actions would bring about the greater good. But we don't similarly have a negative right not to be impacted by an object someone is directing toward least harm in accordance with DDC. The above reflections on reasonable norms and trade-offs explain why.

2.4 The Bystander case, the trolley problem, and its resolution

If the relevant points here turn out to extend equally to Bystander, despite its differences from Driver, then we get the Trolley Problem, as we have seen: For the bystander's turning the trolley will amount to her killing the one in the course of saving the five, which Foot's Precedence Thesis rules out along with the actions in Transplant and Gas; so if the bystander's turning the trolley is in fact permissible then Foot's Precedence Thesis needs revision. We may begin, then, by bringing out why, given what we've said about Driver, we should indeed come to the same verdict about Bystander, showing that there really is a Trolley Problem. At the same time, this will clarify the special factors in Bystander that explain why it is an exception to the Precedence Thesis, thus showing how that thesis needs to be revised and resolving the Trolley Problem.

Recall, then, that all that sets Bystander apart from Driver is that the agent is not responsible for the trolley's movement, as a driver would be, but is merely an unrelated party who is able to take partial control over it. On the face of it, however, it would be extremely surprising if that simple difference could change the moral valence of the shunting all the way from *obligatory* (in Driver) to *impermissible* (in Bystander). It's not implausible that it might make the turning *merely permissible but not obligatory* in Bystander, but this is because the shift in the agent's position and role is relevant to issues surrounding obligation: Drivers have special responsibilities not had by mere bystanders, supporting the claim of obligation in their case; and there are psychological costs for a bystander in going from being uninvolved in the situation to killing someone, which might make it seem too much for morality to demand of them, whereas it can reasonably demand of a driver that she kill fewer rather than more. But what could further transform the status of the shunting all the way to *impermissible* in Bystander?

The natural place to look would be to claims on the part of the one on the sidetrack. But it is hard to see how anything here could change so radically just because of the shift in the *agent's* position from driver to bystander. How could it be that whereas in Driver the trolley may be turned for all the reasons given earlier in connection with DDC, somehow in this variant the one on the sidetrack suddenly acquires a special right that it *not* be turned to save the five, just because the agent wouldn't be the driver? (The oddity of such a claim is even more salient if we imagine the bystander to be a passenger on the trolley, standing next to the driver and intervening after the driver faints.) All of the considerations raised earlier about reasonable norms of social risk and harm management in connection with objects that have become public threats still apply here: It is reasonable to expect the public to accept such risks (given reasonable precautions), and to minimize harm when accidents happen, whether that minimization occurs through the agency of a driver or of someone acting on the driver's behalf. It would be exceedingly odd to suppose that (1) whereas the one has no right against being killed by a driver when in a legitimate deflection zone following brake failure, (2) he does have such a right against *an agent acting on the driver's behalf and doing precisely what the driver would be obligated to do* to limit the damage done in the accident, and so (3) was *perfectly safe* even after the brake failure in the case where only a bystander could turn the trolley, thus objectionably being *put newly in danger* by the bystander, whereas a driver's turning would not have counted as putting him newly in danger.

It's true that the one in Bystander was not in the path the trolley would have taken absent human intervention following the brake failure, but that's equally true in Driver and gave rise to no legitimate complaint there. Similarly, in neither case does the one explicitly consent to being "sacrificed" in this way as part of saving the five. But the point brought out by considering the reasonable set of norms of social risk and harm management that support

DDC was precisely that such explicit consent is not needed in cases like Driver; and the factors in play there do not turn on whether the agent in a position to do something to mitigate an accident happens to be a driver or a bystander acting as a proxy. The same commonsense principles of damage control apply, for the same reasons, as part of socially responsible management of harm.

Indeed, nothing plausibly changes if there is no driver on the scene at all, on whose behalf the bystander might be acting. Imagine that an empty trolley simply broke away from a storage point unwisely located at the top of a hill, and now a bystander can divert it toward lesser harm. Are we to suppose that whereas a driver may (and must) turn it toward lesser harm, and a bystander may likewise do so as long as there were a driver on board who had started it in motion and on whose behalf the bystander is acting, somehow in this "Empty Trolley" case the bystander must just throw up her hands and allow it to do maximal damage? The implausibility of such a thought suggests that although we initially used cases involving agents responsible for the movement of objects under their control (like Driver) to draw out reasonable norms of social risk and harm management, that factor is not actually necessary: The most coherent package of norms will extend beyond "driver-involving" cases and similarly justify *damage control through diversion of a public threat* more generally. As Foot (1994) later recognized, such diversions are just special cases constituting an exception to the Precedence Thesis. Indeed, she took the point to be obvious enough not to require further argument.

Not only would it be morally incoherent to endorse DDC while balking at similar action by a bystander, but the extension of damage control norms to such cases is independently plausible. Just as we all face some risk associated with vehicles and other objects operated in the space we share, we face risks from other objects that can become public threats. It would, I suppose, be possible to respond to such risks with norms that sharply depart from DDC and hold that in these rare "driverless" cases third parties who could similarly divert such threats toward lesser harm must instead allow them to do maximal damage. But what would be the justification for such a departure? Here we are, in a position to minimize accidental harm suffered by innocent people, but we would refuse to do so, instead giving greater normative weight to *mere luck*: The greater number should die rather than the lesser number, on this approach, simply because the former unluckily happen to be in the natural path of the threat if it is not interfered with, while the latter luckily are not on that path. But why should luck be given this decisive role over the value of minimizing loss of life, given that it had no significance in cases where a driver happened to be involved? It's hard to see how, in the context of *shared risks in public space among equally innocent people*, it could make sense to view such matters of luck as grounding moral claims outweighing the value of minimizing loss of life from public threats.

The far more plausible and coherent response is to extend DDC to such cases, allowing for damage control just as before, prioritizing the mitigation of harm from public threats when all else is equal – regardless of whether or not their motion was originally started by a 'driver' – rather than giving normative authority to luck. More precisely, we should accept a version of DDC that, while compatible with DDC, is both more general (applying to a wider range of cases) and weaker (making a claim only of permissibility rather than obligation):

Generalized Deflective Damage Control (GDDC): When an agent faces a situation where an object already in motion will unavoidably cause injury through its continued motion, but she can direct it in such a way as to cause less harm in the accident (where "less harm" is understood to include comparable harms to a lesser number of different people), then all else being equal it is at least permissible for her to do that.

Again, this is just part of the reasonable package of norms governing risk and harm management we have been considering, aiming for an appropriate balance between promotion of welfare and respect for persons. The harm it allows is very limited and stems from a recognition of risks we share from common potential threats, and of the rationality of minimizing the harm done in such rare cases, when all else is equal, rather than giving normative authority to mere luck (such as which direction the object happens naturally to be heading).

To accept GDDC is to accept that among the risks to which we are exposed are not just public threats whose natural paths we happen to occupy, but also public threats whose *legitimate deflection zones* we happen to occupy (if we are in a less populated area to which it can be deflected to save lives). But nothing in this offends against any plausible conception of the inviolability of persons. We are dealing only with special cases where assertions of negative rights against such harm would seem baseless (unlike in Transplant or Driver Topple or Gas), and no person is being viewed or used opportunistically or degradingly, or being treated with callous disregard, or anything of the sort (unlike in those other cases). Even those of us who recognize strong deontological constraints or negative rights of the sort Foot emphasized (and perhaps likewise moral objections to intending harm to innocents as a means or end) can accept GDDC as a reasonable and respectful social arrangement for managing risk and harm from public threats, appropriately balancing all the values in play.

Now if these reflections are roughly correct, then turning the trolley in Bystander is permissible and Thomson was right long ago that there was a problem for Foot's Precedence Thesis: It evidently needs revision, with a principled explanation for that revision. But we have just provided that revision and explanation. The Precedence Thesis simply needs an exception built into it – as Foot (1994) herself later agreed – to handle cases of *deflective damage control*. We should replace the unqualified Precedence Thesis with the:

> **Revised Precedence Thesis**: Negative duties/rights of non-interference are typically more stringent than (or take precedence over) positive duties/rights to aid, where the harms in question are comparable and all else is equal – except in contexts of deflective damage control, which are instead handled by GDDC (and where relevant, by DDC).

Far from being an *ad hoc* solution to the Trolley Problem, this revision is well-supported by all the considerations we have given in support of DDC and GDDC. The Revised Precedence Thesis still rules out the actions in Transplant, Gas, and Driver Topple, reflecting the recognition that we typically owe people more in the way of non-interference than we do in the way of aid (Foot 1967, 1994). But it also allows for commonsense damage control from public threats already underway, as intuitively it should, and we have seen good reasons why the underlying intuitions here make sense.

This leaves open many further questions. Might there, for example, be other cases of permissibly killing one to save five that involve not deflecting a threatening object but instead moving people out of its way as on a giant lazy Susan device, where their being moved to safety incidentally causes a rockslide that kills one (Kamm 2016)? I have no idea, and though I am a robust ethical realist I see no reason to suppose that there must even be determinate ethical facts of the matter about every hypothetical case we might construct. In any event, we were talking about the Trolley Problem and diversion cases, and what we have said about them is not cast in doubt by the possibility of *other* forms of permissible harm in other sorts of cases; nor must it be put on hold until some generalization is found to cover all further cases.

2.5 Thomson's turnabout and where it went wrong

In light of what we've said so far, the bar should be set very high for any case-based argument seeking to show that while a driver's turning the trolley is permissible (even required), a bystander's doing so is impermissible. We should suspect that something has gone wrong in such an argument, unless the support for the intuitions driving it is more compelling than the reasons we've seen for giving the same verdicts in Driver and Bystander.

After decades of defending such parity, Thomson famously abandoned this position, arguing instead that a new case shows that the bystander may *not* turn the trolley. The new case was "Bystander's Three Options," and the twist was again quite simple: All is as it was in Bystander except that now there is a third option; the agent now has the possibility of turning the trolley onto a third track that she herself occupies, thus sacrificing *herself* to save the five in favor of either letting the five die or killing the one (Thomson 2008, 364). According to Thomson, this new option turns out to be deeply illuminating. For given the plausible assumption (at least for non-consequentialists) that the agent may *permissibly refuse* to sacrifice herself to save the five, we now face the question whether in that case she may nonetheless proceed with turning the trolley onto the sidetrack with the one, killing him. Thomson argues that she may not: She must either let the five die or, if she wishes to save them, sacrifice herself; but she may not impose on the one a sacrifice she refuses to make herself, in the course of saving the five.

If that's right, however, and she may not turn the trolley toward the one in that case, then according to Thomson neither can she permissibly do so in the original Bystander case where the self-sacrifice option was not present: If she *wouldn't* have self-sacrificed had the option been available, and so would not have been permitted to impose the sacrifice on the one in that case, then neither may she impose that sacrifice on the one when that is the only way to save the five, as in Bystander (Thomson 2008, 366). And even if she *would* have self-sacrificed had she been in Bystander's Three Options, Thomson says she still may not turn in the original Bystander case, as she lacks consent from the one for the cost she is imposing on him (367). On this revised assessment, then, the turning in Bystander is impermissible after all, and there was never any Trolley Problem to begin with – no burden to explain any exception to the Precedence Thesis, since Bystander wouldn't be an exception after all.

Thomson's argument relies on the intuitions she has both about Bystander's Three Options and about its bearing on the original Bystander case. I will focus on the former, and on what she says about the agent who would refuse to self-sacrifice in it.[6] What support might there be for her claim here? Ultimately, it seems to rest on the following idea:

---

[6] The critique that follows, of Thomson's primary argument (concerning the agent who *wouldn't* self-sacrifice even if she could), equally undermines her argument concerning the agent who *would*: For if I'm right that even the agent who *wouldn't* self-sacrifice in the three-options case may nonetheless

Anti-Hypocrisy Principle (AHP): It is impermissible to impose a sacrifice on someone else without their consent, for the sake of doing good, while refusing the option of voluntarily taking on a similar sacrifice oneself for that same good.

The intuitive thought here is that it seems morally problematic to escape suffering a cost one wishes to avoid by hypocritically imposing that very cost on someone else who equally wishes to avoid it, without their consent. What could give one the right to behave that way? And AHP is indeed plausible in many contexts, as Thomson (2008, 365) notes. For example, although I may voluntarily donate a kidney or half my life savings to save a stranger's life, I may not opt instead to take someone else's kidney or savings without their consent – out of a desire to avoid paying that cost myself – for the same purpose (call those cases "Kidney" and "Bank Account").

The problem, however, is that the plausibility of AHP in such cases is explained simply by the familiar point Foot made at the beginning about negative duties or rights, in connection with the Precedence Thesis: People have strong negative rights against being assaulted and harmed in such ways, even for the sake of aiding others – though of course we are permitted to make voluntary sacrifices ourselves to help others if we wish. That is sufficient to explain why we may not opt for taking someone else's kidney or emptying their bank account, or for that matter toppling them in front of a train, without their consent, rather than making the sacrifice ourselves, even in pursuit of a great good. But the whole point of our discussion of diversion or deflection cases has been to bring out the ways in which the special circumstances of such cases make for an *exception* to the typical stringent negative rights people enjoy against harm. As we have seen, while the inviolability that is plausibly part of our moral status as persons means that people can't ordinarily steal from us or take our organs even to bring about a greater good, it does not plausibly give us moral immunity to harm from public threats being diverted toward lesser harm when all else is equal.

So unless we've been given reason to reject those arguments from Sections 2.3 and 2.4, the fact that AHP is plausible in connection with cases like Kidney and Bank Account provides no support at all for its applicability to the special context of diversion cases like Bystander, where the existence of the usual negative rights is precisely what is in question. Granting that AHP is true *for a*

turn the trolley onto someone else, then the points will obviously extend at least as readily to the case of the agent who would have self-sacrificed if she could have. For a more detailed critique of Thomson's argument, see FitzPatrick (2009), from which I draw here.

certain range of cases, the obvious question, just as with the Precedence Thesis itself from the beginning, is whether it is also true *across the board and without exception*. And it would be plainly question-begging in this context just to assume that it is. What Thomson would need, but does not provide, is a strong argument for believing AHP to hold universally (not just in cases like Kidney and Bank Account), or for thinking that the one in Bystander has a stringent negative right *even* against harm brought about in accordance with GDDC (which would require refuting the considerations given in Section 2.4).

In the absence of any compelling argument along those lines, we should reject AHP in diversion cases, for all the reasons given earlier. There is, in the bystander cases, no violation of any plausible negative rights or of any plausible requirement for consent; and since there is no obligation to sacrifice oneself to save strangers, there is no independent hypocrisy: One is acting within one's rights not to sacrifice oneself, and is also acting in accordance with GDDC to exercise reasonable damage control from a public threat. Someone doing this may not be a hero, but neither is she a hypocrite.

Or at least this is so as long as she accepts that were her position switched with that of the person on the sidetrack, he would likewise be permitted to turn the trolley toward her, and she would have no legitimate complaint against him. That *symmetry* is of course implied by GDDC, so she should accept it to avoid the obvious hypocrisy of imposing this cost on someone else while complaining about the reverse if their circumstances were switched: Recognition of this symmetry is just another part of the set of norms we've been considering, which reasonable people will accept for managing social risk and accidental harm. But this symmetry principle does not provide any support for AHP: It simply tells us that exceptions to AHP, as in Bystander, apply impartially, all else being equal. And even if an agent wrongly rejects this symmetry principle and so acts hypocritically in turning the trolley while being ready to complain if anyone did the same to her, that would not imply that turning the trolley was an impermissible thing to do: It would show only that she manifested a character defect or failed to act well in a certain respect in doing something it was permissible for someone in her position to do.

The bottom line is that Thomson was right about the Trolley Problem the first time, and was later misled into changing course by a misconstrual of the significance of her three-options case (FitzPatrick 2009). Bystander does present a genuine challenge in connection with the unqualified Precedence Thesis, but this challenge can be resolved along the lines proposed here, through a defense of GDDC and the Revised Precedence Thesis, building on Foot's and Thomson's own earlier work.

3   Must we turn the trolley?

Peter A. Graham

3.1 The trolley scenario

Consider the standard Trolley Scenario:

> *Trolley*: An out-of-control trolley is barreling down a track on which five people are trapped. If Bystander does nothing, the five will be killed. Bystander can flip a switch and divert the trolley down a sidetrack, thereby saving the five. However, if Bystander diverts the trolley, it will kill Workman who is trapped on the sidetrack.

Many hold that though it is morally permissible for Bystander to divert the trolley onto the sidetrack, thereby saving the five and killing Workman, it is also morally permissible for Bystander to do nothing, thereby not killing Workman and allowing the trolley to kill the five. In fact, this dominant view was that held by Thomson (1985, 1990), one of the foremost, if not the foremost, theorists on the Trolley Problem – the problem of explaining why it is morally permissible for Bystander to turn the trolley in *Trolley*. Interestingly, Thomson (2008) later came to repudiate her former position on the Trolley Problem; her most recent view is that it is morally impermissible for Bystander to turn the trolley in *Trolley*. Helen Frowe (2018), by contrast, contends that Thomson and the reigning orthodoxy are mistaken. She argues that Bystander is morally required to divert the trolley, thereby saving the five and killing Workman. Thomson's recent position and Frowe's view are both too extreme. The orthodox view that Bystander's turning the trolley in *Trolley* is morally optional is correct. In this chapter, I shall refute Frowe's argument for the impermissibility of Bystander's refraining from turning the trolley as well as advance an argument for the view that it is permissible for Bystander to refrain from turning the trolley in *Trolley*.[1]

---

[1] Elsewhere (Graham 2017) I explain why Thomson's recent position on the Trolley Problem is mistaken.

3.2 Against Frowe's argument

Frowe's argument for the impermissibility of refraining from saving the five in *Trolley* rests upon the following principle:

> *Preventing Harm*: One has a duty to prevent harm to others when one can do so without violating anyone's rights, and without bearing an unreasonable cost (Frowe 2018, 463).

Because turning the trolley would not violate Workman's rights – it would only merely infringe them – and turning does not impose upon Bystander an unreasonable cost, it follows from *Preventing Harm* that Bystander has a duty, and not merely a permission, to divert the trolley in *Trolley*.

First, a couple of preliminary points about *Preventing Harm*. *Preventing Harm*'s antecedent talks of not violating others' rights. Usually, a distinction is drawn between *violating* and *infringing* a right. Infringing a right is just a matter of doing that which the right is a right against one's doing – one infringes another's right against one that one not ϕ just in case one ϕs – and violating a right is a morally impermissible infringement of it.[2] But more than this, a violation of a right is a morally impermissible infringement of a right the moral impermissibility of which is due to the failure of the action which infringes it to satisfy the infringement conditions of the right in question. And the infringement conditions of a right are those conditions *associated with* and *stemming from* the right the satisfaction of which are necessary for the infringement to be permissible. This understanding of the relation between the infringement of and the violation of a right rightly leaves open the possibility of an action which infringes a right being morally impermissible even though the right is not violated in the performance of that action. Here's an example of such a case:

> *Promise*: Chang has solemnly promised Tran that he won't ever harm Bystander even if doing so would be necessary to prevent others from suffering some harm. By punching Bystander in the arm, Chang can prevent some other person from suffering a week-long migraine. Absent his promise to Tran, Chang would be morally permitted to punch Bystander in the arm to prevent the other person from suffering the week-long migraine.

It could well be morally impermissible for Chang to punch Bystander in the arm in this case, and so punching her in the arm could be both morally

---

[2] This understanding of the infringement/violation distinction is due to Thomson (1990).

impermissible and an infringement of Bystander's right not to be punched in the arm, but, plausibly, it needn't be a violation of Bystander's right not to be punched in the arm. And that's because the prevention of a week-long migraine in another is (by stipulation) enough to satisfy the infringement conditions of Bystander's right not to be punched in the arm (and this is evident, given that it would be permissible for Chang to punch her in the arm were he never to have made his promise to Tran). It's because of something else, namely the failure to keep his promise to Tran, rather than the failure to satisfy the infringement conditions of Bystander's right not to be punched in the arm, that makes Chang's punching of Bystander in the arm morally impermissible. And so, Chang's punching of Bystander in the arm in *Promise*, though it might well be both morally impermissible and an infringement of Bystander's right not to be harmed, need not be a violation of that right (though it well might be a violation of Tran's promissory right). So, a right violation is a morally impermissible infringement of the right the moral impermissibility of which is due to the infringement's failing to satisfy the infringement conditions of that right. That's the first preliminary point about **Preventing Harm**.

The second preliminary point is much more straightforward. In saying that we have *a duty* to prevent harm to others when we can do so without violating anyone's rights and without bearing an unreasonable cost, the principle is stating a condition sufficient for its being morally impermissible not to prevent harm to others. The duty to prevent harm to others just means that preventing the harm is morally required.

With these preliminary points onboard, we can understand Frowe's principle preliminarily as:

> **Preventing Harm**: If, by ϕing, one can prevent a harm to others and one's ϕing would both not be a morally impermissible infringement of another's right, in virtue of its failing to satisfy the infringement conditions of that right, or involve bearing an unreasonable cost, then it would be morally wrong not to ϕ.

This principle is the linchpin in Frowe's argument for the conclusion that Bystander must, that is, that she's morally required to, turn the trolley in *Trolley*.

Preventing Harm clearly needs further elaborating, however, for what the infringement conditions on the right not to be killed are is left unspecified. Left unspecified, **Preventing Harm** might well seem to license, and even require, Bystander's turning the trolley in versions of *Trolley* in which it would clearly not be morally permissible for her to do so. Here's an example:

Suicidal Five: Everything is as it is in *Trolley* except the five trapped on the track down which the out-of-control trolley is barreling are the ones who launched the trolley towards themselves in the first place. They did so because they all had a suicide pact and wanted to die by being run over by a trolley. Immediately after having launched the trolley, however, they all have had a change of heart and now want to live. Bystander can redirect the trolley away from the five and onto Workman.

It would not be morally permissible for Bystander to turn the trolley onto Workman in this case.

As turning the trolley would not involve the bearing of an unreasonable cost on the part of Bystander in *Suicidal Five*, the only way for **Preventing Harm** to avoid declaring it morally permissible, even morally required, for Bystander to turn the trolley in *Suicidal Five* is for it to be the case that turning the trolley onto Workman in that case would violate Workman's right not to be killed. But as turning the trolley onto Workman would kill him, clearly doing so would infringe his right not to be killed. So, **Preventing Harm** can avoid saying that it would be morally wrong not to turn the trolley onto Workman in *Suicidal Five* only if turning the trolley would be a morally impermissible infringement of Workman's right not to be killed in virtue of its failing to satisfy the infringement conditions of that right. The particular condition that it fails to satisfy, presumably, is the condition that the harm one would save others from in killing Workman be one they would not have knowingly and freely inflicted upon themselves. For **Preventing Harm** to be fully fleshed out, the other infringement conditions of Workman's right not to be killed would have to be laid out.

Aside from the fact that the infringement conditions of the right not to be killed have not been laid out, there's another preliminary worry for **Preventing Harm** that one might have. Consider the following variant on *Trolley*:

Two Turning Options: Everything is as it is in *Trolley* except that in addition to being able to turn the trolley away from the five and onto Workman, Bystander has another option: She can turn the trolley down a different sidetrack, thereby killing another workman, Workman2.

It follows from **Preventing Harm**, as stated above, that it would be morally wrong not to turn the trolley onto Workman in this case. It also follows from **Preventing Harm** that it would be morally wrong not to turn the trolley onto Workman2 in this case! As stated, then, **Preventing Harm** has the untenable result that *Two Turning Options* is a moral dilemma – that is, a situation in which no matter what one does, one acts wrongly. But surely that's a mistake;

Two Turning Options is not a moral dilemma. Surely, it is morally permissible for Bystander to either turn the trolley onto Workman or onto Workman2 in order to save the five. So, **Preventing Harm** needs further refinement:

> **Preventing Harm**: If, by ϕing, one can prevent a harm to others, h, and one's ϕing would both (i) not be a morally impermissible infringement of another's right, in virtue of its failing to satisfy the infringement conditions of that right, and (ii) not involve bearing an unreasonable cost, then it would be morally wrong not to ϕ (unless there are some other ways of acting, ψing, ωing, etc., by which one could prevent h (or some other harm greater than or equal in magnitude to h^3) which would satisfy (i) and (ii), in which case it would be morally wrong not to either ϕ or ψ or ω or...).

I think it must be something along these lines that Frowe has in mind in putting forward **Preventing Harm** as a premise in her argument that it is morally impermissible for Bystander not to turn the trolley in *Trolley*.

The principle won't do, however. **Preventing Harm** falls prey to counter-examples such as the following:

> *Rollercoaster*: An out-of-control rollercoaster is barreling down a track on which, one behind the other, two people, Hussein and Khan, are trapped. If nothing is done, though the rollercoaster will collide with Hussein, thereby killing him, it will not kill Khan because the weight of Hussein's body will bring the rollercoaster to a halt before it reaches Khan. If Hussein is pulled off of the track, however, he will be saved but Khan will be killed. Bystander can either do nothing or pull Hussein off the track before the rollercoaster collides with him.

Intuitively, it is both permissible for Bystander to pull Hussein off the track and permissible for her to do nothing.[4] Morality does not forbid Bystander's removing Hussein, thereby causing the death of Khan. But, precisely

---

[3] This parenthetical clause is necessary for **Preventing Harm** to avoid yielding the wrong result in the following case:

> *Pond*: A and B are both drowning in a pond. Chang can dive into the pond and save A and she can dive in and save B, but she can't save both.

Without the parenthetical clause, **Preventing Harm** would have the unintuitive result that *Pond* is a moral dilemma.

[4] Frowe would likely claim that it is morally required to pull Hussein off the track because, she would claim, to not pull him off the track would be to intentionally use him as a means to save Khan. This is implausible. In failing to rescue Hussein, Bystander doesn't use him in any way, let alone use him as a means. And even if one thought that an agent's intentions are relevant to the permissibility of her actions (I don't), Bystander's not pulling Hussein off the track needn't involve any objectionable intention, for the fact that not removing Hussein will prevent Khan from being killed is something Bystander can merely foresee, and act on the basis of which, without intending that it happen.

because removing Hussein would cause the death of Khan, morality also does not require removing Hussein. However, were **Preventing Harm** true it would be morally required of Bystander to pull Hussein off the track.[5] And this is because she can prevent harm to someone – viz., Hussein – without violating anyone's rights (Khan does not have a right against Bystander that she not pull Hussein off the track) or bearing an unreasonable cost (Bystander, we might suppose, will suffer no physical or psychological cost as a result of pulling Hussein off the track).[6]

(*Rollercoaster* is importantly different from the following variant of *Trolley*:

Trolley2: Everything is as it is in *Trolley* except that if Bystander does nothing, then only one person will be killed by the runaway trolley.

In *Trolley2*, unlike in *Trolley*, it is not morally permissible for Bystander to redirect the trolley onto the sidetrack. In a one-one version of *Trolley*, such as *Trolley2*, the fact that the harm one prevents is not sufficiently greater than the harm one would cause, makes harming that person a violation of his right not to be harmed, for preventing a harm greater than the one one inflicts is presumably one of the infringement conditions of the right not to be harmed. In a one-one case like *Rollercoaster*, however, though Bystander's removing Hussein from the track does cause Khan to suffer the harm of death, it doesn't count as Bystander's harming Khan in a way such that Khan has a right against Bystander that she not harm him in that way, and so it is permissible in that case for Bystander to remove Hussein from the track.[7] (Because Khan has no right against Bystander that she not pull Hussein off the track, in pulling Hussein off the track Bystander doesn't even permissibly infringe anyone's rights; by contrast, Bystander does infringe (permissibly) Workman's right against her that she not kill him when she redirects the trolley onto him in *Trolley*.))

---

[5] **Preventing Harm** has the perhaps even more counterintuitive consequence that it would be morally required of Bystander to pull Hussein off the track in a version of *Rollercoaster* in which not only Khan, but also four other innocent people are trapped behind Hussein, all of whom will be run over and killed were Hussein removed from the track. Now, it might be morally permissible to remove Hussein from the track in such a version of *Rollercoaster* (though I don't take it to be at all obvious that it is) but it is surely not morally required to do so. Frowe (2018, 477) explicitly embraces the consequence that it would be morally required of Bystander to pull Hussein off the track in this version of *Rollercoaster*. (She does so in her discussion of her *Bus* case.)

[6] Were Bystander to pull Hussein off the track in *Rollercoaster* she would engage in what Hanser (1999) calls preventing someone from being saved from being harmed, a third relation, one that he claims falls in between doing and allowing harm.

[7] The comparison between *Rollercoaster* and *Trolley2* nicely establishes that the right not to be harmed is not a right simply not to be harmed, but rather a right not to be harmed in particular ways.

In *Rollercoaster*, Bystander can prevent harm to Hussein without infringing anyone's right not to be harmed – in pulling Hussein off of the track Bystander prevents Hussein from saving Khan; as noted above, though she causes Khan to suffer a harm, she doesn't harm him in a way such that Khan has a right against her that she not harm him in that way. Another way in which someone may lack a right not to be harmed is by way of consent. Accordingly, **Preventing Harm** is also subject to counterexamples involving consent:

> *Train*: An out-of-control train is barreling down a track on which one person, Nguyen, is trapped. If Bystander does nothing, Nguyen will be killed. Bystander can flip a switch and divert the train down a sidetrack, thereby saving Nguyen. However, if Bystander diverts the train, it will kill Chen and Ruiz who are both trapped on the sidetrack. Chen and Ruiz do not want Bystander to divert the train onto them – they'd prefer, and have made their preferences known, that Bystander do nothing and allow the train to kill Nguyen – however, they have, nonetheless, freely and fully informedly consented to Bystander's turning the train onto the both of them in order to save Nguyen. (Why have they jointly consented to their both being killed? Because they want Bystander to have the moral option of killing them to save Nguyen should she so wish.)

In this case, though it would be permissible for Bystander to divert the train onto Chen and Ruiz, it is not morally required of her to do so. Bystander may refrain from turning the trolley onto Chen and Ruiz, and allow the trolley to kill Nguyen. Chen's and Ruiz's consent waives their rights against Bystander that she not kill them, thereby removing that moral barrier to Bystander's killing them, but, intuitively, the removal of that barrier does not entail Bystander's having an obligation to kill them. But, if that's right, then, once again, **Preventing Harm** is false. Though Bystander can prevent a harm to someone – viz., Nguyen – without violating anyone's rights (Chen and Ruiz have both waived their rights not to be killed) or bearing an unreasonable cost (Bystander, we might suppose, will suffer no physical or psychological cost in turning the train onto Chen and Ruiz), she needn't prevent that harm.[8]

---

[8] One might contest the claim that it is permissible to kill Chen and Ruiz as a side effect of saving Nguyen in *Train* because, even though, because of their consent, turning the trolley onto them wouldn't wrong them, nonetheless, killing them would be the infliction of more harm than would be allowed by allowing Nguyen to die. I think it is intuitive, however, not only that it wouldn't violate their rights not to be killed for Bystander to turn the train onto Chen and Ruiz in *Train* but also that it would in fact be permissible for her to do so in such a scenario.

Another way in which someone may lack a right not to be harmed is by way of forfeiture. Accordingly, **Preventing Harm** is also subject to counter-examples involving forfeiture:

> *Train2*: Everything is as it is in *Train* except that instead of consenting to be killed to save Nguyen, Chen and Ruiz were the ones who unwittingly launched the out-of-control train toward Nguyen in the first place. (They mistakenly, though non-negligently, thought that the track on which Nguyen is trapped was empty.)

In this case, though it would be permissible for Bystander to divert the train onto Chen and Ruiz, it would not be morally required of her to do so.[9] But, if that's right, then, once again, **Preventing Harm** is false. Though Bystander can prevent a harm to someone – viz., Nguyen – without violating anyone's rights (Chen and Ruiz, by initiating the lethal process that threatens Nguyen's life, have both forfeited their rights not to be killed as a side effect of saving Nguyen) or bearing an unreasonable cost (Bystander, we might suppose, will suffer no physical or psychological cost in turning the train onto Chen and Ruiz), she needn't prevent that harm.

As **Preventing Harm** is false, and Frowe's argument for the moral impermissibility of refraining from diverting the trolley in *Trolley* relies on **Preventing Harm**, Frowe's argument for the moral impermissibility of Bystander's refraining from diverting the trolley in *Trolley* fails. And if her argument fails, then Frowe has given us no reason to abandon the intuitive verdict that it is merely permissible, and not required, for Bystander to redirect the trolley onto Workman in *Trolley*.

Now, mightn't Frowe be able to dodge my argument by weakening **Preventing Harm**? Consider:

> **Preventing Harm 2**: If ϕing, of all the options one has which will neither violate anyone's rights nor involve one's bearing an unreasonable cost, would reduce to a unique minimum the amount of harm suffered by others overall as compared with those other options, then it would be morally

---

[9] If one is dubious of the permissibility of diverting the train onto Chen and Ruiz in this case, suppose instead that Bystander can, before Chen and Ruiz unwittingly launch the train toward Nguyen, press a button which will, unbeknownst to Chen and Ruiz, switch the tracks the train will go down once they launch it so that it will instead go down a sidetrack and loop back around and kill Chen and Ruiz themselves instead of Nguyen should they launch it. It would be morally permissible for Bystander both to press the button and not to do so in this version of the case. I believe the points I make in the text with *Train2* could equally be made with a so-modified version of the case.

wrong not to ϕ (unless there is some other such option one has the taking of which would reduce to a unique minimum the harm suffered by others overall).

Rollercoaster, *Train*, and *Train2*, you might think, pose no threat to **Preventing Harm 2**. As both of Bystander's options in *Rollercoaster* would result in the same amount of harm suffered overall – both result in one person being killed – **Preventing Harm 2** does not require Bystander's pulling Hussein off the track in that case.[10] And, as Bystander's diverting the train onto Chen and Ruiz actually causes more harm to be suffered by others than would be suffered were Bystander not to do so in *Train* and *Train2*, **Preventing Harm 2** does not require Bystander's turning the train in those cases. What's more, **Preventing Harm 2**, you might think, can do all the work Frowe puts **Preventing Harm** to in her argument – in *Trolley* not only does Bystander's diverting the trolley prevent harm to the five, it also minimizes harm overall compared to not turning the trolley. So perhaps Frowe can dispense with **Preventing Harm**, in favor of **Preventing Harm 2**, and still run her argument for the impermissibility of refraining from turning the trolley in *Trolley*.

This won't do. **Preventing Harm 2** still gets the wrong answer in *Train* and *Train2*, for in those cases, **Preventing Harm 2** has the consequence that it is morally impermissible for Bystander to redirect the trolley onto Chen and Ruiz. This is because, in not diverting the train, Bystander would be minimizing harm suffered overall and doing so without violating anyone's rights or bearing an unreasonable cost. But it is not morally impermissible for Bystander to turn the train on Chen and Ruiz in *Train* and *Train2*.

Preventing Harm 2 may also be subject to further counterexample. A three-option case involving consent might pose problems for it:

> *Tram*: An out-of-control tram is barreling down a track on which five people are trapped. If Bystander does nothing, the five will be killed. Bystander can flip a switch and divert the tram down a left-hand sidetrack, thereby saving the five. However, if Bystander diverts the tram down the left-hand sidetrack, it will kill Chen and Ruiz who are both trapped on the left-hand sidetrack. Chen and Ruiz do not want Bystander to divert the

---

[10] If, however, in a version of *Rollercoaster* in which the number of people Bystander could pull off the track were greater than one and it were permissible for her not to pull them off the track, then such a version of *Rollercoaster* would make trouble for **Preventing Harm 2**. Though it seems plausible to me that Bystander wouldn't be morally required to pull two in front of Khan off the track in such a version of *Rollercoaster*, I leave it open whether this is the case, and thus do not rely on it in my argument against **Preventing Harm 2**.

tram onto them – they'd prefer Bystander to do nothing and allow the tram to kill the five – however, they have, nonetheless, freely and fully informedly consented to Bystander's turning the tram onto them in order to save the five. (Why have they jointly consented to their both being killed? Because they want Bystander to have the moral option of killing them to save the five should she so wish.) Bystander can also press a button and divert the tram down a right-hand sidetrack, thereby saving the five. However, if Bystander diverts the tram down the right-hand sidetrack, it will kill Mbeki who is trapped on the right-hand sidetrack. Mbeki has *not* consented to Bystander's killing him as a side effect of saving the five.

It's plausible that it is morally permissible for Bystander to divert the tram down the left-hand sidetrack, thereby saving the five and killing Chen and Ruiz. However, were **Preventing Harm 2** true, this might not be permissible. Were **Preventing Harm 2** true, it's plausible that it would entail that Bystander would be morally required to divert the tram down the right-hand sidetrack, thereby saving the five and killing Mbeki; and that's because only in doing so she would be minimizing the harm suffered overall most, without violating anyone's rights or bearing an unreasonable cost, herself.

Now there might be a response that Frowe could make here. Perhaps, she might argue, turning the trolley onto Mbeki would violate Mbeki's right not to be killed in this case. Why might this be? Well, it might be that one of the infringement conditions of the right not to be harmed is that the harm one prevents in infringing that right not be preventable by means that would not involve the infringing of anyone's rights. And, as the harm Bystander would prevent by turning the trolley onto Mbeki, viz., the saving of the five, is a harm that could be prevented without infringing anyone's rights, viz., by turning the trolley onto Chen and Ruiz, that infringement condition on Mbeki's right not to be killed would not be satisfied, and so turning the trolley onto him would indeed be a violation of his right not to be killed.

This reply might work. However, it will do so only if it is not morally permissible for Bystander to turn the tram onto Mbeki in *Tram*. If, on the other hand, it is permissible to either turn the trolley onto Chen and Ruiz or turn it onto Mbeki, then this reply won't work. And one might well think that it is morally permissible to turn the trolley either onto Chen and Ruiz or onto Mbeki. One might think that what makes it morally permissible to turn the trolley onto Chen and Ruiz is that they've consented and that what makes it permissible to turn it onto Mbeki is that doing so will minimize harm overall most and do so only by harming Mbeki as a side effect.[11] If that's right, and I'm inclined to think that it is, then *Tram* is indeed a counterexample to **Preventing Harm 2**.

Because these arguments against **Preventing Harm 2** involve consent, there's another maneuver Frowe might make in response to them. She might suggest that in *Train* and *Tram*, consent works in a way that doesn't threaten a suitably modified version of **Preventing Harm 2** and so her argument remains unscathed by my attacks on it. You might think that in *Train* when Chen and Ruiz consent to Bystander's killing them to save Nguyen they exercise a normative power they have to make their interests count for nothing in Bystander's determination of what to do. And, as they take their interests out of consideration, killing them would be permitted by a lesser-evil justification in *Train*. A similar point might be made with respect to *Tram*. If this is right, then Frowe might appeal to something like the following principle in her argument:

> **Preventing Harm 3**: If ϕing, of all the options one has which will neither violate anyone's rights nor involve one's bearing an unreasonable cost, would reduce to a unique minimum the amount of *morally relevant harm* suffered by others overall as compared with those other options, then it would be morally wrong not to ϕ (unless there is some other option one has the taking of which would reduce to a unique minimum the morally relevant harm suffered by others overall...).

Where "morally relevant harm" is harm to those who haven't exercised their normative power to make their interests count for nothing in the determination of what it is permissible for others to do.

There are two problems with this maneuver. First, **Preventing Harm 3** has intolerable consequences: It has the consequence that it is morally required of Bystander to kill Chen and Ruiz in both *Train* and *Tram*, whereas, intuitively, in both cases that only seems merely morally permissible. Second, and more important, it is simply false that consenting to be harmed entails exercising a power to eliminate one's interests in the determination of what the one to whom consent has been given may do. While it is plausible that people do have the normative power to alter the impact their interests have on what

---

[11] That Mbeki is harmed as a side effect of preventing the greater harm to the five is clearly crucial to the permissibility of Bystander's turning the trolley onto him, for if the only way of preventing the trolley from hitting the five were to fatally hurl Mbeki at it, it would clearly not be permissible to do so.

others may permissibly do, it isn't plausible that this is what is going on in *Train* and *Tram*. Recall that in both *Train* and *Tram*, Chen and Ruiz would prefer, and have made their preferences known, that Bystander not kill them, and they've only consented to being killed in order to give Bystander the moral option of killing them in order to save the others should she so wish. We might suppose, further, that in each of these cases they expressly do not eliminate their interests from consideration in the determination of what Bystander may permissibly do: Suppose they say "though we consent to your killing us, we prefer that you not kill us and that you do take our interests fully into account in determining what to do." In such versions of the cases, it would still be permissible, though not required, for Bystander to turn the trolley onto Chen and Ruiz in order to save Nguyen (in *Train*) or the five (in *Tram*).

Note, also, that holding that in consenting to be killed in order to give Bystander the option to save Nguyen, Chen and Ruiz have exercised a normative power to take their interests out of consideration in the determination of what Bystander may permissibly do has counterintuitive consequences in a slight variation of *Train*:

> *Train3*: Everything is as it is in *Train* except that Bystander has another option. She can turn a knob thereby diverting the train onto an empty sidetrack, thereby saving Nguyen and killing no one.

If it were thought that in consenting to Bystander's turning the train onto them in *Train* Chen and Ruiz were eliminating their interests from consideration, then it would follow that it is permissible for Bystander to divert the train onto Chen and Ruiz, thereby killing them to save Nguyen, in *Train3* – because in making their interest count for nothing, they remove any and all reasons against turning the train onto them. But it is patently not morally permissible for Bystander to do that in *Train3*: in *Train3*, Chen's and Ruiz's consent notwithstanding, Bystander is morally required to turn the knob and divert the train onto the empty sidetrack.

Consent is just different from the normative power people do in fact have to alter the impact their interests have in the determination of what other people may permissibly do. Consent operates purely at the deontic level. It doesn't work by way of affecting the weight one's interests have. Consent to be harmed simply is the waiving of a right not to be harmed, but that waiver is just that, a waiver. And the waiving of the right not to be harmed needn't do anything except make it the case that harming the one harmed doesn't wrong her. (Such a waiver doesn't always succeed in making the option in question morally permissible, of course, as witnessed by *Train3*.) Conflating consent with the power to alter the impact of one's interests in the determination of what others may permissibly do, then, can't be used to salvage Frowe's argument.

Preventing Harm is false and so too are any variants of it that might do the work Frowe puts it to in her argument for the conclusion that Bystander is morally required to turn the trolley in *Trolley*. I submit, then, that Frowe has not given us reason to ditch the intuitive verdict that it is permissible, but not required, for Bystander to turn the trolley in *Trolley*.

3.3 An argument for the permissibility of not turning in the trolley scenario

Not only does Frowe's argument not give us any reason to give up the intuitive verdict that it is permissible for Bystander both to turn and to not turn the trolley in *Trolley*, there are independent positive grounds for thinking that this is the case. Below I present an argument for the claim that it is permissible for Bystander not to turn the trolley in *Trolley*. This argument was originally given by Kamm (2007, 168).[12] It, in addition to the intuitive verdict that it is permissible to turn the trolley in *Trolley*, suffices for a defense of the moral optionality of Bystander's turning the trolley in *Trolley*.

The argument for the permissibility of Bystander's not turning the trolley in *Trolley* has two premises:

1. It is morally permissible for Workman to kill Bystander to prevent her from turning the trolley onto him in *Trolley*.
2. If it is morally permissible for Workman to kill Bystander to prevent her from turning the trolley onto him in *Trolley*, then it is morally permissible for Bystander not to turn the trolley in *Trolley*.
3. Therefore, it is morally permissible for Bystander not to turn the trolley in *Trolley*.

This argument is clearly valid. Premise 1 I take to be intuitively true. It is not morally required of Workman to stand back and allow Bystander to kill him as a side effect of saving the five in *Trolley* if he can (even lethally) prevent her from doing so.[13] And premise 2 I take to be supported by the general principle:

---

[12] Kamm also presents it in (Kamm 2016).

[13] It's even more intuitively clear that it would be permissible for Workman to kill Bystander to prevent her from turning the trolley onto him if his doing so would also save the five from being killed by the trolley.

Requirements Protect Against Permissible Defensive Killing: Necessarily, if S_1 would be morally permitted to kill S_2 to prevent S_2's ϕing or its consequences on defensive grounds, then it is not the case that S_2 is morally required to ϕ.[14]

The basic thought behind ***Requirements Protect Against Permissible Defensive Killing*** is, as its name suggests, that morality can never require one to act in a way such that were one to act in that way it would be permissible for others to kill one in defense of themselves or others precisely because of one's acting in that way.[15] And that's because it would be unfair and potentially incoherent of morality to require people to act in ways that rendered them susceptible to being defensively killed to prevent them from acting in those very ways, and morality is neither unfair nor incoherent.[16]

It would not be unfair or incoherent of morality, on the other hand, to permit Workman's killing Bystander to prevent her from turning the trolley onto him in *Trolley* were Bystander's turning of the trolley onto him merely permissible. Whereas morality's requirements do grant one immunity from defensive killing, its permissions don't. If Workman permissibily kills Bystander to prevent her from turning the trolley onto him, there would be nothing unfair or incoherent in that if Bystander had been morally permitted not to turn the trolley onto Workman in the first place. Bystander could easily, and morally permissibly, have avoided susceptibility to being defensively killed by not being such as to be about to turn the trolley onto Workman.

If ***Requirements Protect Against Permissible Defensive Killing*** is correct, then we can directly test the claim that it is morally required of Bystander that she turn the trolley in *Trolley* by seeing whether it would be permissible for

---

[14] ***Requirements Protect Against Permissible Defensive Killing*** is a consequence of the more general and independently plausible ***Requirements Protect Against Permissible Defensive Harming*** according to which it is not morally permissible to harm others in order to prevent them from doing what they're morally required to do.

[15] Frowe seems to accept ***Requirements Protect Against Permissible Defensive Killing***. She writes: "Moreover, it's particularly implausible that [Bystander] might become liable to harm by doing what morality compels her to do . . . Moreover, it seems straightforwardly incoherent that morality might pronounce [Bystander] liable to be harmed to protect her from doing the very thing that morality requires her to do" (2018, 476). Frowe would also clearly reject premise 1 of the argument for the permissibility of Bystander's not turning the trolley in *Trolley*.

[16] Arguably, ***Requirements Protect Against Permissible Defensive Killing*** follows from an even more general principle, to the effect that morality never requires one to put oneself in a position to be permissibly killed in the course of some other good's being promoted. (The world may of course put one in a position such that one may be permissibly killed in the course of some other good's being promoted; it's just that morality doesn't ever force one into such a position when one wouldn't otherwise be in it.) Though I think such a principle is plausible, I don't have the space to argue for it here.

Workman to kill Bystander to prevent her from doing so. As it would be permissible for him to do so, we can conclude that Bystander wasn't morally required to turn the trolley in the first place. And that's the argument for the permissibility of Bystander's not turning the trolley in *Trolley*.

A valid argument is, of course, only as strong as its premises. And I realize that one might not share the intuition that it is morally permissible for Workman to kill Bystander to prevent her from turning the trolley onto him in *Trolley*. Fair enough. But I think the argument can be run with an even less potentially controversial premise. For not only would it be permissible for Workman to kill Bystander to prevent her from turning the trolley onto him, he would also be morally permitted to lethally redirect the trolley onto Bystander after Bystander redirected it toward him in a suitably modified version of *Trolley*.

> *Double Redirection*: Everything is as it is in *Trolley* except that Bystander, herself, is trapped on a track onto which Workman can lethally redirect the trolley after Bystander redirects the trolley away from the five innocent people and toward him.[17]

I take it to be clear, even more clear than that it would be morally permissible for Workman to kill Bystander to prevent her from killing him in *Trolley*, that it would be morally permissible for Workman to redirect the trolley onto Bystander, thereby killing her as a side effect of saving his own life in *Double Redirection*. Workman is permitted to make Bystander pay the cost of saving the five innocent people, instead of himself, if he can do so by redirecting the trolley onto her.[18]

But note, other things being equal, it is not morally permissible for a person to redirect a trolley away from killing herself and lethally onto another innocent person in order to save her own life. It would patently not be morally permissible for one innocent person to redirect a runaway trolley

---

[17] McMahan (2014) agrees that it would be permissible for Workman to redirect the trolley onto Bystander in *Double Redirection*. Kamm (2007, 2016) agrees as well and also thinks this shows that Bystander is not morally required to turn the trolley in *Trolley*.

[18] The thought here might seem reminiscent of Thomson's thought in "Turning the Trolley" (2008, 365) to the effect that "if A wants to do a certain good deed, and can pay what doing it would cost, then – other things being equal – A may do that good deed only if A pays the cost himself." In fact, I think what's going on here is distinct from that thought. What's going on here is that Bystander's impending morally optional infringement of Workman's right not to be killed justifies his redirecting the trolley onto Bystander in *Double Redirection*. It's a good thing that my argument does not rely on Thomson's thought, for, as I show in "Thomson's Trolley Problem" (2017), that thought is mistaken.

away from herself and onto another innocent person if she could do so. What makes it permissible for Workman to redirect the trolley onto Bystander, after Bystander turns it toward him in *Double Redirection*, is that were he not to redirect it, Bystander would have morally optionally infringed his right not to be killed and that impending optional infringement licenses Workman to make Bystander pay the price of saving the five rather than himself.[19]

If all of this is right, then we can reformulate the argument for the permissibility of Bystander's not turning the trolley in *Trolley* with this weaker premise as follows:

1. It is morally permissible for Workman to redirect the trolley onto Bystander after she turns it toward him in *Double Redirection*.
2. If it is morally permissible for Workman to redirect the trolley onto Bystander after she turns it toward him in *Double Redirection*, then it is morally permissible for Bystander not to turn the trolley in *Double Redirection*.
3. Therefore, it is morally permissible for Bystander not to turn the trolley in *Double Redirection*.
4. If it is morally permissible for Bystander not to turn the trolley in *Double Redirection*, then it is morally permissible for Bystander not to turn the trolley in *Trolley*.
5. Therefore, it is morally permissible for Bystander not to turn the trolley in *Trolley*.

As I've indicated, I think it's intuitive that premise 1 is true. Premise 2 is supported by **Requirements Protect Against Permissible Defensive Killing**. And premise 4 also seems plausible: How could the addition of Workman's option to redirect the trolley back at Bystander make Bystander's initial redirection toward Workman go from being morally required in *Trolley* to merely morally permissible in *Double Redirection*? What's more, if **Requirements Protect Against Permissible Defensive Killing** grounds the mere permissibility of turning the trolley in *Double Redirection*, it likewise does so in *Trolley*, for even though, in *Trolley*, Workman can't redirect the trolley back at Bystander, Bystander would nonetheless be susceptible to

---

[19] Further evidence of its not being an infringement of Khan's right not to be harmed for Bystander to remove Hussein from the track in *Rollercoaster* is that it would not be morally permissible for Khan to (lethally) prevent her from doing so in such a case. It would, however, be permissible for Workman to (lethally) prevent Bystander from redirecting the trolley onto him in *Trolley2*, and that, once again, this is because Bystander's doing so would be an infringement, and even a violation, of Workman's right not to be killed in that case.

having it redirected to her in such a case, and that's all that's needed, given *Requirements Protect Against Permissible Defensive Killing*, to make not turning the trolley in *Trolley* morally permissible.

So, because, intuitively, Bystander is susceptible to being killed defensively by Workman in *Trolley*, that supports the thought that it is morally permissible for Bystander to not turn the trolley in that case. As it is clearly permissible for Bystander to turn the trolley in *Trolley*, Bystander's turning the trolley in *Trolley*, contra Frowe, is morally optional, not required.[20]

---

[20] Many thanks to Kerah Gordon-Solmon, Theron Pummer, and Hallvard Lillehammer for comments on earlier drafts of this chapter.

4 Non-consequentialism in light of the trolley problem

F. M. Kamm

4.1

The aim of this chapter is to understand non-consequentialism's (NC) view of harming some as a consequence of helping others, specifically when the harm caused is the death of innocent nonthreatening people who would otherwise not soon die.[1] (Hence, what is said is limited to discussing interpersonal harm and benefit and may not apply at all to intrapersonal harm and benefit.[2] It is also limited to discussing cases in which everyone involved knows their own and others' positions, such as who would be harmed, who saved, and who would act.) NC is ordinarily thought to involve individual rights against harm and to hold that we have a stronger duty not to harm others than we do to aid them. Why then may a trolley driver redirect his out-of-control trolley so it kills one person on the sidetrack rather than five other people to whom it is headed (Driver Case)? Why may a bystander redirect a trolley so it kills one person rather than omit to save five other people to whom the trolley is headed (Bystander Case)?[3]

Some, however, think the bystander may not turn the trolley. Judith Thomson argues[4] that if the person on the sidetrack has no duty to turn the trolley to himself and has not consented to do so to save the five when it will kill him, then the bystander may not turn the trolley toward the person without his consent either. Challenging Thomson's view involves showing

---

[1] Non-consequentialism denies that *only* consequences matter in determining what is morally right to do. It does not deny that consequences can matter. This chapter draws on, modifies, and adds to my previous work (Kamm 1996, 2007, 2016, among others).

[2] Hence, it may be permissible to harm a person for his own greater good when it is not permissible to harm a person for the greater good of others.

[3] Philippa Foot introduced the Driver Case in her "The Problem of Abortion and the Doctrine of Double Effect" (Foot 1967/2002). Judith Thomson introduced the Bystander Case in her "Killing, Letting Die, and the Trolley Problem" (Thomson 1976). Thomson also introduced the title "Trolley Problem" in 1976 to refer to Foot's Driver Case but then used it to refer solely to the Bystander Case in her "The Trolley Problem" (Thomson 1985). See Kamm (2016) for discussion of this change.

[4] In her article "Turning the Trolley" (Thomson 2008).

that in NC what someone may sometimes permissibly do to another for a greater good may go beyond what either person is morally required or has agreed to do to himself or has agreed to have done to him for the greater good.[5] Even to justify the driver turning the trolley at least part of this must be shown because the one person hit by the driver has no duty to turn the trolley on himself and has not consented to have it done to help the driver avoid killing others. However, it not being wrong of someone to do this to the one person is consistent with NC implying that the person is wronged by what is done. An indication that he is wronged is that he may resist the trolley being turned to him even by turning it back on whoever turns it to him though this interferes with saving the five.[6] I will assume it is permissible to redirect in both Driver and Bystander Cases and focus on explaining why this is so on non-consequentialist grounds.

4.2

My basic view is that it is permissible for the driver or the bystander to turn the trolley in part because it satisfies what these and other cases show to be a (defeasible) requirement of NC, namely, that given our actions it is possible for harm to be justified (in whole or part) by *what produces it*. If a harm cannot be justified in this way, it cannot be justified by *what it produces* alone nor should it be used to help produce other goods. Goods brought about improperly are themselves not justified. I call this the Doctrine of Productive Purity (DPP).[7] It concerns how both good (where this includes reducing harm) and harm may permissibly be brought about. It contrasts with a Consequentialist (C) view that whatever we can do to achieve the greater good is inherently justified, meaning that harm can be justified by the greater good it produces.

Section 4.4 details my view of the DPP by considering intuitive judgments about cases that have been important in discussing the trolley problem.

---

[5] For a defense of this view, see Kamm (1987).

[6] For a defense of these views see Kamm (2007, 2016). A desire to avoid wronging someone may be why it is only permissible and not obligatory for the bystander to turn the trolley.

[7] The DPP should be understood to hold up to a threshold on how much good (including avoiding bad) would be lost if harm that violates the DPP is not done. For the acts permitted by the DPP meeting that threshold is not required. The DPP is also consistent with what I call the Principle of Secondary Permissibility (PSP) which claims that an act that would be impermissible considered on its own may be permissible as a substitute for an otherwise permissible act that would otherwise be done and cause more harm to the same person. (For a more complex account of the DPP, see Kamm 2007, 164. It relates to what I called the Principle of Permissible Harm (PPH) in that the principles I claim it encompasses are parts of the PPH (see Kamm 1996, 2007 on the PPH and PSP)).

The judgments illustrate and support several summary principles that yield the DPP when synthesized.

However, not all cases that satisfy the DPP will involve permissible harm. Section 4.5 investigates conditions other than the DPP sometimes needed to make turning the trolley permissible and their relation to a moral distinction between killing and letting die. Section 4.5 also considers what deeper moral ideas underlie or supervene on the DPP and how they relate to our moral idea of persons and their relations to each other.

4.3

Before considering my view further, consider alternative proposals for NC's justification of turning the trolley in the Driver and Bystander Cases.

4.3.1

The Doctrine of Double Effect (DDE) claims that one may turn the trolley because the harm to the one person is only foreseen, not intended. Harm (or at least putting in harm's way) would be intended in toppling a fat man from a bridge so that he falls in front of the trolley to stop it hitting the five.[8] The DDE is what I call a "state of mind" theory distinguishing the moral permissibility of acts depending on whether a harm is actually intended or merely foreseen by the agent who kills (or lets die).[9] But in what I call the Bad Man Trolley Case it remains permissible for someone to turn the trolley, foreseeably saving five people from it, even if he only acts because he intends to kill the one other person to whom the trolley is redirected. Furthermore, Philippa Foot noted that it is impermissible to use a gas to save five people even if it kills one other person only as a foreseen side effect. (I call this the Gas Case.)[10] Hence, that in

---

[8] Rather than imagining someone pushing the man "up close and personal" as Thomson did when she introduced this "Fat Man Case" (Thomson 1976), I will imagine toppling him by pressing a switch from a distance. This holds constant the distanced, mechanical cause of death in redirecting a trolley. Intentionally involving someone in a way foreseen to cause his death (which is what may actually happen in toppling the man) would also be ruled out by a somewhat revised DDE.

[9] This is different from claiming that an act would be impermissible only if no reasonable agent could do it without intending a harm even if the actual agent intends a harm. I do not think such an interpretation of the DDE is correct. For one reason, see Fruge (2019).

[10] See Foot (1967/2003). However, consider a Gas Case variant in which the gas used to save the five is harmless but its presence will foreseeably move some germs that were safely closeted so that they now kill one other person (Germ Case). I think that it would be permissible to save the five in this case. This suggests that doing what foreseeably causes death can be permissible more often than Foot may have thought. I discuss this further below.

the Driver and Bystander Cases causing the death of the one is only foreseen seems neither necessary nor sufficient to make turning the trolley permissible.

4.3.2

Foot claimed that the trolley driver may permissibly turn the trolley killing one person because otherwise he would kill a greater number of other people impermissibly since he started the trolley. This is a non-state-of-mind theory of permissibility. One problem with her proposal is that it rules out the *bystander* turning the trolley since he would only let five die, not kill them. It also raises the question whether a driver who is thrown from the trolley and lands near a trolley-turning switch may use it. In such a Bystanding Driver Case, the driver faces a choice between killing one and letting five die. (This is so even though he would become their killer in virtue of both letting them die and having started the trolley.) Another problem with Foot's proposal is that it incorrectly implies that the driver may topple a fat man from the bridge or explode a bomb that stops the trolley but directly kills one other person (Bomb Case). It also incorrectly implies that if turning the trolley from the five when it would kill two other people were permissible for both the driver and the bystander, each should topple one other person from the bridge instead to reduce the number of people they each kill from two to one. That they may not do this is important because it has been suggested that an agent's duty to respect rights is "time relative." That is, it can be impermissible for an agent to *now* transgress one person's right (e.g., not to be toppled from the bridge) to prevent the consequences of his *past* act that would transgress the rights of a greater number of other people. But the driver is not permitted to topple one person when it would be the alternative to, *at the very same time,* turning the trolley toward killing two people. So it can not only be impermissible for him to transgress someone's rights now to prevent the consequences to others of his past transgressive act. It can be impermissible for him to reduce the number of people whose rights not to be killed he would transgress at a given time.[11]

4.3.3

In her earlier work Thomson suggested that the trolley may be redirected by a bystander because (i) it better distributes an existing threat rather than

---

[11] I use "transgress" to apply to impermissible violations as well as permissible infringements of rights.

creating a new threat and (ii) it does not do this *by* infringing anyone's rights.[12] However, consider my Lazy Susan Case:[13] The five are moved on a swivel table away from a trolley that would otherwise hit them, causing rocks to fall killing another person. Turning the Lazy Susan seems permissible for the same reason as turning the trolley even though it doesn't redistribute an existing threat and creates a new one (falling rocks). Furthermore, consider another version of this case in which the Lazy Susan pushes another person into the trolley when it turns to save the five. This too seems permissible even if it is impermissible to topple someone from a bridge into the trolley.

4.4

My positive proposal for NC (the DPP) is a non-state-of-mind theory for the permissibility of harm that synthesizes the principles below. While I present the principles separately, it must be understood that no principle should be violated in satisfying another principle and that, other things equal, it may be wrong to bring about a certain amount of harm without violating any of the principles if it were possible to cause *less* harm without violating any. The order of presentation is a principle first and then cases that support it even though the order of discovery is from cases to principles.

Principle A. Greater good that involves elimination of greater harm may permissibly cause lesser harm. (This assumes that the way the greater good is brought about does not violate any of the other principles.)

Example to clarify Principle A: We may permissibly move the five away from the trolley to a safer area where their presence moves one other person to his death. (The harm is caused only by the first temporal component of the greater good; this is because the greater good is really the five living sufficiently long after avoiding death-by-trolley to justify the one other person's death. We should not act unless we reasonably expect the greater good, of which the first time period is a component, to occur. This is to be understood in all further discussion when we speak of the greater good causing or being caused by something.) The greater good in these cases involves eliminating a greater harm that consists in a greater number of people each suffering the same harm that, because of our actions, will now be inflicted onto someone else instead. Hence, "greater good" and "greater harm" should be understood in this way in this discussion.

Principle B. Means that have a noncausal relation to the greater good (e.g., means that in the context actually constitute the greater good) may permissibly

---

[12] Thomson (1976).   [13] Introduced in Kamm (1989).

cause lesser harm. (This assumes that the means are brought about in a way that violates no other principle.[14])

Examples to clarify Principle B: The movement of the trolley away from the five, which is the means of saving them, constitutes their being saved given that the trolley is the only threat they face. The movement of the trolley and the saving of the people are like two sides of one coin: the one side does not cause the other. Another way to say this is that the movement of the trolley away from the five has their being saved as its noncausal flip side. Note that the movement of the trolley away is different from what is *done* to move the trolley away (e.g., flipping a switch) which has a mere causal relation to the five being saved by causing the trolley to move away.

The redirected movement of the trolley involves the trolley becoming a direct threat to the one person it kills. By "direct" I mean that it, not something in the environment independent of the redirected trolley, kills the person. (By contrast, in the Germ Case discussed in Footnote 10, germs independently in the environment kill someone after they are moved by the released gas that saves five other people. The gas indirectly causes the death.[15] Using the gas in this case seems permissible.)

Consider how turning the trolley in both the Bystander and Driver Cases compares with what I call the Crosspoint Case in which someone must choose between directing a trolley to five people or toward one. In the Crosspoint Case the means that has a noncausal relation to the five not being threatened (i.e., the trolley turning toward the other track) constitutes the greater good. This is the same as in the Bystander and Driver Cases where the means that has a noncausal relation to the five not being threatened (i.e., the trolley moving away) constitutes the greater good. But in the Crosspoint Case someone faces a choice between doing an act that will kill five or kill one. In the Driver Case, the choice is between doing an act that will kill one or refraining to act and killing five by the driver not redirecting the trolley that he started toward the five. In the Bystander Case, the choice is between doing an act that kills one or letting five people die. Suppose it is permissible in all these cases to do what kills one person (though it may be obligatory only in Driver and Crosspoint). This would show that some differences in how the five would come to die are less important than that (i) means that constitute (rather than cause) the five's

---

[14] Henceforth, I will not repeat this condition when discussing each principle.

[15] As I use "independently" in the environment it is not purely a matter of how many distinct links there are in a causal chain. Suppose A sets up all the elements in a "Rube Goldberg" device for killing B. The presence of the elements in the chain is not independent of what A does.

surviving (i.e., the trolley turning away) eventually cause the one person's death and (ii) this one person's being threatened constitutes the five not being threatened given that he cannot escape the trolley.[16]

Notice that in the Crosspoint Case there would be reason to turn the trolley toward killing one person even when doing so would save only two other people. I suspect this would also be true in the Driver and Bystander Cases had they involved the trolley about to kill two people rather than five. This would show that the permissibility of harming the one person in trolley cases is not a matter of the amount of harm avoided having gone beyond a threshold in "threshold deontology."[17] That theory implies that the right of a person not to be harmed in certain ways (e.g., toppled from the bridge) hold up to a threshold beyond which the number of those who could be saved is large enough to override the right.

Redirecting the trolley that threatens the five can also be contrasted with the following Second Trolley Case: If we redirect a second trolley that threatens no one, it will push away the trolley headed to the five. However, on its way the second trolley directly kills someone else. Here the trolley that directly kills someone else has a mere causal relation to the greater good since it causes the trolley threatening the five to move away. It is this latter trolley's moving away that constitutes (and so has a noncausal relation to) the five being saved. Redirecting the second trolley seems impermissible (for reasons to be given below).

In the Lazy Susan Case, the means of saving the five is the Lazy Susan turning; those five being away from the trolley is merely an aspect of the Lazy Susan turning, not something it causes. Their being away from the trolley constitutes the greater good of their being saved. The turning swivel table indirectly kills one other person when it creates a new threat by moving nearby rocks which then kill him. In a different version of the case, the Lazy Susan would itself be a new threat that directly kills a bystander by banging

---

[16] Suppose the choice in all three cases was between one person and one other person rather than between one and five. Then there may well be a moral distinction between the Crosspoint Case where an act of killing must be done either way and this revised version of the Bystander Case where not killing one may take precedence over not letting one die. Even in this revised version of the Driver Case not killing one person by redirecting the trolley might take precedence over the driver not stopping the trolley he started from heading to another person. Those who conceive of the original Driver Case as involving a choice between killing one or killing five have not, I believe, compared it with the original Crosspoint Case which has more claim to involving a choice between killing one or killing five.

[17] I have made this point elsewhere, arguing that it is how the killing comes to pass that is morally crucial (Kamm 1996).

into him. Suppose the Lazy Susan moved one other person (seated on the table opposite the five) into the trolley that threatened the five. Then it would move the one person into a preexisting threat that kills him. Presenting these new and preexisting threats to the single person is permissible because they are caused by a means to saving the five (the Lazy Susan turning) that has as its aspect (and so has a noncausal relation to) the greater good of the five being saved.[18] When means that have a noncausal relation to the greater good cause a death, it is almost as if the greater good itself (as described by Principle A) caused the death of the other person.

In these cases illustrating Principles A and B, the lesser harm seems causally downstream from the greater good or means that constitute it.[19] But suppose the Lazy Susan turning to get the five away from the trolley also pushes one other person seated on the other side of the Lazy Susan into the trolley. Is the lesser harm then an aspect of the same means that also has greater good as an aspect? If so, then to be permissible lesser harm needn't be causally downstream from the greater good or means that have a noncausal relation to the greater good. That might be one reason why the view of NC being presented here is only "downstreamish." However, this view could still require that a harm not already justified by what produces it not have an upstream causal role in producing a greater good. A harm that is already justified may permissibly have a role in producing goods that are greater or lesser than it is. For example, suppose turning the trolley away from the five justified the death of one other person it hit. Then there would be no moral problem if his death had the direct effect of preventing someone else's leg from being broken even though this is a lesser good than the harm that caused it which could not itself justify the death of the one other person.

Principle C. What could become the greater good or means that constitute it may permissibly cause a lesser harm that stops threats that would interfere with what caused the harm becoming the greater good. This is so when such threats arise from what could become the greater good itself or what produces it. (A particular instance of this is when what I call a "structural equivalent" of the greater good [or means that constitute a structural equivalent of the greater good] may permissibly cause lesser harm that causally sustains that structural equivalent so that it becomes the greater good.)

---

[18] For ease of presentation, henceforth I will include cases in which the means have the greater good as its aspect under the rubric of cases in which the means constitute the greater good.

[19] I believe Jonathan Bennett was the first to describe NC as a "downstream" theory (Bennett 1980). I try to distinguish between downstream and downstreamish views below.

Examples to clarify Principle C: In the Loop Case,[20] the trolley turning away from the five will loop back to hit them unless it hits the one person on the other track. His being hit is causally required and sufficient to stop the trolley from looping back and the hit kills him. In this case, the greater good of the five surviving or means that constitute it cannot be the cause of the one's death since it is the one's being hit that is needed to cause the survival of the five for a significant enough period of time to justify killing another person. How can turning in the Loop Case be permissible on my view of NC that involves the DPP?

What causes the one person's being hit and killed is not a mere causal means to the greater good (like the bomb in the Bomb Case or the second trolley in the Second Trolley Case). What causes his death is the moving away of the trolley as it faced the five when we first had to act if they were to survive. Furthermore, it is the initial moving away of the trolley from the five that also causes the new threat of the looping back of the trolley. This means that when we abstract from the threat to them of the looping trolley, the trolley turning away is a means that constitutes what I call the "structural equivalent of the greater good": It constitutes what would be the greater good were it not for the threat of the trolley looping created by turning the trolley. The trolley hitting the one person causally sustains the structural equivalent of the greater good (i.e., what exists when we turn the trolley away abstracting from the new threat of the looping trolley). It does this by defeating a potential defeater (the looping trolley) of the structural equivalent becoming the greater good (i.e., the five saved for long enough to justify the harm to the one person). This allows the structural equivalent of the greater good to become the greater good itself.

However, recall that the downstreamish theory of NC holds that harms are not justified by what they cause but by what causes them and only already justified harms may play a causal role in producing goods. If this theory is correct, then turning the trolley in the Loop Case can be permissible only because the harm that the redirected trolley causes is already sufficiently justified by what causes it. This is required for it to be permitted to play its causal role in sustaining the structural equivalent. How this is possible must be due to there being a "justificatory loop" as well as a physical loop. A condition on permissibly causing the harm to the one person is that what causes the harm (the trolley being away from the five) would justify the harm if the five are expected to continue to survive. An effect of the trolley turning is to bring about the five's continued survival by causing a harm that eliminates the looping trolley threat also caused by the trolley turning. This makes what causes the harm (namely, the trolley turning away from the five that constitutes the structural equivalent) capable of justifying that harm.[21]

Even if the harm itself did not defeat the defeater caused by moving the trolley away initially, what causes the harm could justify it. Consider a Loop Case variant in which the turning trolley kills the one other person as a mere side effect. Afterward the trolley would still loop back to the five unless it is stopped by a large rock (independently in the environment) after the person is killed. Is this also a case in which the structural equivalent of the greater good could justify the harm it causes given that the structural equivalent would be sustained by the rock only after the trolley kills the one person? Suppose it is. Then if lesser harm can here be justified when it is caused by only the structural equivalent of the greater good, it should be similarly justified in the original Loop Case. Thus, the lesser harm (in the original version of the Loop Case) could permissibly cause the structural equivalent to be sustained and become the greater good.[22]

Further, suppose that in yet another variant of the Loop Case the trolley turning originally would not kill the one person but only break his leg. It is the additional pressure on his body of stopping the trolley from looping that foreseeably would cause his death. In this case, lethal harm comes to him only because he stops the trolley from looping. I do not think this makes it impermissible to turn the trolley. To see this, consider: if it is permissible (as we are assuming it is) to turn the trolley in one of the original trolley cases when the trolley itself kills the one person, then it is permissible for a further effect of the trolley turning to kill him instead. (This would be so, for example, if the redirected trolley not only broke his leg but it also caused an electrical discharge that killed the person.) Now suppose turning in the Loop Case is permissible even if the redirected trolley kills the person when it first hits him. Then turning should also be permissible when the trolley at first only breaks

---

[21] It must be true that the five are expected to continue to survive to make it permissible to do what kills the one person (i.e., turn the trolley in the first place). Hence, it is not sufficient to say about the Loop Case (i) that it is permissible to turn the trolley despite the turning trolley killing the person (as shown by the original trolley cases) and then point out (ii) that no further harm comes to him if his dead body stops the trolley from looping. This is because in the original trolley case the five are saved with the expectation of continued survival once the trolley turns away but without the one person being hit. That will not be so in the Loop Case. Below I will also consider a case in which further harm does come to the one person in stopping the trolley from looping.

[22] However, we will consider another principle (D) that may also account for this case.

his leg but a further effect of its turning is that it starts to loop and this puts pressure on the person that both stops the looping and kills him.[23]

In evaluating this explanation of why the harm in the Loop Case is sufficiently justified by what causes it, consider how it draws a moral distinction between the Loop Case and the Tractor Case.[24] In the Tractor Case, the five are threatened not only by a trolley but by a deadly tractor. If the trolley turns away, it will move one other person in front of the tractor thus stopping it from killing the five. The tractor will kill that one person if he has not already been killed by the trolley. The structural equivalent of the greater good does not already exist when we turn the trolley away because abstracting from any effects of our turning the trolley, a deadly threat (the tractor) is still headed to the five and that state of affairs does not have the structure of the greater good.

This other threat to the five exists independently of anything we do to get rid of the trolley threat and its elimination causally requires the single person to be hit. In the Loop Case, getting the initial threat facing the five away from them does not causally require the hit on the other person. Rather eliminating this initial threat on the five results in the threat of the trolley looping, a type of threat whose elimination requires another effect of the turning trolley, namely the one person's being hit.[25] The Loop and Tractor Cases differ even though we foresee in both that someone's being hit must play a causal role in bringing about the greater good. What seems significant is whether the threat to the five that can only be eliminated by the hit exists independently of turning the trolley and what this implies.

However, another version of the Tractor Case challenges the view presented so far that focuses on whether turning the trolley results in a structural equivalent of the greater good. Suppose that flipping a switch is a necessary causal means to moving the trolley away from the five but doing this immediately starts up a tractor that threatens the five before the trolley starts moving away from them. The trolley's moving away hits the one person; this moves him in front of the tractor, saving the five from that second threat.

---

[23] The DPP does not base permissibility on an agent's state of mind. A state-of-mind theory that might be offered to explain the Loop Case is what I call the Doctrine of Triple Effect (DTE). For more on this see my "The Doctrine of Triple Effect and Why a Rational Agent Need not Intend the Means to his End" (Kamm 2007).

[24] The DTE need not distinguish morally between Loop and Tractor.

[25] In the original Loop Case by the time the person stops the looping he will already have been killed by the redirected trolley. Hence, no further harm comes to him in blocking the looping trolley. However, I have already suggested that this is neither sufficient nor necessary to justify turning in the Loop Case.

In this case, if we abstract from further effects of the trolley moving away, we don't have the structural equivalent of the greater good any more than we have in the original Tractor Case. This is because the tractor threat to the five is not caused by the trolley moving away but by what causes the trolley to move away. Yet intuitively it seems as permissible to turn the trolley in this second Tractor Case as in the Loop Case and for the same reason.

This suggests that while a focus on a structural equivalent is sometimes sufficient to justify turning the trolley, it isn't necessary and so doesn't get to the heart of the matter. The remaining difference between the two Tractor Cases is that only in the second is the tractor threat caused by what we do to turn the trolley from the five. So a potential defeater of saving the five (the tractor coming at them) is caused by trying to save the five. (In the second Tractor Case saving the five from the initial threat of the trolley also causes the lesser harm that defeats the defeater of the five's sufficiently long survival.) The existence of the additional threat is not independent of what we do to stop the first threat and the hit of the one person that defuses the additional threat is also caused by what stops the initial threat of the trolley.

In sum, a harm justified by what causes it in an otherwise threat-free environment (as the harm to the one is justified by the trolley turning away from the five in the original Trolley Case) does not become unjustified if the cause of the harm gives rise to new threats to the five that the harm is needed to defeat. By contrast, suppose it is impermissible to turn the trolley in the first Tractor Case. Then a harm that would be justified by what causes it in an otherwise threat-free environment could become unjustified if another threat to the five exists independently and the harm caused by removing the trolley threat to the five is needed to defeat that other threat.

This pattern of justification may be related to the fact that in the first Tractor Case, the five are actually better off by being exposed to the trolley threat than they would have been without it. This is because without the removal of the trolley and the harm to the one to which it leads, the five would have been killed by the tractor. By contrast, in the second Tractor Case, the five are no better off by being exposed to the trolley threat and the harm to which the trolley's removal leads than if these had never occurred. This is because without having to remove the trolley, they wouldn't face a tractor threat whose being stopped requires the one to be harmed. They are no better off than they would have been if no threats that needed to be eliminated had arisen.

One way to sum up what has been said about all these cases is Principle C: What could become the greater good or means that constitute it may permissibly cause lesser harm that stops threats to its cause from becoming the greater good. This is so when such threats arise from what could become the greater good itself or what produces it (e.g., flipping a switch to turn the trolley). (A particular instance of this is when what I call a "structural equivalent" of the greater good (or means that constitute a structural equivalent of the greater good) may permissibly cause lesser harm that causally sustains that structural equivalent so that it becomes the greater good.)

When Principle C is satisfied, a harm is initially sufficiently justified to have a causal role in sustaining a structural equivalent, or more generally helping what causes the harm to become the greater good itself. Because of this, NC would not require that the lesser harm be causally downstream from the fully accomplished greater good. This is another reason to say that NC is a downstreamish rather than a downstream theory.

Principle D. A component of a greater good may even directly cause side-effect harm that the component alone cannot justify if innocent means (including that component of the greater good or some otherwise already sufficiently justified harm) produces the rest of the greater good and that greater good can justify the side-effect harm.

Example to clarify Principle D: Suppose we could move a trolley headed to kill five people only enough to save one of them from being hit by it, yet as it swerves to avoid him the trolley kills two others not previously threatened. The good of saving one person does not justify this greater harm. However, suppose we know that once he is saved, the one person will move the trolley completely away from the remaining four so that they will survive unharmed, but the two others will still have been killed. Intuitively, the five being saved in this way could justify the bad side effect of the two others being killed. By contrast, the trolley should not be moved away from the one person when it will kill two if those very deaths are needed to cause the trolley to move further away from the remaining four. This is because the continued survival of the one person saved could not even initially sufficiently justify the two deaths. Yet the possibility of such justification is needed for the deaths to play a permissible causal role in bringing about the greater good (according to Principle C).

In discussing Principle C, we considered a variant of the Loop Case in which the death of the one person is a mere side effect that occurs before a rock stops the looping trolley. Suppose what results from the trolley being turned from its initial hit on the five should be conceived as a particular component of the greater good rather than a structural equivalent of it. Then the death that does not play a causal role in producing the rest of the greater good could be justified by Principle D without relying on Principle C. But then that case could not be used (as we used it) to justify turning the trolley in the original Loop Case where hitting the one person has a causal role in stopping the looping trolley.

Principle E. A mere causal means to producing a greater good – which is not a component of it but causally upstream from it – may not directly produce a lesser harm nor may a lesser harm that is not caused by what justifies it be a causal means to producing a greater good. However, mere causal means to producing a greater good may permissibly produce lesser harm indirectly by affecting something that is in the environment independently of what we do.

Examples to clarify Principle E: In the Bomb Case, a bomb may not be set to redirect the trolley from five if the bomb would also kill a bystander. Similarly, a gas may not be used to save five people in the Gas Case when it also kills a bystander, and the second trolley in the Second Trolley Case may not be redirected when it will kill the one person. Principle E also specifically rules out as-yet unjustified harm itself being a mere causal means to the greater good. (This rules out toppling the man from the bridge to stop the trolley.)

The greater good that these mere causal means produce cannot justify the lesser harm they either constitute or directly cause. Hence, there is a more stringent requirement on mere causal means to the greater good causing harm than on components of a greater good causing harm (as discussed in Principle D). The components may sometimes permissibly directly cause side-effect harm when the greater good of which they are components can justify what the components alone cannot.

It is consistent with Principle E that a gas that itself is not lethal to anyone may be used when necessary to save the five even if this moves germs already in the environment but heretofore safely closeted so that they then kill one other person (in the Germ Case). Similarly, a bomb may be used to move the trolley away from the five if it will foreseeably move rocks independently in the environment that fall on and kill someone.

How should we treat the following Worse Than Dead Case? The five toward whom the trolley is headed will shortly die of organ failure unless they receive organ transplants. We can acquire these by completely innocent means but first we must move the trolley away from them and this will kill another person as a mere side effect. Additionally, the short time period between the trolley being away and when the five receive transplants would be worse than death for them due to rays emitted from the redirected trolley.

If it is otherwise permissible to turn the trolley, it is clearly permissible to do so in the Worse Than Dead Case since it hitting the five would prevent their surviving by the transplants. But since the trolley moving away constitutes the five being worse off (before they become better off) how can we say that its turning away is the first part of the greater good rather than a mere means to it? If the trolley moving away were a mere means to the greater good, it shouldn't be allowed to directly harm the one person according to Principle E.

In this case, the trolley threat moving away is not a mere means to the greater good. It is a means that constitutes the five being alive for a short time which is a temporal part of the greater good of their long-term survival even if during the short time they are worse off than dead.[26] Its badness will be compensated by their eventual survival at a level sufficiently above worse-than-dead.

Principle F. Modality enters into all these principles about permissible harm. This is because it only has to be *possible* for the principles to be satisfied given our actions even if sometimes, given our actions, permissible routes to an outcome are preempted by routes that would ordinarily be impermissible.

Examples to clarify Principle F: Consider Thomson's case of bombing a munitions factory to end a war when this would cause permissible side-effect deaths and fear.[27] Suppose we know that the role of destroying munitions to end a war will be preempted by people surrendering out of fear of the side-effect deaths. As Thomson notes, bombing the factory does not become impermissible (though causing death and fear as a means to end the war would be) just because fear of side-effect deaths is what actually causes the war to end. This is because (it is assumed) our act of bombing the munitions could have ended the war without the bad side effects occurring; they were not causally necessary.

Now consider a trolley case illustrating Principle F. Suppose using the only device that can turn a trolley away from five people causes vibrations. The vibrations foreseeably will cause a boulder to loosen, which will push someone into the path of the trolley and his being hit will stop the trolley before our device can turn it away. Using the device does not become impermissible just because it is the person's being hit by the trolley that will actually stop it from killing the five. This is because (a) using the device to turn the trolley would have saved the five even if the device hadn't loosened the boulder that pushed

---

[26] A temporal part of the greater good should be distinguished from a component of the greater good (e.g., one of the five being saved).

[27] Thomson (1991). Whether, when, and why bombs having such direct side-effect harm in war is permissible is an important question since it seems to conflict with Principle E. It may have to do with the people harmed having to bear risks as citizens at war (see Kamm 2012).

the person into the trolley and (b) according to Principle E it is permissible to use the device even if it affects something independently in the environment that then causes harm to a person (here by pushing him into the trolley). This is consistent with its being impermissible to use the device when it physically could not be a means to turn the trolley but only be a means of loosening the boulder so that it pushes someone into the trolley to stop it.[28]

4.5

4.5.1

I believe the DPP captures and synthesizes the principles in Section 4. Principles A and B say that the greater good and means that constitute it can justify lesser harm they produce. Principle E says that harm is not justified alone by the greater good it is causally necessary to produce. Suppose we should morally distinguish between (a) producing a greater good and causally sustaining a structural equivalent of it so that it becomes a greater good, and between (b) defeating threats that arise from attempting to produce a greater good and defeating threats that arise independently of that. Then the DPP is consistent with Principle C that allows harms produced in certain ways to help cause the greater goods that justify those harms. Principle D says that side-effect harms directly caused by a component of (by contrast to a mere means to) a greater good may be justified by the good of which the component is a part. However, such harms should not play a causal role in producing that greater good and until justified should not have a role in producing other goods.

4.5.2

What morally significant ideas about persons and their relations to each other underlie or supervene on the DPP? One suggestion is that sometimes harm to fewer people may permissibly *substitute* for harm to a greater number of other people. In particular, people may be substituted for each other when harm not coming to some people is what causes the harm to fewer other people.

By contrast, causing harm would be impermissible when the relation created between people would not be *substitution* but *subordination*. Subordination is clearest when the death of someone is brought about (in a way that doesn't involve permissible substitution) to be the necessary causal

---

[28] The DPP was presented in Section 4.2 to capture modality.

means to fewer deaths of others (as might occur in a version of the Fat Man Case). How does subordination occur when mere causal means to the greater good have only the direct side effect of killing someone else (as in the Bomb Case)? Suppose we must send a destructive threat either to one person or to a tool (Tool Case). Ordinarily we would send it to the tool. But what if the tool is a required causal means to save five lives? Though the tool is instrumentally important, we should still destroy it rather than kill the one person. While killing the person would not be a causal means to saving the five, he would be subordinated to them if the importance of the tool for saving their lives implied that we should kill him rather than destroy the tool. Something similar happens if we would use a tool to save five lives though as a direct side effect it will kill someone (as in the Bomb Case).[29]

4.5.3

The Tool Case also bears on how killing some to save others in accord with the DPP relates to the NC view that not killing is a more stringent duty than not letting die. In discussing Principle B, we argued that it was as permissible for the bystander who would otherwise only let the five die to turn the trolley as for the driver who would otherwise kill the five. But now suppose a trolley will kill eight people. A bystander can save them either by (1) redirecting the trolley so that it kills one other person or (2) redirecting the trolley toward a tool that he alone could (and would) use to save five other people from a different deadly threat to which he is also a bystander. Intuitively, it may seem that rather than kill the one person, the bystander should save the eight by doing what will lead to his letting the five die (i.e., destroying the tool). (I call this the Saving-by-Letting-Die Case.[30])

This is so even though turning the trolley from eight to one satisfies the DPP as much as turning from five to one in the Bystander Case. Furthermore, suppose the driver of the trolley headed to the eight is the one who could use the tool to save five people. It may seem that he too should turn the trolley to the tool, even if for him it would be a choice between killing eight or killing

---

[29] What if we had to choose between saving the tool or the person? Subordination may only occur when the person's right not to be harmed rather than a duty to save him is overridden to save the tool that can help others. Indirect harms of mere means such as the tool are dealt with differently because we are assuming such harms come about when what we introduce (e.g., our means) has an effect on things independently in the environment. However, if a greater good is not at stake, the difference between a means directly versus indirectly harming may not be morally relevant in the same way.

[30] I introduced it in *The Trolley Problem Mysteries* (Kamm 2016).

one. (We could call this the Not-Killing-By-Letting-Die Case as it involves the driver.) These judgments would imply that even if satisfying the DPP were necessary to justify killing innocent nonthreatening people, it is not sufficient for doing so.

Could a moral direction to let five die rather than kill one in the Saving-by-Letting-Die Case be consistent with the permissibility of killing one rather than letting five die in the Bystander Case? These conclusions seem consistent but showing why is a new puzzle related to the Trolley Problem.

One proposal claims that all these cases are consistent if the five who would die from aid not being given in the Saving-by-Letting-Die Case either have no right or a weaker right to that aid than the five in the Bystander Case have not to be hit by the trolley, even if they do not have such a right against the bystander. For suppose that in different versions of the Bystander and the Driver Cases the trolley was headed toward disconnecting five people whom the driver had attached to his life support machine when he had no duty to do so. Since the five have no rights that would be violated if he disconnected the machine, even the driver should not turn the trolley away from terminating aid (a form of letting die) to those five and toward killing the one other person who has a right not to be killed.

According to this proposal, the crucial issue is whether the five made worse off by the trolley hitting them would have a right against that being done and whether that right is as stringent as the right of the one person not to be killed. In the standard Driver and Bystander Cases they have such a right. Then their right may be counted against the right of the one person who would be hit, and the DPP could be used to explain the permissibility of redirecting as a way of preventing the five from being killed.

Thomson argued that since there was no right of the five that the *bystander* would transgress in letting them die but there was a right had by the one not to be killed that the bystander would transgress, the bystander should not turn the trolley.[31] The current alternative analysis suggested by considering the Saving-by-Letting-Die Case suggests that what is crucial is not whether the bystander's letting die would violate the five's right, but whether those who could be saved by the Bystander have a right that would be violated in being hit by the trolley. The violation of the right is embedded within the scope of what would happen if the bystander were to let die. Hence, his letting five die *from a killing* could be morally different (i.e., not required) from his letting

---

[31] Thomson (2008).

five die *from a letting die* (required) when the alternative is his killing one other person with a right not to be killed.

Here are two separate objections to this proposal. First, suppose there were a naturally occurring threat (like germs) headed toward killing five people. The current proposal would rule out redirecting the threat toward one other person because redirecting would transgress the one person's right not to be killed yet not prevent any violation of the five's rights. (This assumes that germs cannot violate rights and no persons were involved in causing the threat.) If redirection were permissible in this case, the proposal we have been considering for consistency of the Bystander Case and the Saving-by-Letting-Die Case would be wrong.

Second, it might be that the five people in the Saving-By-Letting-Die Case are about to be killed by a second trolley whose conductor has lost control of it. Then if the bystander turns the trolley headed to the eight toward the one other person, this will also allow him to use the tool to save the five from having their rights violated. According to the proposal for consistency we have been considering, it should be permissible for the bystander to do this *for the same reason* it is permissible for the bystander to turn the trolley in the original Bystander Case. If one thinks this is not so, one will either have to (i) find a different proposal for the consistency of turning the trolley toward the one person in the Bystander Case and not turning it in the Saving-By-Letting-Die Case or (ii) find a different reason for the permissibility of turning the trolley toward the one person in the Saving-By-Letting-Die Case.

Here is a new proposal that may deal with the second objection: It is turning the trolley from the eight people that could result in killing the one person in the Saving-By-Letting-Die Case. But since there is another way to save the eight that does not require killing the one person (turning the trolley so it destroys the tool that would save the five), it must be shown that there is no need to use that alternative because aiding the five by not destroying the tool also makes killing the one permissible. To use the DPP to show that, in the same way we show that we may aid the five in the Bystander Case, we would have to show that saving the five is a greater good (or is constituted by means) that causes the lesser harm. But in the Saving-By-Letting-Die Case it is not saving the five from the trolley that would hit them that would kill the one person. It is turning the trolley from the eight that would do that. So it is not true that the greater good (or means that constitute it) that is to justify the harm to the one (saving the five) causes that harm. This difference between the Bystander Case and the Saving-By-Letting-Die Case might make it consistent to save the five by killing the one in the first case but not in the second.

However, suppose saving five people would justify turning a trolley from them to hit one other person were that possible (as in the Bystander Case). Then might it be argued that it is permissible to save a group of people (the five in the Saving-By-Letting-Die Case) by saving another group (the eight) in a way that conforms to the DPP so long as the number saved in each group is sufficiently greater than those harmed? This would allow us to reject the judgment about the impermissibility of killing the one in the Saving-By-Letting-Die-Case but it would also go beyond using the DPP to justify killing. It would provide a different reason for the permissibility of killing in the Saving-By-Letting-Die Case than is available for the permissibility of killing in the Bystander Case.

Even when not killing does not take priority over not letting die, efforts morally required of an agent not to kill may still be greater in general than those required not to let die. In that sense the duty not to kill is more stringent than not letting die. So the driver may be morally required to make greater efforts not to kill the five than the bystander is required to make to save them. However, doing what morally requires less effort from an agent (not letting die) sometimes permissibly takes priority over doing what morally requires more effort (not killing). (Similarly, we may be morally required to make more effort to meet a business deadline than to save a life yet do the latter rather than the former.)[32]

---

[32] Kamm (1985, 1996).

5   Non-consequentialist principles under conditions of uncertainty

A framework

Dana Kay Nelkin and Samuel C. Rickless

5.1 Introduction

In an early variation on a pair of classic Trolley cases (Foot 1967, 1984; Thomson 1986e), a runaway trolley is on course to kill five people tied to the tracks. In one scenario, a bystander can push a single large man onto the track which would stop the trolley, killing the man. In the other, a bystander can turn the trolley onto a sidetrack on which a single person is tied to the track, killing that person, but saving the five in the original path of the trolley. Many share the intuitions that it is impermissible to push the man into the path of the trolley and permissible to turn the trolley. What explains these intuitions? One hypothesis is that we are relying on the Doctrine of Double Effect (DDE), which states, roughly, that intending harm in pursuit of a good is harder to justify than merely foreseeing it. But there is another difference in the two scenarios that is also a good candidate for moral salience. In the scenario in which the bystander pushes the man into the path of the trolley, the bystander does harm to him; in the scenario in which the bystander turns the trolley, he allows or enables harm to come to him without actually *doing* harm (Foot 1984, 1985b; Rickless 1997). Thus, we could also appeal to the Principle of Doing and Allowing (DDA), which states, roughly, that doing harm in pursuit of a good is harder to justify than allowing it. It is possible that both principles are operative in the classic Trolley case. Fortunately, we can accept both. Other pairs of cases isolate one of the two differences.

For example, consider two scenarios involving bombing during a war:

Strategic Bomber: A pilot bombs an enemy factory in order to destroy its productive capacity. But in doing this he foresees that he will kill innocent civilians who live nearby.

Terror Bomber: A pilot deliberately kills (the same number of) innocent civilians in order to demoralize the enemy. (Quinn 1989b, 336)

In this case, many have the intuition that the bombing in Strategic Bomber is permissible while in Terror Bomber it is not. Or, more cautiously: It is more difficult to justify the bombing in the second case. Since in these scenarios we have two cases of doing harm, the DDA is inapplicable. But appeal to the DDE seems to explain our intuitions nicely.

To test the distinction on which the DDA rests, consider the two courses of action provided by the following case:

> Rescue: Roger is driving across a mountainous region to save five innocent people who are being slowly crushed to death by a large pneumatic press. If Roger reaches the press, he will be able to shut it off and the five will walk away unharmed. As Roger reaches a narrow mountain pass, he discovers that there is one innocent person trapped on the road ahead. (Rickless 2011, 67; see Foot 1984)

Roger has two options: he can stop the car, in which case he will allow five innocent people to be crushed to death; or he can continue driving, in which case he will crush one person to death in order to reach the five in time to save them. Intuitively, it seems permissible for Roger to stop the car and thereby allow harm, but impermissible for him to continue driving and thereby do harm (even if only to prevent greater harm).

All of these cases involve stipulations about the outcomes given certain actions (or inaction). But in real life, we are very often faced merely with some degree of risk of harm and some chance of doing good. For example, real-life cases are often more like a probabilistic version of the Trolley cases in which we are faced with, say, a .9 chance that the pushed man or the single person on the track will die.[1] Similarly, for the other cases. In this chapter, we explore whether there are plausible probabilistic versions of the DDE and the DDA, and more generally pursue the question of how probabilistic outcomes affect the application of moral principles like the DDE and DDA to particular cases. We will focus on the DDE for ease of exposition, but we believe similar lessons can be drawn concerning the DDA.

On a version of the DDE that we favor (Nelkin and Rickless 2014), and following Quinn (1989b), the key moral distinction is one between harmful direct agency, in which one intentionally involves another person in one's plan in a way that they are harmed, and harmful indirect agency, in which the other person is not a part of the plan at all:

---

[1] See Ryazanov et al. 2018 for experimental results that show that people tend to substitute their own prior judgments of (less than 1) probabilities even when presented with scenarios in which outcomes are stipulated.

Harmful Direct Agency: Agency in which harm comes to some victims, at least in part, from the agent's deliberately involving them in something in order to further his purpose precisely by way of their being so involved.[2]

Harmful Indirect Agency: Agency in which harm comes to some victims, but in which either nothing in that way is intended for the victims or what is so intended does not contribute to their harm. (Quinn 1989b, 343)

With this distinction in mind, we can state the principle:

(DDE-R) In cases in which harm must come to some in order to achieve a good (and is the least costly of possible harms necessary), the agent foresees the harm, and all other things are equal, a stronger case is needed to justify harmful direct agency than to justify equally harmful indirect agency.

The principle helps to explain and justify our intuitions in the Bomber cases, as well as the Trolley cases. This is because it is harder to justify intentionally involving someone in a plan in such a way that harm comes to them than to justify merely foreseeing harm in pursuit of some good. The principle as stated does not say that either form of agency is forbidden; simply that one is harder to justify than the other. But it opens the door to the idea that in some cases, perhaps the Bomber cases, it is not simply *harder* but *impossible* to justify terror bombing over strategic bombing. Similarly for the Trolley cases.

Further, it would seem to follow as a kind of corollary that given a forced choice between leading the person onto the track so that he will stop the trolley and thereby be killed, and turning the trolley onto a sidetrack on which one person is tied and will be killed in order to save the five, one ought to turn the trolley. Another way of putting the point is as follows: Keeping the extent of the harms and all else equal, harmful direct agency is disfavored relative to harmful indirect agency. A powerful explanation for this principle is the Kantian idea that there is something especially problematic about being used as a means without one's consent. It seems that one has a right against being used in this way, and that this is a morally salient consideration beyond the mere bad outcomes that are equally bad in this case.

---

[2] One reason for appeal to this sort of agency rather than agency in which the harm itself is aimed at is to avoid the so-called closeness problem. One might try to deny that there is intention to harm even in the Terror Bomber case, insofar as the bomber would be happy if the "victims" returned to life after the end of the war. Nevertheless, there is no denying that the bomber intentionally involved them in a way that harm came to them. See Nelkin and Rickless 2014 and 2015 for further discussion.

Now consider a probabilistic case: Suppose that we can choose between involving a person in our plans in such a way that we impose a 0.9 risk of harm on them in order to save two others and simply foreseeing that there will be a 0.9 risk of harm on them in order to save two others. Here, too, it seems that it is harder to justify imposing the 0.9 risk of harm as a means to our end than to merely foresee it as the result of one's pursuit of the end. To put it in a way that parallels the corollary above: Keeping the *degree of risk of harm* and all else equal, direct agency that results in risk is disfavored relative to indirect agency that results in risk.

Not only does this probabilistic version seem as plausible as the original, but it seems equally plausible for just the same reason, namely, the Kantian injunction not to use others as means without their consent in a way that brings them disadvantage. This is all to the good, because it appears that many real-life situations are ones in which outcomes are not certain, and where we face risk. Ideally, our principles will apply to and provide guidance for us in real-life scenarios. So far, so good.

But this leads to two sets of further questions, one about the relationship between harm and risk and one about what happens when we vary the risk of harm. First, it has been argued that pure risk is not itself a harm. Thus, we can ask whether, if this probabilistic version of the principle is correct and for similar reasons as the original, it presupposes that pure risk is itself a harm. If so, can the presupposition be defended? If not, can the Kantian injunction be modified in a plausible way?

Second, it is often the case that risks are *not* equal. It is possible, then, that there are other related principles that can help us with real-life cases where risks are not equal. For example, we can ask: Does it make a difference if one of our options is to lead a person onto the main track believing that there is only a *small to moderate chance* he will be killed or harmed (given that he is, say, heavily padded)? Does it become permissible – or even required – to lead someone, or perhaps even more than one person, onto the track, knowing that there is a chance, but not a certainty, that they will be killed or harmed rather than turning the trolley onto a track, which will result in the certain death of one person? More generally, how do we weigh varying probabilities of harm due to involvement in plans and probabilities of harm that are merely foreseen?

In the remainder of this chapter, we make a start in answering these questions. In Section 5.2, we set out our general account of the morality of risk, which has multiple components: We have both duties corresponding to others' rights against the imposition of risk of harm, as well as duties of beneficence that enjoin us not to impose risk of harm in many circumstances even if rights are not salient.[3] In Sections 5.3 and 5.4, we consider the first set of questions related to the relationship between risk and harm, and show how our theory can be developed in different ways depending on the answers. Then, in Section 5.5, we respond to a set of challenges to the idea that any sort of right not to have risk of harm imposed can sort cases properly when it comes to overall moral permissibility. We refer to these as *sorting challenges*. Here we argue that our particular way of understanding rights – with lessons learned from the debate about the DDE – can provide unique resources. Finally, in Section 5.6, we address the second set of questions about how to respond to cases in which risks are not equal.

Before turning to our account, we should clarify that we are presupposing the possibility of providing a defensible theory of objective risk. There are two varieties of risk: The subjective risk of A is the probability that a particular individual assigns to A, whereas the objective risk of A is the probability that A will occur regardless of anyone's beliefs about A's likelihood. Notoriously, it has been difficult for probability theorists to arrive at an acceptable account of objective risk (for details, see Hájek 2019). And yet, it seems difficult to deny that there is such a thing as objective risk, risk that is a fact about the world rather than a fact about one's beliefs about the world. This is what explains why casinos are generally profitable, and why it is more rational to drive with a seat belt than without one. In the sequel, we will assume that there is such a thing as objective risk, *the* objective risk of a particular (type of) event, even if there is as yet no convergence among probability theorists on the proper interpretation of risk. At the limit, we invite the reader to read the sequel as one very long conditional whose antecedent is the claim that there is such a thing as objective risk.

5.2 A first pass at a simple pluralistic answer: Rights and beneficence

Our proposal is to adopt a deontological moral framework in which rights have a prominent but nonexclusive role to play. On this picture, people have rights, including the right not to be harmed. But our duties outstrip respect for the rights of others. Sometimes we have duties to promote the good, and sometimes we have very particular duties of assistance even when no one has

---

[3] There are also principles concerning the distribution of risk, and while we discuss these briefly, we leave a fuller discussion for a different occasion.

a right to it. We will not defend this picture here, but instead will ask how much we can explain of the morality of risk within it.

At the same time, if the picture is able to accommodate our intuitions about the morality of risk, this provides a kind of support for the picture itself. This is significant because it might seem at first that alternative pictures can easily handle questions about permissibility and risk. For example, on a consequentialist picture, according to which *all* moral considerations are comparisons of consequences of courses of action, it seems that any question of permissibility will be settled by which course of action has the highest expected value. Questions concerning risk are simply absorbed into the calculation of expected value.[4] Alternatively, on a contractualist picture, questions concerning the permissibility of imposing risk will be settled by whether imposing said risk accords with principles that cannot be reasonably rejected.[5] While these apparently simple answers obscure complications beneath the surface, our aim here will not be to criticize these directly, but rather to point to the most promising way of developing the deontological picture in light of the ubiquity of questions concerning risk.

Thus, in what follows, we assume that people have rights, including the right not to be harmed, and that the tricky task for thinking about risk in connection with rights is to defend the idea that we have a right against what is sometimes called "pure" risk, that is, risk in which the risked harm does not come to pass. On the one hand, that we have such rights seems very intuitive. For example, it seems obviously wrong to play Russian Roulette on one's flatmates while they are asleep; and even if all goes well and no bullet is fired, it seems that one's flatmates have a legitimate complaint, and it is plausible that this would be based on a stringent right not to be so treated. As described above, when it comes to a right not to be used as a means without one's consent, it seems just as plausible that the right is in play whether harm is certain to come to one as a result, or merely whether harm is very likely to come to one as a result. In other words, it seems we have rights not just that others not harm us but that they not impose risks of harm either. Despite its intuitive pull, there have been a number of serious challenges to this thought, and the account will require elaboration to meet them.

We also make room for duties not to impose risk that are not based on rights that others have against us. Just as we have duties of beneficence, including perfect ones that require particular action (such as in the case of

---

[4] See, e.g., Railton 1985, Hurd 1996, and Fried 2012b.
[5] See, e.g., Scanlon 1998, Kumar 2015, and Oberdiek 2017.

saving a drowning person) or omission (such as in the case of not holding a previous transgression against a good friend who has sincerely resolved not to do it again), we sometimes also have duties not to impose risks even when there is no right of others that we are called to respect. To take a simple case, our neighbors might have explicitly waived their right against our setting off fireworks very close to their house, but we could still have a duty not to impose on them the kind of risk that doing so would represent.

If one is already sympathetic to the kind of deontological account in the background here, this might all seem very easy to accept. However, as we explain below, things are not so simple, and elaboration will be needed as we respond to challenges.

5.3 Risk, harm, and compensation

The first set of questions poses a challenge to the very simple account we have given thus far. The account seems to presuppose that when a person A imposes a risk of harm on another B, A has thereby caused harm to B. Call this the Risk=Harm thesis. We believe that there is much support for this thesis, but at the same time recognize that there are powerful challenges to it.

There is a great deal at stake in this debate. If the thesis is true, then we can adopt an already well-established framework of beneficence, rights, and the distribution of harms and apply it to the particular wrong of risking. But if being put at risk is not itself a harm, we are left without an explanation of several things. First, how do we have what looks like a duty of beneficence not to impose risk on others? Beneficence seems to presuppose that we are avoiding harm, and promoting people's good. Further, it is not clear why we would have a duty not to use people as means to our ends by imposing *pure* risk on them. As stated earlier, the Kantian injunction specifies that what is prohibited is using people in such a way that *harm* comes to them. And this qualification is supported by the fact that there seems nothing wrong with, say, standing in someone's shadow to find some relief from the sun at a bus stop. Not every case of using someone as a means is problematic, as the shadow case makes clear, and a natural way of constraining the problematic subset is by the fact that using someone as a means where harm comes to them is an essential requirement for being in the disfavored category.

In fact, we take it that the kind of parsimony we achieve by categorizing the imposition of risk as a harm is itself an argument for doing so. It seems that the entitlement we have to demand that others not treat us as a means in imposing a serious risk of harm on us is the same kind of entitlement to demand that others not harm us as a means to some further good. Dovetailing with this kind of reason is the fact that it is intuitively appealing to treat particular instances of risk imposition as harms. As both Thomson 1986b and Finkelstein 2003 point out, we very often prefer actual material harm to the risk of a greater harm. For example, we would prefer to suffer an awful one-day headache to a game of Russian Roulette where we are the target, even in a gun with thirty-six chambers instead of six.[6] It seems very natural in cases like this to trade off a risk of harm with a harm, and that by itself suggests a common currency at the least. A natural explanation for our preference in this kind of case is that we take the imposition of a serious risk to be a kind of harm in itself.

Despite these strong reasons in favor of the Risk=Harm thesis, it is important to consider objections and alternatives. In this section, we consider one such argument that we call "the No Compensation Argument," reconstructed from Thomson (1986d, 165) (see also Hurd (1996, 262)), and in Section 5.4, we consider a second, which we call "the Classification of Harm Argument."

Before laying out the No Compensation Argument in detail, it is important to note a distinction that Thomson makes between "market" and "non-market" harms. Though she does not offer a definition or analysis of either, she offers illustrations of both. A market harm is caused, for example, when one person invents a machine that efficiently produces lace, thereby driving down the value of another person's hand-made lace business. This is a harm, but not one that we have a right against others not to suffer. In contrast, we have a right not to be killed. If risk of harm is itself a harm, it appears that it would be in the "non-market" category, and so be the sort of harm that we have the right not to suffer. So, just as we would have a right not to be killed, we would have a right not to be the target of a game of Russian Roulette with a single bullet in a six-chambered gun, without our knowledge. As Thomson suggests, there is a general principle connecting harms and rights supporting this point: If A causes B a (nonmarket) harm, then A infringes or violates a right of B's (Thomson 1986d, 164). But, if A infringes or violates a right of B's, then A owes damages to B (Thomson 1986d, 165). And yet, nothing is owed if the risked harm does not come to pass. After all, what would one pay damages for? There was no medical treatment needed and no pain or suffering. Thus, we reach a contradiction, and our assumption that risk imposition is itself a harm has led to it and should be rejected.

---

[6] Interestingly, both Thomson and Finkelstein consider an argument from symmetry: Chances of benefits are benefits; therefore risks of harms are harms. For example, many would select a lottery ticket over a plum (Thomson 1986d: 164). Both agree that chances of benefits are benefits. But they diverge on what follows from this. Finkelstein endorses the symmetry argument, while Thomson rejects symmetry on the grounds of the No Compensation Argument to be discussed shortly.

To spell out the No Compensation Argument in step-by-step form:

(i)   Assumption for *reductio*: for A to impose a risk of harm on B is for A to cause B a (nonmarket) harm.

(ii) If A causes B a (nonmarket) harm, then A infringes a right of B's.

(iii) If A infringes a right of B's, then A owes damages to B.

Therefore,

(iv) If A imposes a risk of harm on B, then A owes damages to B (from (i), (ii), and (iii)).

(v)   But the imposition of mere risk of harm does not lead to any owing of damages. (Intuition)

Contradiction; so the assumption for reductio should be rejected.

There is surely something right about the idea that appropriate responses to the causing of a death and to the imposition of a one-sixth chance of death differ in some ways. But we do not believe that the argument is sound. The argument could as easily be seen as a reductio of (ii), (iii), or (v), none of which is obvious. Let us start with (ii), which we believe can easily be shown to be false. For there are many harms that A may cause B without A infringing a right of B's, and these are not limited to what Thomson seems to think of as "market" harms. For example, if A tells B that A does not want to be friends with B, this might be very hurtful to B and constitute a kind of harm to B. But, at least in many circumstances, B does not have a right to A's friendship or to avoid that sort of harm. Or, to take a case of Thomson's, A's planting plastic geese in front of B's yard might cause B tremendous unpleasantness, presumably a harm, but B have no right that A not do it. Thomson (1986d, 164–165) bites the bullet here, and suggests that the geese-planting does not cause harm. But we believe that this is to depart considerably from not only an ordinary folk notion of harm, but also a philosophical analysis of harm that is often invoked as a kind of sharpening of the concept in related contexts, namely, the undermining of a person's legitimate interests (see Feinberg 1984, 34–38 and Finkelstein 2003, 971). Thus, we could simply deny (ii), reject the argument and move on, concluding that the Risk=Harm thesis is safe.[7]

---

[7] One might defend Thomson here in the following way: Her claim is most plausible when it is read as presupposing a use of "harm" as a term of art, and not as the – folk concept (or one of an overlapping set of folk concepts). And there are good arguments that what we really need here is not the (or a) folk concept, but instead the concept that makes true many simple moral claims, such as that we have a right not to be harmed, period (see Hanser 2019). As interesting as this methodological

But that would be too fast given our ultimate aims. For imposing a risk of harm seems like the *kind* of harm which we could have rights to avoid (as in the Russian Roulette case). If Thomson is right that (iii) and (v) are true, these premises would be enough to generate an argument that risk impositions are – at the least – not the sorts of harms against which we have rights. And this seems counterintuitive to us. Fortunately, neither of these premises is clearly true either. In the Russian Roulette case, it seems that *something* is owed even if no death results. We do not always require material harm for damages (consider payment for pain and suffering); and we do not find it implausible that some sort of restitution might be owed in compensation for having put someone's life at risk. Thus, (v) could be false.[8] But even if (v) is true, the idea that the target of the Russian Roulette game has the very same *kind* of claim against the player suggests that there is a right being asserted. It isn't simply that the player ought not to play (as Thomson (1986d, 165) concludes); it is that the target is in a special position to demand that the player not play, by asserting a right. This seems to be the most fundamental feature of a right, even more clearly than its association with compensation, and certainly more clearly than its association with material compensation.

debate is, we believe it is possible to be ecumenical here. "Harm" might be taken to mean "whatever we have a right against"; alternatively, one might offer a more substantive account that purports to capture just what it is that we have a right against (or that which we have a stringent duty not to do, as does Hanser, for example). Our claim here, which we develop below in a different way, is that whatever the best way of understanding the notion, there is good reason to accept that risk of harm is itself a harm: Whatever sort of right against being harmed we have, we have the very same sort of right against the imposition of risk of harm. Having said that, we adopt for present purposes the characterization in the text as an undermining of legitimate interests, in part because it is often and naturally appealed to in discussions of risk.

[8] McCarthy (1997, 218) argues that (v) is false, and provides a formula for how much compensation is owed, namely, whatever would be owed for actual harm that is equivalent to the expected value provided by the risk of harm as a function of probability and magnitude of harm risked. For example, if X imposes a .1 risk of ten units of harm, then X owes compensation corresponding to one unit of actual harm. Interestingly, McCarthy does not commit to risk of harm itself being a harm, though he does sometimes speak of the target of risk as being thereby made "worse off." While we too see the appeal of rejecting (v), it is not clear to us that the formula McCarthy provides is correct. One challenge is that the formula appears to have some counterintuitive results, such as that admittedly small, but still real compensation is owed even for trivial risk impositions. McCarthy (1997, 221–225) attempts to sidestep these results, by appeal to a lottery system in which rather than directly paying people for the risks we impose, we give them a guarantee that we will pay for the harm if it comes to pass (in a kind of lottery system). While this is a clever suggestion, it remains the case that technically what is owed to those on whom we impose risk is the equivalent of the direct payment, and intuitions to the contrary must be confronted. We believe that the better approach has one or both of the following elements: (1) reject the formula, while acknowledging that something is owed, even if not always in material form; (2) restrict the scope of the right not to have risk imposed so that not every risk imposition is a rights infringement, if not a violation. We take up the second element on independent grounds in Section 5.5.

If that is true, then we can reject (iii), consistently with retaining a robust conception of rights and including a right against risk imposition. Thus, either (iii) or (v) must be false.

For this reason, we believe that considerations about compensation do not undermine the Risk=Harm thesis or the idea that risk imposition can be the kind of causing of harm against which we have rights. But the thesis faces a second challenge, and it is to this that we now turn.

5.4 What kind of harm is risk imposition?

The Classification of Harm Argument takes the form of a challenge to say what *kind* of harm risk is. In cases of pure risk, as we have seen, it is not material harm, nor is it psychological harm (though it might often be accompanied by such harm). Here, we briefly take up two alternative suggestions.

One conception of a person's interests (or, equivalently, their good) takes them to be exhausted by preference-satisfaction. And, as we noted earlier, people do not generally prefer to be at serious risk of harm, all else equal. So, one suggestion is that risk imposition is a causing of harm insofar as people prefer to avoid it. But just as preference-satisfaction theories of individuals' good face serious general challenges independent of discussions of risk, they face challenges when it comes to accounting for intuitions about cases of risk. For example, some risk-seeking people seem to be quite mistaken about what is in their interests. And some people for whom we judge that their being under a new risk is a harm might not have considered them. This undermines the idea that risk imposition is only a harm insofar as alternatives are preferred. While one might take Finkelstein 2003 to be endorsing a preference-satisfaction view (see, e.g., Perry (2007, 200) and Oberdiek (2017, 75–78)), we believe that the best argument concerning preference-satisfaction takes preferences to be *evidence* of interests. Very often we prefer what is in our best interests, and, where what we prefer is among a range of good options, satisfying our preferences can add to a good life. If we understand the role of preference-satisfaction in this way, we have not yet explained *why* risk undermines interests, but we have an explanation of what appears to be a great deal of rational behavior, and an evidentiary argument *that* risk of harm often undermines our interests.

Is there an alternative way to understand the nature of the harm that risk imposition causes? A natural thought is that the lesson of the failure of preference-based accounts points us toward an objective list account of well-being. In this spirit, Oberdiek 2017 argues that risk imposition causes a kind of harm that undermines a particular item on a perfectionist, objective list account of well-being. That item is autonomy, understood as requiring "plotting one's own life and having a range of acceptable options from which to do so" (Oberdiek 2017, 86).[9] As Oberdiek explains it, imposing risk impacts our normative lives "in virtue of narrowing the risked person's otherwise 'open future'. . . thereby narrowing the risked person's set of worthwhile opportunities" (Oberdiek 2017, 85).

The way that autonomy is undermined is understood through an analogy: laying a trap (Oberdiek 2017, 86). Laying a trap on a path can take away that path as an option, and certainly a safe one, even if one avoids that path. In this way, argues Oberdiek, one's options are narrowed, and one's autonomy is diminished, even if one wouldn't have gone down that unsafe path anyway. There is no material harm, but there is harm in the form of a diminishment of autonomy (Oberdiek 2017, 87). While it is true that undermining autonomy, as Oberdiek understands it here, is surely possible without material harm, the details of the analogy bear closer scrutiny. The best way we can understand it to work is that possible worlds correspond to paths. (This is borne out by Oberdiek's claim that it is the entailment of possibility, not probability, that is relevant in understanding why risk narrows options (Oberdiek 2017, 87).) If a person is put at risk, say, by the fact that an unexploded mine is buried under some leaves somewhere on her property, then in a possible world in which she walks on precisely that spot, she will be greatly and materially harmed. Insofar as that particular path is no longer a safe option, her safe options for where she walks are constricted as a result, whether or not she knows there is a bomb in her vicinity. The analogy seems to work well in this sort of case. But risk is not always imposed in this way. In a Trolley case, in which a person is tied to a track and faces a .1 risk of death, it is not clear that their autonomy has been constrained any further than it already is. In a Russian Roulette case in which the target does not know that someone is playing on them and no bullet is fired, there appears to be no narrowing of the target's safe options, and hence no diminution of the target's autonomy. Or suppose Tonya has a higher chance of developing cancer as the result of chemical dumping by a nearby factory owner. Tonya's propensity for developing cancer is greater, but it is not clear what corresponds to a "path" she might have otherwise chosen to walk that would result in material harm. One way to proceed is to say that in the event that one has, say, a .3 higher propensity to develop cancer, then for

---

[9] Oberdiek (2017, 86) here follows Raz (1986, 398). Note that there are numerous other conceptions of autonomy (see Buss and Westlund 2018).

every hundred possible worlds accessible from the actual one, one suffers great material harm in thirty of them, thereby reducing the number of possible worlds that are safe. But it is not clear how this maps onto *options* in the context of a Raz-inspired notion of autonomy. Options would seem to include things like pursuing a career in medicine or in peace studies. It doesn't seem that these options, or others like them, are precluded if we think in terms of possible worlds. And in a world in which one does not get cancer and goes about life as one would have without the heightened risk, it is not clear what particular option has been precluded, or, intuitively, that one's autonomy has been undermined. Of course, there is a sense in which every option, including one's actual path through life, is less "safe" in the sense that there is a higher likelihood of any one of them not working out in so far as one's likelihood of getting cancer is increased. But it is not clear to us that thinking in terms of autonomy adds to the explanation of why it seems bad for one to have risk of harm imposed. Saying that all of one's choices are "less safe" appears to be merely a way of saying that one is at risk.

Another intriguing possibility is that the imposition of risk is not reducible to *another* sort of harm, but is instead simply a fundamental kind of harm. On this picture, alongside our bottom-line interests in autonomy, the exercise of rational capacities, relationships with others, and so on, is to not be put at risk of harm. Though we find this idea intriguing, we can see that it might not be satisfying, at least not without being able to say more about why it should have this status.

Where does this leave us? While we are still left with the challenge of explaining *why* pure risk imposition is the causing of a harm, we do not believe that this provides good reason to reject the Risk=Harm thesis. For, along the way of considering candidate explanations, we have been able to add to the considerable support for the thesis. The *evidentiary* argument from preferences is itself a significant reason in support of the thesis, and when we add that to the intuitiveness of risk as something that it is good for us to avoid, and to the parsimony and elegance that attaches to the theory that takes risk imposition to be a causing of harm, we have strong reason overall to accept the Risk=Harm thesis.

We realize, however, that the remaining challenge to classify the harm might result in resistance to acceptance of the thesis. And here we note that there are two alternatives that, while requiring modification of the simple pluralistic account we put forward earlier, preserve much of its spirit as well as its verdicts.

The first is to modify the claims of the account in a way that depends not on the Risk=Harm thesis, but on a thesis that we call the Risk *Like* Harm thesis. On this account, risk imposition plays a very similar role to the causing of harm. For example, we have duties that are perfectly parallel to our duties of beneficence, such as duties not to put people at risk of harm where easily avoidable. In general, there is a disjunctive approach to each of rights, beneficence, and distributive justice. We have rights not to be harmed, but also not to be risked; we have duties of (quasi-)beneficence not to impose risk even where there are no rights-bearers in a position to make claims on us; and there are principles of distribution of risk that parallel those of the distribution of burdens and benefits. This alternative avoids the Classification Challenge, but only at the expense of introducing another unanswered question, namely, why should there be these two parallel kinds of duties? They seem closely related in a way that points toward a more explanatorily linked connection. The risk of harm seems bad precisely because of its connection to the harm risked.

The final alternative, then, is to flip the script. On this account, material harm is just a limit case of risk imposition.[10] Actual causation of material harm is simply pure risk imposition where the harm also comes to pass. There is something pleasing about the simplicity of this picture, but in the end, we find it not entirely satisfying. The problem is that the badness of being harmed materially is not, intuitively, exhausted by the badness of being subjected to risk. It is more plausible to us that we have rights against risk imposition, and the right against being harmed is a limit case of such rights.[11] But it is less plausible that there is no more to the badness of being harmed materially than to having been subjected to risk of harm.

In conclusion, we tentatively favor adopting the Risk=Harm thesis, but we believe that, on any of the three alternatives, something in the spirit of the simple pluralistic deontological account proposed can be made to work in a way that accounts for our intuitions.

5.5 Sorting challenges

There remains a set of challenges to the simple pluralistic account that share the core idea that accommodating risk in a non-consequentialist picture cannot be both extensionally adequate and principled. To see why, recall that

---

[10] Within the conception of culpability as a function of actus reus and mens rea, the counterpart of interpreting the actus reus of causation of material harm as a limit case of risk imposition is interpreting the mens rea of intention or knowledge as a limit case of recklessness (see Alexander and Ferzan 2009).

[11] McCarthy (1997, 224) takes this approach to rights, without addressing the Risk=Harm thesis.

we have appealed to a right not to be the object of risk imposition. But it seems counterintuitive that we have a right against *all* risk imposition. Thomson presents a series of cases that make this point. On the one hand, it does not seem impermissible to turn on our stoves, even if by doing so we impose a tiny risk of a house fire on our neighbors. But however small the risk, say, one in a billion, it seems impermissible to play a variant of Russian Roulette on our neighbors with the same odds of harm. Thomson concludes that there is no plausible way of constraining a right against risking to accommodate the permissibility of one and not the other, and so takes it that we must seek an alternative explanation altogether.

In a different way, Railton (1985) and McKerlie (1986) worry that rights against risk imposition won't work in cases where they should be expected to.[12] Here is a variation of a case that seems especially resistant to explanation in terms of rights:

> River: A farmer can dispose of a toxic substance by throwing it in the river or by recycling it in a way that would be safe but expensive. Each member of a large set of people, say one million, who live on the river would bear a small chance of death as a result of the toxic substance landing in their vicinity, say one in a million. And though it is likely that one person will die, it is possible that no one will. There is only a .9 probability that some person will die.[13]

It seems impermissible for the farmer to throw the substance in the river. Can we explain this within the simple account offered earlier?

While we do not have a complete account of how to sort every case, we hope here to say enough in answer to the challenges to show that the simple pluralistic account remains promising. Our first response is directed to those who already accept a fundamental role for rights in moral theory, by pointing out that both claims about rights against harm and about rights against risk imposition need qualification in one way or another, at least when it comes to most rights theories.[14] It can be permissible for others to do things that cause us harm without our consent, but also without violating or even infringing our rights (such as when our neighbors paint their house a color that makes us unhappy when we look out). Likewise, it is sometimes permissible for others to

---

[12] Presumably their conclusion is that we ought to turn to a consequentialist picture to accommodate such cases.

[13] This case is adapted from a scenario described by McKerlie (1986, 247–248).

[14] As we saw in footnote 7, one solution is to circumscribe harm in such a way that no further qualification of a "right not to be harmed" is necessary. But we take it that this is not to eliminate the work, but to relocate it.

impose a risk of harm without our consent, but also without violating or even infringing our rights (such as when they use stoves of the type Thomson imagines). Getting clear on exactly when we have a rights violation and when we do not is a serious challenge, but our first response is to point out that we are not obviously in a worse position than most theorists who recognize rights against harm. Still, one might respond by concluding that rights, rather than risk, are the ultimate problem. And, in any case, it would be good to be able to address what are presented as special challenges for accommodating risk. We aim to make a start here and sketch some directions for further work.

Assuming for the moment that imposing risk of harm is imposing harm of a sort, we can appeal to extant approaches for constraining the right in intuitively plausible and principled ways, and then apply them to the specific case of risk. A first strategy is to distinguish between violations of rights (which are impermissible) and infringements of rights (which are sometimes permissible, though they may lead to a moral "residue" that must be addressed by compensation) (Thomson (1986a, 40–41), Thomson (1986b, 54), Thomson 1986c, Thomson (1986d, 165), Thomson (1990, 84 and 93–96), and McCarthy (1997, 209)). This clearly helps support the existence of a right not to be harmed without the counterintuitive result that imposing any harm is impermissible.[15] While we believe that any adequate account ought to accept this distinction, there is an alternative way to proceed, and that is simply to treat any action opposed to a right as impermissible. In order to handle cases like Thomson's stove case and many more, then, such views must make the content of the right in question exactly as narrow as would match claims of impermissibility. Oberdiek (2017, 122–126) takes this maximally "specificationist" approach, which includes all of the circumstances that would make an action impermissible when expressing the content of the right. This specificationist approach faces a variety of challenges, as Oberdiek notices, including the fact that it appears to make the appeal to rights otiose. Why not simply speak of what is permissible or not? But one challenge in particular stands out, given the present discussion, and it is that the specificationist approach makes no room for moral residue. If there are no permissible rights infringements, then there is no residue when it comes to any permissible risk imposition. But this seems counterintuitive. Suppose that it is

---

[15] The distinction between right-infringement and right-violation makes room for the claim that rights are not absolute (or, at the least, that not all rights are absolute). This addresses objections, such as those raised by Hurd (1996, 264) and Hansson (2013, 34–37), which presuppose that rights, if they existed, would have to be absolute.

permissible to put ten people at a .01 risk of serious bodily harm to save one person from certain death. It nevertheless seems that there is some moral residue. Oberdiek recognizes the intuition, but rather than explain residue arising from the infringement of rights, he appeals to what he calls "value pluralism" (Oberdiek 2017, 118). Just as taking one job over another leaves one with a kind of negative residue related to the path not taken, similarly here we have a negative residue because people were subject to risk. There has been a loss of value – of autonomy on Oberdiek's own account – and this can explain the residue. While this suggestion is responsive to the challenge of accounting for moral residue, we believe that it does not rest on a full appreciation of the nature of that residue. It is not a mere loss of a certain kind of value for which we could feel a sense of regret; rather, it seems that those put at risk have a certain claim on us. It would be appropriate to apologize at the least and to owe an explanation, if not more. This suggests to us that it is a distinctive kind of residue, associated with rights infringements. For this reason among others, we believe that adopting the infringement/violation distinction has more explanatory value than the specificationist alternative.

But appealing to the distinction between violation and infringement does not answer all questions. For there is an important further choice point. One can be maximally inclusive and treat the right not to be harmed (or the right not have risk of harm imposed) as referring to any kind of harm (or risk of harm), and then be very capacious in the scope of when rights are permissibly infringed (see McCarthy 1997). So, for example, on this view, turning on your stove infringes your neighbors' rights, although it is permissible to do so. Or, alternatively, one can constrain the kinds of harm that we have rights against and be less capacious in the scope of when rights are permissibly infringed.[16] On either of these approaches, it is possible to end up with an intuitive and extensionally adequate account of what is permissible and impermissible. Where the two approaches differ, however, is in how much moral residue there is left in the world after rights infringements are taken into account. On the maximally inclusive approach, you have infringed your neighbors' rights when you turn on your stove, and thereby owe something in compensation. Of course, it is a very small something that you owe, and there are other ways to soften the counterintuitive implication here. But softening is not the same

---

[16] Or, one can constrain the use of "harm" in a stipulated way (Hanser 2019). This might be seen as equivalent to limiting the harms we have rights against to a subset of harms. The key is to get the right category of what we have rights against (or for), and the labeling is less important.

thing as eliminating, and we believe that if there is an alternative and principled way to accommodate intuitions, that would be preferable.[17]

Here we return full circle to what we take to be the lessons of Trolley Cases, Bomber Cases, and others introduced earlier. Focusing specifically on the cases that most plausibly implicate the Doctrine of Double Effect as an example, it seems that our rights are individuated more specifically than simply rights against harm in general. For example, we have a right not to be used as means in ways that harm comes to us without our consent. Our rights are not rights that things happen (or not happen) to us; rather rights are rights to be treated (or not treated) in certain ways. In this case, it seems that we have a special right not to be used, a right that people not harm us for a particular set of reasons. If this is correct, then it can be used to sort just the kinds of cases Thomson thought were intractable. Playing Russian Roulette, even with a many-chambered gun, is imposing risk on another for the fun of it. It is involving someone in one's plans in a way that a risk of harm is imposed on them. Notably, such involvement is absent from the case in which one turns on one's stove. Of course, this is not to say that it is permissible to turn on one's stove no matter the probability of harm, just as the most plausible version of the DDE does not imply that it is permissible to harm whenever one merely foresees it. But it is to mark a relevant difference between the two kinds of cases that will often underwrite different bottom-line permissibility judgments.[18]

What to make of other hard cases? Consider River, where it appears that the farmer has no intention to use anyone; his only aim is to get rid of the toxic substance. It appears impermissible to put others at risk even as a foreseen side effect in this case. Here we acknowledge that there are many impermissible risk impositions that are not explained as violations of the right not to be used as a means. Indeed, we can ask: How is this case different from Stove? Suppose that none of the people at risk in River faces a greater risk

---

[17] For example, one might appeal to a lottery system (see footnote 8) to distribute compensation, so that you are not required to have a separate transaction for each risk imposition. One might also appeal to the fact that your neighbors, too, will turn on their stoves and that you cancel each other's compensation out. But this will not work in all cases: consider your neighbors who do not cook, or people who live in neighborhoods that receive disproportionate amounts of pollution. (See Railton 1985, who is especially concerned with how to explain the impermissibility of risk for future generations who cannot possibly reciprocate risk imposition.)

[18] McCarthy (1997, 212) also expresses openness to an intend/foresee distinction, but notably he takes it to be relevant not for constraining the contents of rights themselves, but for indicating when infringing them is permissible. While this might result in indistinguishable bottom-line permissibility judgments, as long as one takes there to be a moral residue with permissible rights infringements, this approach will likely yield different answers about obligations to compensate.

(measured on either the dimension of probability or the dimension of harm) than one's neighbors in Stove. If there is no violation – or even infringement – of rights in Stove, it seems that there cannot be in River. Our response here is to appeal to the fact that morality is not exhausted by rights.[19] Just as we ought to rescue a child we see drowning in a pond as we walk by, regardless of any rights they have, we have room to explain the case in a similar way. The most salient difference between Stove and River is that in River, while there is a low chance of any particular person suffering harm, there is a high chance that someone will. This contrasts with the case of Stove, in which the chance of any person being harmed is very low.[20]

Our aim here has not been to offer a complete theory, but we hope to have shown that risk does not pose uniquely novel problems for the general moral theory we favor, and, indeed, that the theory is supported by its resources, including principles that take into account the intentions and reasons for which people act in determining permissibility and that allow for intuitively plausible sorting of risk cases.

5.6 Frameworks for varying risk cases

It remains to address the question of what to do when the probabilities for imposing harm are not all equal, so that principles like the Doctrine of Double Effect do not apply in their current form. In particular, does it become permissible – or even required – to lead someone, or perhaps even more than one person, onto the track, knowing that there is a chance, but not a certainty, that they will be killed or harmed rather than turning the trolley onto a track that will result in the certain death of one person? More generally, how do we weigh varying probabilities of harm due to involvement in plans and probabilities of harm that is merely foreseen?

If imposing a risk of harm is itself a harm, but a lesser harm than certainly causing harm, then, at least on one level of generality, we have a clear framework for handling cases where probabilities are not equal. Suppose, for example, that we could lead one person on to the track where he thereby

---

[19] This might help to answer the worries about deontological theories of risk imposition expressed by Railton 1985 and McKerlie 1986, who seem to suppose that rights theorists can't accommodate risk because rights are all there is to morality on these views. And anyway, won't consequentialists have to treat these cases in the same way?

[20] As the Russian Roulette case with a very large number of chambers shows, restricting the impermissible to *high* risk imposition does not work. But degree of risk can still be *relevant*, and this is one such example.

faces a .01 risk of death, or we could turn the trolley onto a sidetrack, which would result in one person's certain death, or we could allow the trolley to continue on its current path, which would result in the certain death of five people. The idea that we ought to turn the trolley becomes much less intuitively plausible as the risk of death decreases for the person led onto the track. And this is predicted by the account in which people have a right not to be involved in someone's plan in such a way that harm comes to them without their consent. Because the harm here is less than the harm of death, and at some point, the harm becomes small enough that such a right is permissibly infringed, it is to be expected that imposing a very low risk will become permissible to achieve a great gain. For comparison: If the only way to save the five without turning the trolley onto the one were to give someone a paper cut, we should surely do it, despite the fact that we would be infringing someone's right to bodily integrity.

There is much work to be done in assessing how to compare the severity of harm – and so the stringency of the corresponding right – of a .n risk of death to a risk of death of 1. One idea that immediately suggests itself is that it is simply equivalent to .n times the harm that is risked. On this formula, being subjected to .1 risk of death is to experience one-tenth the harm of death.[21] This is a neat formula, but it is far from obvious that our intuitions match this simple formula, and it is also true that in real life things are more complicated still, insofar as there is often a *shift* of probability of harm depending on our actions from some nonzero number to another. Do we subtract the probability if we do nothing from the probability if we act to determine the risk that we compare to certain harm? In experimental work, we have found some evidence that people's intuitions follow a linear algorithm neither in their disvaluing of risk of harm nor in their views of whether it is permissible to impose risk in order to save others. In particular, people are sensitive not only to changes in expected value, but also to the location between 0 and 1 where the change in expected value takes place (e.g., whether the increase in risk is from 0 to .25 or from .50 to .75 – see Ryazanov et al. 2021). Some shifts in probability appear to be judged as more "harmful" than others, even when the change in expected value is identical, and this seems to contribute to bottom-line judgments of permissibility. It might be that the right not to have one's risk of death increased from seventy-five percent to ninety-five percent is more stringent than the right not to have one's risk of death increased from

---

[21] As we saw, McCarthy 1997 suggests something like this formula when it comes to *compensation*, though, notably, he does not commit to the risk of harm being a harm.

ten percent to thirty percent. While we are not able to offer a complete explanation here, we note that a framework – like the deontological one we have sketched – that does not exclusively feature differences in expected value has an advantage over traditional consequentialist theories from the start. Of course, intuitions are only one kind of support for a theory, and it might be that some intuitions ought to be explained away in a fully defended theory. But, for now, we see them as posing a challenge for any theory that takes the imposition of risk to be a harm to explain the particular patterns of intuitions, and as favoring something like the deontological account we provide over traditional consequentialist accounts insofar as the patterns diverge from a consistent appeal to expected value.[22]

We believe that something similar will hold true even if the imposition of risk is not a harm, but either, as described in Section 5.4 above, something *like* harm, or the larger category of which harm is a subset. As long as there is a common currency for measuring harm and risk of harm, we should be able to explain why, when we lower the risk of harm sufficiently, it becomes permissible to involve someone in our plans without their consent rather than causing certain harm to another.

Thus, though we do not have a complete theory to offer, and cannot assign specific probabilities, or probability shifts, as the tipping point for when infringing the right not to be used as a means becomes permissible, we do not take this to undermine the promise of the general framework.

5.7 Conclusion

We began with Trolley Cases that are naturally thought to support a version of the DDE, according to which the permissibility of an action can depend on whether harm comes to the victim as a result of their involvement in the agent's plans or only as a foreseeable consequence. To the extent that the DDE is plausible, it appears that a probabilistic variant is also plausible. In this chapter, we have defended a deontological theory that includes such a principle from challenges, by appealing to what we see as the foundational justification of the DDE itself, among other resources. Although the deontological theory we defend faces challenges that alternative views do not face, such as the demand to identify the relationship between harm and risk of

---

[22] In other work (Ryazanov et al., in preparation), we find another way in which participants do not follow a simple formula tracking expected value. People prefer to distribute risk over more people than to cause certain harm, even when the expected disvalue is considerably greater.

harm, we have sought to show not only that these challenges can be met, but that the deontological principles themselves gain support by being able to not only accommodate but also explain our reflective intuitions about the permissibility of risk imposition. We also set some new tasks, namely, to offer more precise contents for principles that apply in the hard cases in which we must weigh varying probabilities of harm due to involvement in plans and probabilities of harm that are merely foreseen. While we cannot complete these here, we hope to have made progress by laying out a range of cases and intuitive responses to be accounted for, and by offering some reason to believe that the deontological theory has better prospects in the long run for being able to do so.[23]

---

[23] For very helpful comments on the chapter, we owe many thanks to Hallvard Lillehammer, and for excellent discussion of the issues, we are very grateful to the participants in a UC San Diego seminar we led in Winter 2021 on Risk, Responsibility, and Morality, including William Albuquerque, Saba Bazargan-Forward, Samantha Berthelette, Weixin Cai, Craig Callender, Aaron Chipp-Miller, Ryan Hayes, Emily LaRosa, Dafna Mark Ben Shabbat, Sam Ridge, Ann Thresher, and Keyao Yang.

6 The trolley problem and the doing/allowing distinction

Fiona Woollard

6.1 Introduction

For some years, the main focus of my research was the moral nature and significance of the distinction between doing harm and merely allowing harm. When I told other philosophers what I was working on, they would often smile and nod, "Ah, yes. Trolleys." The trolley problem is one of the most famous thought experiments, both inside and outside philosophy. A lot of people associate it strongly with the doing/allowing distinction. However, as I will argue, the relationship between the trolley problem and the doing/allowing distinction is complex.

Before I begin, a word about terminology. I will use the term "trolley case" to refer to a hypothetical case usually involving a trolley where the agent must choose whether to harm one person to save a different, and usually larger, group of persons. In the classic trolley cases, you must choose whether to turn a runaway trolley that is heading toward five innocent people. If you turn the trolley, the five will be saved, but another innocent person who is trapped on the sidetrack will be hit by the trolley and killed (Foot 1967/2002a, Thomson 1976, 1985).

A lot of people think the trolley problem is whether you ought to turn the trolley in these cases. But that is not the real trolley problem. The real trolley problem starts from the observation that, intuitively, you are at least permitted to turn the trolley and save the five in the classic trolley cases. The trolley problem is to explain *why* you are permitted to turn the trolley when there are many cases where intuitively you are not permitted to kill one person to save five. We need to find a morally relevant difference between the classic trolley cases and these other cases. That has proved extremely tricky.[1]

---

[1] Of course, an alternative way to solve the trolley problem is to argue that our intuitions are wrong. Peter Unger has argued that our intuitions that it is impermissible to kill one to save five in the other cases are wrong. He argues that those intuitions are subject to various types of distortion and that features of the classic trolley cases cancel out this distortion, leading to more accurate

I will begin by discussing the origin of the trolley problem. The original version of the trolley problem was introduced by Philippa Foot who argued that the problem could be solved by appeal to the doing/allowing distinction. Judith Jarvis Thomson presented a modified version of the case, which became the canonical trolley case, to show that appeal to the doing/allowing distinction would not solve the problem. Thomson's seminal discussion of the trolley problem is in a pair of articles, "Killing, Letting Die, and the Trolley Problem" published in 1976 and "The Trolley Problem," published in 1985. I will show that in the 1976 article, Thomson's overall aim is not to argue that the distinction between doing and allowing harm is not morally relevant, but to raise questions about precisely what we mean when we say this distinction matters morally. In the 1985 paper, Thomson does seem to be arguing against the moral relevance of the doing/allowing distinction, but I will argue that this should not be taken to undermine her claims in the 1976 paper.

I will then discuss my own understanding of the relationship between the trolley problem and the distinction between doing and allowing harm. I start by arguing that the claim that the distinction between doing and allowing matters morally should be understood as a claim about justification. The claim is that, other things being equal, doing harm is harder to justify than merely allowing harm. With that understanding, it becomes clear that cases in which it is permissible to do harm instead of merely allowing harm are not counterexamples to the moral relevance of the doing/allowing distinction. To say that doing harm is harder to justify is not to say that it is never justified.

I then address the issue of whether the trolley problem presents a more serious challenge for the distinction between doing and allowing harm because it may make it seem as if the defender of the doing/allowing distinction cannot give a consistent and intuitively acceptable answer to *how* much harder doing harm is to justify than merely allowing harm. I argue that this concern is misguided because we should expect there to be other morally relevant features that interact with the doing/allowing distinction, strengthening or weakening constraints against doing harm. What the trolley problem shows is not that we should abandon the doing/allowing distinction but that we need some additional deontological distinction to make sense of our intuitions about cases. This deontological distinction should be seen as a supplement, rather than a rival, to the distinction between doing and allowing harm.

intuitions (Unger 1995). More recently, Judith Jarvis Thomson, creator of the canonical trolley case – the Bystander case which will be described in the next section – has changed her mind and argued that in fact it is not permissible to turn the trolley in that case (Thomson 2008).

This chapter is about the relationship between the trolley problem and the distinction between doing and allowing harm. Some of the authors I discuss talk instead about the distinction between killing and letting die. I take the distinction between killing and letting die to be merely the doing/allowing harm distinction applied to the specific harm of death. Sometimes I will follow an author in discussing the killing/letting die distinction. Where I do so, I take it the discussion can be applied more widely to the doing/allowing distinction.

6.2 Trams and trolleys: The origins of the problem

The original trolley was a British tram. It first appeared in a case put forward by Philippa Foot in 1967. In this case:

> Driver [The agent] is the driver of a runaway tram which he can only steer from one narrow track on to another; five men are working on one track and one man on the other; anyone on the track he enters is bound to be killed (Foot 1967/2002a, 23).[2]

Foot introduces this case in discussion of the doctrine of double effect: the principle that it may be permissible to cause a harm to another as a merely foreseen side effect of pursuing a good end when it would not be permissible to strictly intend the same harm for the same good end. Foot argues that we may think that we are forced to accept the doctrine of double effect to explain the intuitive moral difference between the Driver case and the following case:

> Rioting Mob: Rioters are demanding that a culprit be found for a certain crime and threatening otherwise to take their own bloody revenge on a particular section of the community. The real culprit being unknown, the [agent] sees himself as able to prevent the bloodshed only by framing some innocent person and having him executed (Foot 1967/2002a, 23).[3]

Foot notes that intuitively it is permissible for the driver to turn the tram away from five and toward one, but not permissible for the agent to frame one innocent person to save five other innocent people from the mob. The doctrine of double effect seems to offer us a way out of this puzzle. We can

---

[2] It is difficult to get hold of a copy of the original paper. For that reason, I use references to the version reprinted in Foot's *Virtues and Vices.*

[3] Foot originally makes the agent a judge but later changes him to a private citizen in order so that the difference cannot be explained by the fact that the riot case involves corruption of justice.

say that the driver of the tram foresees – but does not strictly intend – the death of the innocent person on the tracks: That death is a mere side effect of the way that he saves the five. In contrast, when the agent frames the innocent man, he strictly intends the man's death: The death is the means by which he achieves his goal of saving the five. Foot uses this pair of cases to show why we may be tempted to accept the doctrine of double effect.

However, Foot argues that we do not need to accept the doctrine of double effect to explain this puzzling pair of cases. Instead, she argues, the difference in intuitions can be explained by appeal to an associated but different distinction: the distinction between doing harm and merely allowing harm (or in her terms the distinction between positive duties to aid others and negative duties not to harm them). As Foot argues, these distinctions are not the same:

> To see this one has only to consider that it is possible deliberately to allow something to happen, aiming at it either for its own sake or as part of one's plan for obtaining something else. So one person might want another person dead and deliberately allow him to die. And again one may be said to do things that one does not aim at, as the steering driver would kill the man on the track. (Foot 1967/2002a, 25)

Foot argues that the driver faces a conflict of negative duties: He must choose between doing harm to one person and doing harm to five people. As the driver has to do harm to someone, he should minimize the amount of harm he does. This explains why the driver should turn the tram toward the one. In the riot case, the citizen is faced with a negative duty not to harm the innocent man and a positive duty to save the victims of the rioters. Negative duties not to harm are stronger than positive duties to aid. This explains why the citizen should not frame the innocent man (Foot 1967/2002a, 27–28).

Judith Jarvis Thomson's response to Foot transformed the British tram into a North American trolley, produced the canonical version of the case, coined the term "the trolley problem" and secured trolleys a place in philosophical history.[4]

Thomson's crucial move is to adjust the case so that the agent is not the driver. In her 1976 paper, she makes the agent a passenger on the trolley.

---

[4] Thomson's 2008 paper includes this rather lovely explanation of the name change: "Since trams are trolleys on this side of the Atlantic, I call this the 'trolley problem.' (Besides, that is more euphonious than 'the tram problem')" (Thomson 2008, 363). I have known British students to be slightly confused by the term "trolley," thinking that the puzzle referred to a runaway shopping trolley (which an American would call a "shopping cart"). Differences between US English and UK English are a source of continued delight.

In her 1985 paper, a bystander is out for a stroll beside the track. It is this latter case that has become the canonical trolley case:

> Bystander: The agent is strolling by the trolley track when he sees a runaway trolley heading towards five innocent people who are trapped on the track ahead. There is a side-track on which one innocent person is trapped. The agent can pull a switch which would turn the trolley onto the side-track, saving the five and killing the one. The agent can do nothing, in which case the trolley will kill the five and the one will live (Thomson 1985, 1397).[5]

As Thomson points out, this version of the case shows that Foot's solution will not work. It seems permissible for the bystander to turn the trolley. But the bystander does not face a conflict between negative duties not to kill. If the bystander turns the trolley, they will kill the one. If the bystander does not turn the trolley, they will not kill the five. The bystander faces a choice between killing one and letting five die. We cannot explain the permissibility of the bystander turning the trolley by appeal to a conflict of negative duties (Thomson 1976, 207; 1985, 1398).

It can be tempting to see the Bystander case as showing that the distinction between doing and allowing is not morally significant. In her 1976 article, Thomson is at pains to show that this is a mistake. Her aim is not to undermine the doing/allowing distinction but to get clearer on what those who say that doing harm is worse than allowing harm (or as she puts it that killing is worse than letting die) have in mind and to urge caution about what we try to deduce from this claim.

The article opens with a beautiful discussion of the use of contrast cases to undermine the killing/letting die distinction. Contrast cases are pairs of cases where the only difference is that in one case the agent kills and in the other, he merely lets die: All other factors are held equal. We can construct contrast cases where letting die seems just as morally reprehensible as killing. Some people use these cases to argue that there is no morally relevant difference between doing and allowing harm. Thomson shows that this argument does not work:

> Compare the following argument for the thesis that cutting off a man's head is no worse than punching a man in the nose. "Alfrieda knows that if she cuts off Alfred's head he will die, and, wanting him to die, cuts it off; Bertha knows that if she punches Bert in the nose he will die – Bert is in peculiar physical condition – and, wanting him to die, punches him in the

---

[5] I have redescribed the case in my own words.

nose. But what Bertha does is surely every bit as bad as what Alfrieda does. So cutting off a man's head isn't worse than punching a man in the nose." (Thomson 1976, 204)

As Thomson points out, the Bertha and Alfrieda argument does not work. The claim "cutting off a man's head is worse than punching him in the nose" is not disconfirmed by the existence of a pair of cases where a nose-punching is as bad as a head-cutting-off. Similarly, the claim "killing is worse than letting die" is not disconfirmed by the existence of a pair of cases where a letting die is as bad as a killing. This shows us something important: It shows us that the claim that "killing is worse than letting die" should not be understood to mean anything that entails that every case of killing is worse than every case of letting die (where other factors are equalized).

Thomson finishes the paper by arguing that the claim that "killing is worse than letting die" should *also* not be understood to mean anything that is disconfirmed by the existence of cases where you may choose to kill rather than letting die (Thomson 1976, 217). The trolley cases do not undermine the killing/letting die distinction. Instead, they show that certain overly simplistic ways of understanding what is meant by this claim are unacceptable and challenge us to get clearer on what exactly is meant. Importantly, they also undermine use of the distinction "in any simple mechanical way" to reach conclusions in applied ethics.

> If nothing else comes out of the preceding discussion, it may anyway serve as a reminder of this: that there are circumstances in which – even if it is true that killing is worse than letting die – one may choose to kill instead of letting die (Thomson 1976, 217).

It seems clear that in Thomson's 1976 paper, she uses the trolley case not to undermine the claim that the doing/allowing distinction matters morally, but to enrich our understanding of what this claim could mean and to caution us against careless use of the distinction in applied ethics.

Almost a decade later, in 1985, Thomson published another paper, "The Trolley Problem." In this paper, Thomson does seem to be arguing against the doing/allowing distinction. She says:

> I have been arguing that
>
> (I) Killing one is worse than letting five die,
> is false, and a fortiori that it cannot be appealed to to explain why the surgeon may not operate in the case I shall call *Transplant*. (Thomson 1985, 1399)

The Transplant case involves a surgeon who has five patients each of whom will die unless they receive an organ. As they each require a different organ, the surgeon could save all five lives by killing a healthy person and redistributing his organs (Thomson 1976, 205). Intuitively, it is impermissible for the surgeon to operate in this case.

Thomson's grounds for arguing that thesis (I) is false are that "If thesis (I) were true, it would follow that the bystander may not throw the switch and that I am taking to be false" (Thomson 1985, 1398).

This conflicts with Thomson's own earlier conclusion that those who say that killing is worse than letting die do not have anything in mind that is disconfirmed by the existence of cases where the agent may kill rather than let die. Moreover, while the 1976 paper contains some persuasive arguments to support her conclusion, the 1985 paper simply includes the statement above about what "would follow" "if thesis (I) were true".

In addition, in the next section of her 1985 paper, Thomson discusses an amended Transplant case with a surgeon responsible for the plight of the five and thus facing a choice between killing five and killing one. She argues that we should say that thesis (II) - the claim that killing five is worse than killing one - is true but that it does not imply that this surgeon ought to operate because "the assessments of which acts are worse than which other acts do not by themselves settle the question what it is permissible for an agent to do" (Thomson 1985, 1400).

This argument does not automatically transfer over to the defense of the killing/letting die distinction. First, the claim that killing five is worse than killing one has a firmer place in our intuitions than the claim that killing is worse than letting die. To argue that killing one is no worse than killing five would be really deeply counterintuitive. It would be to say that the number of deaths you cause does not matter morally. I have argued elsewhere that rejection of the doing/allowing distinction would require radical revision of commonsense morality (Woollard 2015, 4). Nonetheless, this seems to pale in comparison to the radical overhaul of our intuitions required to cease seeing the number of deaths one causes as mattering morally.[6] Second, as Thomson argues, it does seem as if the surgeon's act of killing the five is worse than his act of killing the one – even if it is not permissible for him to kill the one to prevent his having killed the five. In contrast, it does not seem that the bystander does what is worse if he kills the one rather than allowing the five to die. Nonetheless, in this discussion we see Thomson being careful about the

---

[6] It is true that some philosophers have denied that the number of people to be saved matter morally, most famously Taurek (1977). However, this claim is still I think seen as deeply counterintuitive.

implications of claims that one type of act is worse than another type of act. She notes that we have an intuitive judgment that may seem to disconfirm a claim that one type of act is worse than another type of act. But she cautions us not to accept such judgments at face value, but instead to reflect on what our original claim meant. This is the same care that we saw Thomson applying to the claim that killing is worse than letting die in 1976. It is not clear to me why in 1985, Thomson kept this care in the case of the claim that it is worse to kill more people but concluded so quickly that the Bystander case disproves the claim that it is worse to kill than to let die.

Overall, it seems to me that we should take Thomson's discussion in 1976 to show Thomson's most plausible account of what the trolley case implies for the moral relevance of the distinction between doing and allowing harm.

6.3 Trolleys and the doing/allowing distinction[7]

Thomson argues that care is needed to understand just what is meant by the claim that doing harm is worse than merely allowing harm (or in her terms that killing is worse than letting die). I agree with this – but I would go further. I think we should question whether this claim about the badness of acts is really the claim that we should make if we want to defend the moral significance of the doing/allowing distinction. I do not think that it is. I follow Warren Quinn (1989a) in holding that it is much better to focus on claims about justification rather than on how bad acts of a given type are.

If the doing/allowing distinction is morally significant, doing harm will be *harder to justify* than merely allowing harm (other things being equal). Factors that would justify allowing another person to suffer a certain harm may not be enough to justify doing that same harm to the person. More than this, the difference in justification should be attributed to the distinction between doing and allowing. We should be inclined to say that Fred's behavior is justified while Bob's is not *because* Fred would be merely allowing harm whereas Bob would be doing harm.

To say that there is a morally significant difference between doing and allowing harm, meaning that doing harm is harder to justify than merely allowing harm, does not entail that unjustified cases of doing harm will be worse than unjustified cases of merely allowing harm. Warren Quinn made this point beautifully in 1989:

---

[7] Some parts of this section overlap with Woollard (2015) pp. 11–16, others, overlap with Woollard (2017).

Your right of privacy that the police not enter your home without permission, for example, is more easily defeated than your right that I, an ordinary
citizen, not do so. But it seems morally no better, and perhaps even worse,
for the police to violate this right than for me to. (Quinn 1989, 290)

Quinn's point bears repeating. Failure to bear it in mind can lead to the moral
relevance of the doing/allowing distinction being dismissed too quickly on
inadequate grounds. Just because someone has found a pair of cases where
merely allowing harm is just as bad – or even worse – than doing the same
harm, does not mean they have shown that the doing/allowing distinction is
morally irrelevant. The pair of cases may both involve unjustified behavior –
and even if merely allowing harm is easier to justify than doing harm,
unjustified allowing harm may be no better than unjustified doing harm.

Moreover, to say that there is a morally significant difference between
doing and allowing harm, meaning that (other things being equal) doing
harm is harder to justify than merely allowing harm, does not entail that there
will never be cases where it is permissible to kill rather than letting die. We are
claiming that doing harm is harder to justify not that it is never justifiable.

It might seem as if the trolley problem presents a more serious challenge for
those who would defend the doing/allowing distinction. After all, the trolley
problem presents us with pairs of cases. The first case of the pair is a case like
Transplant. In this case, it is impermissible to kill one to save five. The second
case is a case like Bystander Trolley, where it is permissible to kill one to save
five. This pair of cases may make it seem as if the defender of the doing/
allowing distinction cannot give a consistent and plausible answer to *how*
much harder it is to justify doing harm than to justify merely allowing harm.
If saving five people *is not* enough to justify killing one person, then it seems
as if it *should not* be permissible to turn the trolley in the Bystander Trolley
case. If saving five people *is* enough to justify killing one person, then it seems
as if it *should* be permissible to save the five in the Transplant case.

I think this concern is misguided. We claim that the doing/allowing
distinction matters morally. We do not claim that it is the only thing that
matters morally. It should not be surprising that there can be other factors
that interact with the doing/allowing distinction.

There are two possible ways to think about what is happening here with
respect to the doing/allowing distinction. First, we might say that the
Bystander case shows that it is permissible to kill one to save five. As noted
above, we were not defending an absolute constraint against killing. On this
way of thinking, there must be some factor present in the Transplant case that

strengthens the constraint against doing harm. Even though it is normally permissible to kill one person to save five, when this additional factor is present, the constraint against killing is stronger and it is not permissible to kill one to save five.

Alternatively, we might start with the Transplant case and say that this case shows it is not normally permissible to kill one to save five. On this way of thinking, there must be some factor present in the Bystander case that *weakens* the constraints against doing harm. Even though it is not normally permissible to kill one person to save five, when this additional factor is present, the constraint against killing is weaker and it is permissible to kill one to save five.

Both these ways of thinking are compatible with the moral significance of the doing/allowing distinction. One way of thinking may prove to be more appropriate: It may be that the best way to explain the difference between the Bystander case and the Transplant case is by pointing to something that is best understood as a feature that strengthens the constraint in Transplant. In my view, that is beyond the scope of a defense of the doing/allowing distinction.

Whichever way we think about it, the trolley problem shows that the doing/allowing distinction alone cannot make sense of our intuitions about cases. Some additional distinction is needed.

So far, we have learned two things about the relationship between the trolley problem and the doing/allowing distinction. First, the trolley problem does not undermine the moral relevance of the doing/allowing distinction. Second, the doing/allowing distinction on its own cannot solve the trolley problem. I will now argue that the trolley problem, when seen as an argument for a new deontological distinction, implicitly assumes the moral relevance of the doing/allowing distinction. In addition, potential solutions to the problem – or at least any potential solutions that attempt to explain our intuitions about cases – will need to either accept the doing/allowing distinction (or some replacement) as a background assumption or incorporate the distinction (or some replacement).

I've argued elsewhere that the use of cases like the Bystander case to motivate principles such as the doctrine of double effect (DDE) tacitly presupposes the moral relevance of the distinction between doing and allowing:

In Trolley and Bridge we must choose whether to kill one person to save five. We do not try to motivate the DDE by looking at cases where we must choose whether to kill one to save two, because we assume that it is not permissible to kill one to save two, even when the killing would be merely foreseen. We tacitly assume that there is a constraint against killing and take this into account when choosing the cases we use to support the DDE. (Woollard 2017, 153)

I think this applies to the trolley problem more generally when seen as an argument for an additional deontological principle. The examples that are put forward to convince us that we require some additional principle to solve the trolley problem are chosen with the doing/allowing distinction as a background.

Shelly Kagan has argued against the doctrine of double effect on the basis that it cannot give an appropriate account of due proportion. The argument begins with the observation that appeal to the doctrine of double effect should not provide an unlimited license to harm people where this is merely foreseen. In Kagan's example, a factory owner plans to increase his profits by using a new chemical process. As a side effect, poisonous waste will be released into the river, killing people nearby. These deaths will be foreseen but not strictly intended. Nonetheless, the factory owner's behavior is impermissible (Kagan 1989, 151). Kagan concludes that a requirement of "due proportion" is needed. The doctrine of double effect should hold that merely foreseen harm can be justified but only if there is due proportion between the various aspects of the outcome countenanced by the agent: The good aspects of what he countenances must be enough to justify countenancing the bad (Kagan 1989, 152).

Thus far, Kagan's argument should not find any objection from defenders of the doctrine of double effect: It is widely recognized that this doctrine is not meant to imply an unlimited permission to countenance merely foreseen harm. However, Kagan argues that there is no way the defender of the doctrine of double effect *can* give a consistent account of due proportion. To see why, consider the following cases:

Mosquito Poison: In an effort to free my backyard of mosquitoes, I release a smoke bomb – foreseeing that it will pollute the river, causing an elderly man in the next town to die from drinking poisoned water.

Mosquito No-Donation: I could have used the money spent on the smoke bomb to fit a water filter to the house of an elderly man in the next town. Without the water filter he dies from drinking poisoned water. (Woollard 2017, 150)

These are modified versions of cases originally put forward by Kagan (1989, 154). I modified the original pair of cases to equalize for distance and manner of death. Intuitively, Mosquito No-Donation is permissible while Mosquito

Poison is impermissible. But, as Kagan points out, we cannot explain this by appeal to a principle of due proportion: Both cases involve merely foreseen harm and the proportion between this harm and the good to the agent is equal (1989, 155). As Kagan notes, the obvious response is to appeal to the doing/allowing distinction. We can say that constraints against doing harm are stronger than constraints against merely allowing harm, even when the harm is merely foreseen. This would explain why a cost to the agent that cannot justify doing harm to the old man may justify allowing that same harm.

Now Kagan does not think that appeal to the doing/allowing distinction will work, partly because he believes that he has already provided arguments against the moral relevance of that distinction. He therefore takes this as an argument against the doctrine of double effect. I have responded elsewhere to Kagan's concerns.[8] In my view, appeal to the distinction between doing and allowing can allow the doctrine of double effect to have a coherent understanding of due proportion. For that reason, I take Kagan's argument to show that anyone who endorses the doctrine of double effect should also endorse the moral relevance of the distinction between doing and allowing.

Of course, Kagan's examples focused on cases where the harm to the victim was supposed to be justified by what it would cost the agent to avoid the harm. Trolley cases typically concern cases where harm to one is justified by appeal to the greater good: We are permitted to turn the trolley toward the one because in doing so we will save five lives. Kagan's argument still applies: We can come up with a pair of examples where the harm is supposed to be justified by appeal to the greater good.

> Two Lives and Two Legs Turn: In the familiar story, you are a bystander who can turn the runaway trolley from the main track to a sidetrack where one innocent person is trapped. This time, however, the trolley is headed toward two innocent persons, one of whom is almost out of the way. If you do not turn the trolley, it will kill one of the persons on the main track and remove the legs of the other. If you do turn the trolley, it will kill the person on the sidetrack.[9]

---

[8] See Woollard (2017), footnote 22 for a summary of how I believe my work provides a convincing rebuttal to Kagan's general argument against the moral relevance of the distinction between doing and allowing and Woollard (2017), 150–151 for a response to Kagan's argument that appeal to this distinction cannot resolve the proportionality issue.

[9] Kamm (2020b, 21) argues that "whatever could account for the permissibility of turning the trolley to save five and kill one could account for the permissibility of turning to save two and kill one or to save five and kill four. If we could not account for the latter two cases, I doubt we could account for the original case." See also Parfit 2017, 388. It seems to me that it is only permissible for the

Two Lives and Two Legs Rescue: Two runaway trolleys are heading towards innocent persons trapped on the tracks. One track has one innocent person. The other track has two innocent persons, one of whom is almost out of the way. If you rescue the person on the first track, the other trolley will kill one of the persons on the second track and remove the legs of the other. If you rescue the group on the first track, the second trolley will kill the person on the second track.

I think it is intuitively permissible to rescue the greater number of people in Two Lives and Two Legs Rescue, but intuitively impermissible to kill the one for the greater good in Two Lives Two Legs Turn. Again, in both cases, the harm is merely foreseen and the proportion between harm and good are the same. It seems as if the distinction between doing and allowing – or something like it – is needed to explain the difference between the two cases.

I think considering these cases shows that any solution to the trolley problem should either accept the doing/allowing distinction (or some replacement) as a background assumption or incorporate the distinction (or some replacement). In my view, the most promising option is to endorse both the doing/allowing distinction and a separate solution to the trolley problem.

First, the moral relevance of the doing/allowing distinction seems to me to be part of commonsense morality. This is not just because our intuitive moral verdicts about cases seem to treat the distinction as morally relevant. We also tend to appeal to the moral relevance of the distinction when justifying those verdicts. We say things like: "It would be wrong for the agent to turn the trolley in Two Lives and Two Legs Turn *because he would be doing harm*." I also believe that the moral relevance of the distinction can be defended – but that is certainly beyond the scope of this chapter.[10]

But it also seems to me as if in order to solve the trolley problem we are looking for a deontological distinction that cuts across the doing/allowing

---

bystander to turn the trolley when the number of lives to be saved is great enough. I am not sure at what point the number of lives does become great enough. I do not think that saving two lives is enough to kill one person. However, as there seems to be disagreement on this point even amongst deontologists, I have set the example so that it is one life versus one life and one pair of legs rather than one life versus two lives. I wanted to choose an additional good where it is clearly impermissible to switch, but where the additional good is not so trivial in comparison to the loss of life as to be irrelevant. I think the loss of both legs fits these criteria. See Kamm (2007, 6165) for discussion of irrelevant goods. Thank you to Henrik Ahlenius, David Edmonds, and Charlotte Unruh for helpful discussion on this footnote.

[10] For a defense of the moral relevance of the distinction between doing and allowing harm, see Woollard (2015).

distinction. I noted above Foot's argument that the doing/allowing distinction is not the same as the intended/merely foreseen distinction. Foot argues that one person might want another person dead and deliberately allow him to die (Foot (1967/2002, 25). I think that we can find at least some cases of deliberately allowing harm to others that seem to be morally similar to the Transplant case. For example:

> Bait: I have many guns but due to my position I cannot shoot my way out. I could easily throw a gun to Fred who is closer to an exit and could use it to shoot his way out. If I do so, Fred will escape and I will die. If I do not give Fred a gun, the zombies will overpower him and the resulting feeding frenzy will allow me to escape. I do not give him the gun. I escape. Fred dies. (Woollard 2017, 151)

My behavior in Bait seems to me to be impermissible, even though the harm is merely allowed. We might hope that the solution to the trolley problem would also explain why it is impermissible for me to allow Fred to die in Bait even though I am not normally required to prevent another's death at the cost of my own life.

Thus, I think, any solution to the trolley problem should explain a moral difference between cases that is clearly different from the doing/allowing distinction, while also responding to a difference between cases that matches the doing/allowing distinction. In my view, the most promising avenue is to explain this by appeal to the doing/allowing distinction plus some other morally relevant distinction. In this case, the solution to the trolley problem would take the moral relevance of the doing/allowing distinction as a background assumption. However, it might also be that the solution explains all cases in one fell swoop. I would say that in this case, the solution should be seen as incorporating the doing/allowing distinction or some replacement.

6.4 Conclusion

I have argued that the relationship between the trolley problem and the doing/allowing distinction is complex. The distinction between doing and allowing should not be understood as a candidate solution to the trolley problem, nor should the trolley problem be seen as showing that the doing/allowing distinction is morally irrelevant. Instead, the trolley problem shows that an additional deontological distinction, alongside the distinction between doing and allowing, is needed to explain our intuitions about cases. This additional deontological distinction should be seen as a sister of, rather than as a rival to, the distinction between doing and allowing. Both distinctions working together are required to explain when it is permissible to countenance harm to one in order to avoid greater good to others.

This complex relationship is reflected in the history of trolley problem. The first version of the trolley case was first introduced by Philippa Foot. In this case, it is the driver of the runaway trolley (or rather tram) who must choose whether to steer the trolley on to the sidetrack, saving five and killing one. Foot argues that our intuitions can be explained by appeal to the doing/allowing distinction: The driver will kill the five if he does not turn the trolley; he thus faces a choice between killing one and killing five. It is thus permissible for him to choose to kill the smaller number. Thomson introduced the Bystander case in which there is a switch beside the tracks and a bystander must decide whether to turn the trolley. Thomson argues that Foot's solution will not work for the Bystander case as the bystander does not kill the five if they do not turn the trolley. Thomson's version has become the canonical trolley case. I have argued that Thomson's work is not best interpreted as an attempt to undermine the relevance of the doing/allowing distinction. Instead, she is best interpreted as showing that we must be careful in thinking about what is meant by the claim that doing harm is worse than allowing harm – and that we cannot draw practical conclusions from this claim in a simple straightforward way.

7   Virtue ethics and the trolley problem

Liezl van Zyl

7.1 Introduction

Judith Thomson's paper "Killing, Letting Die, and the Trolley Problem," published in 1976, initiated what has since become known as the Trolley Debate.[1] At the time, virtue ethics was still very much in its infancy. A few ethicists were sympathetic to the call, by Elizabeth Anscombe (1958), John McDowell (1979), and Alasdair MacIntyre (1985), for a return to Aristotle's moral philosophy. But it remained to be seen whether thinking about the virtues could form the basis of a complete normative theory, and whether such a theory could (or should) include an account of right action. Virtue ethicists (or virtue theorists) were simply not ready to make an attempt to reconcile the intuitions that lie at the heart of the Trolley Problem: that it is acceptable to divert a runaway trolley, thereby killing one in order to save five, but unacceptable to push a big man onto a track in order to save five others. Participation in the Trolley Debate was therefore limited to supporters of the two dominant normative theories – deontology and consequentialism.

However, since the publication of Thomson's paper virtue ethics has firmly established itself as the third major normative theory, and the Trolley Problem remains "a particularly vexing problem in ethics," as Peter Graham (2017, 168) puts it. It therefore seems entirely reasonable to wonder whether virtue ethics, as the new kid on the block, can contribute anything useful to the debate. To date, however, and somewhat surprisingly, virtue ethicists have not shown any interest in the Trolley Problem. It is for this reason that I begin this chapter by briefly discussing possible explanations for this apparent lack of interest. The most obvious of these is that virtue ethicists reject the very idea that there are universal moral rules and principles, that we have moral duties, and that actions

---

[1] An early version of the Trolley Problem was introduced by Philippa Foot in her seminal paper, "The problem of abortion and the doctrine of double effect" (1967), but as I discuss below the Trolley Debate commenced with Thomson's 1976 paper, in which she shows that Foot's solution does not succeed.

can be evaluated as permissible or impermissible (Section 7.2). It is possible to frame the Trolley Problem in terms of what a virtuous person would and wouldn't do, but then a further problem emerges, which is that trolley experiments (even realistic ones) are not good tests of character. They rule out many of the ways a virtuous person might distinguish themselves from the non-virtuous (Section 7.3), and the various constraints on the agent make it difficult for a virtuous person to act in character in these circumstances (Section 7.4). In the second part of the chapter, and with a few reservations and qualifications in mind, I argue that a virtue ethicist can support our commonsense intuitions in the two central cases – *Bystander* and *Footbridge* – while also offering a response to Thomson's "loop challenge" (Sections 7.5–7.7).

7.2 Virtue ethics and moral duties

One of the reasons why virtue ethicists have not shown an interest in finding a solution to the Trolley Problem is that the debate is focused on the correct formulation, application, and relative stringency of two moral duties: the duty not to kill an innocent person, and the duty to rescue. The earliest version of the problem, introduced by Philippa Foot (1967), involves a pair of cases like these:

> *Driver:* A runaway trolley is heading towards five men working on the track ahead. The driver must decide whether to steer onto a sidetrack, where there is one man working. If he does nothing, five men will be killed, and if he steers onto the sidetrack, one man will be killed.

> *Footbridge:* A runaway trolley is barreling toward five men working on the track ahead of it. If nothing stops the trolley, the five men will be killed. A thin man is standing on a footbridge and must decide whether to push a big man onto the track, thereby stopping the trolley but killing the big man, or to do nothing, and let the five men die.[2]

The question, then, is why it is permissible for the driver to turn the trolley, thereby killing one man, but impermissible for the thin man to push the big man onto the track. One solution is to appeal to the doctrine of double effect and to argue that the driver doesn't *intend* the one's death. His intention is to save the five, and the one's death is a merely foreseen effect of doing this.

---

[2] *Footbridge* (or *Fat Man*) was introduced by Thomson (1976, 207) in her formulation of the Trolley Problem. Foot herself contrasts *Driver* with the case of the judge who has to decide whether to frame and execute an innocent person to prevent an angry mob from killing others.

By contrast, the thin man intentionally kills the big man as a means to saving the five. Foot (1967) rejects this solution and gives an explanation that appeals to the distinction between negative and positive duties, together with a generally accepted "ranking rule," namely, that negative duties are more stringent than positive duties: The thin man faces a choice between killing one (violating a negative duty) and letting five die (violating a positive duty), whereas the driver faces a choice between two negative duties: not killing one, and not killing five.

Thomson (1976) rejects this solution, on the grounds that it doesn't explain why it is permissible to turn the trolley in a modified version of Foot's original trolley case:

> *Bystander:* A runaway trolley is heading toward five men working on the track ahead. A bystander must decide whether to flip a switch, thereby diverting the trolley onto a sidetrack. If he does nothing, five men will be killed, and if he steers onto the sidetrack, one man will be killed.

Like *Footbridge*, *Bystander* involves a conflict between a negative and a positive duty. But unlike *Footbridge*, it seems permissible for the bystander to redirect the trolley. The Trolley Problem, as defined by Thomson, is whether it is possible to formulate a general moral principle that can account for our differing moral intuitions in cases like *Bystander* and *Footbridge* (1976, 206–207; 1985, 1401). Why is it permissible to turn the trolley but impermissible to push the big man onto the track?

When asked to consider this question, the virtue ethicist would respond as follows: We cannot be expected to shed light on questions about the correct formulation, application, and relative stringency of moral principles and duties, given that we object to the assumption that we have a set of *moral* duties, that it makes sense to try to rank these in some hierarchical order, and that particular actions can be described as morally permissible, impermissible, obligatory, and so on.[3] Simply put, the Trolley Problem is none of our business.

I suspect this is the main reason why virtue ethicists have not become involved in the debate. Nevertheless, I think it is entirely reasonable to ask how one might apply virtue ethics (or, more specifically, a virtue-ethical account of right action) to the trolley cases. That is, dropping all talk of moral duties, principles, permissibility, and so on, we can simply ask: What would a

---

[3] For discussion, see Anscombe (1958), Annas (2015), and Van Zyl (2018, 124–144).

virtuous person do in these circumstances? Would they turn their trolleys in *Driver* and *Bystander*, and would they push the big man onto the track? Why, or why not?[4]

It is worth noting that virtue ethicists have participated enthusiastically in discussions of everyday moral dilemmas, in part to demonstrate that they can respond to the frequent objection that virtue ethics doesn't provide action guidance.[5] Instead of applying moral rules and principles to cases, they consider the complexities of every situation and consider how a virtuous (courageous, generous, honest, etc.) person would act in the situation. And whereas consequentialists and deontologists tend to focus exclusively on the agent's decision (in these cases, whether or not to divert the trolley, or to push the big man), virtue ethicists also consider the agent's motives, reasoning, emotions, demeanor, and attitude to be relevant when deciding whether (and to what extent) they succeed to perform a right or virtuous action. But this brings us to another difficulty. Trolley experiments have been designed with a very specific purpose in mind, which is to test the relative stringency of two moral duties. As such, the cases have been stripped down to their bare minimum. The kinds of complexities and uncertainties found in real-life moral dilemmas have been removed in order to focus our attention on the decision the agent has to make. But this has also made it very difficult for virtue ethicists to contribute anything useful to the debate. In the following two sections, I discuss some of the reasons why trolley experiments are not good tests of character.

7.3 The realism problem

As many critics have pointed out, trolley cases are very unrealistic. It seems highly unlikely that any of us would ever find ourselves in these situations. This complaint is usually brushed off by moral philosophers, as they are interested in testing a set of moral principles and intuitions. For the virtue ethicist, however, the lack of realism poses a more serious problem, for it rules out, right from the start, many of the ways in which virtuous people distinguish themselves from non-virtuous or vicious ones. Virtues are character traits that allow human beings to respond well to the demands of this world (Swanton 2003, 19). There are many different features of the situations we

---

[4] Virtue ethicists have put forward different accounts of right action. In this chapter I will apply a relaxed version of an Aristotelian "qualified-agent" account, as outlined in Van Zyl (2020).

[5] For an overview of some of the literature in this area see Axtell and Olson (2012, 183–203).

encounter in the course of our everyday lives that make demands on us, and, in many cases, make it difficult to respond well. But there are at least three such features that are noticeably absent from the dilemmas faced by the hypothetical agent in trolley experiments. The first is that actual moral dilemmas are not labeled as such. Rather, we find ourselves in a messy and complicated situation, and before we can even turn our attention to the question of what we are to do in this situation, we first have to figure out that we are facing a moral dilemma, and that our options are limited to x and y. This task often requires a significant amount of thought, moral sensitivity, and insight. The second is that we have to make decisions under conditions of uncertainty – more often than not, we don't have access to all relevant information needed to make a good decision. In particular, we hardly ever have certainty about the expected long-term (or even short-term) consequences of possible actions. The third feature of everyday moral dilemmas is that they often evoke strong feelings and emotions, such as fear, anxiety, doubt, and confusion. By contrast, thought experiments are, of course, purely intellectual exercises.

To appreciate the significance of these differences it is useful to consider an attempt by Michael Stevens, a documentary film maker, to create a realistic version of the bystander's dilemma for an episode of the television series, *Mind Field* (2017). The experiment was highly contentious, for scientific and ethical reasons, but it highlights some of the differences between trolley thought experiments and actual dilemmas. Stevens was interested in discovering whether people would actually divert a trolley in a real-life scenario. The participants were invited to take part in a survey about the development of a new high-speed train. Upon arrival they are told that the experimenter is running late, and asked to wait in a nearby train-switching station. Here they meet a friendly operator, who tells them about the project he is working on – one that requires him to watch the monitors for oncoming trains and to operate a switch to divert these from one track to another. He then goes outside to take an important call, leaving them in charge of the station. Soon, a computerized voice alerts them to the presence of the workmen on the track (five on the track ahead, and one on the sidetrack), and a bit later on it warns them that a train is approaching. They now face the decision of whether to pull the switch to divert the train onto the sidetrack with only one workman on it.

Stevens was reasonably careful to set up the experiment in such a way that it would be immediately obvious to participants that they were forced to make a choice between two options. For instance, they were told that the train was "many miles away" and weren't given any information about how to avert disaster by sounding an alarm or hitting an emergency brake. Nevertheless, at least four of them tried to find a way out of the dilemma by opening the door and calling for help. This points to an obvious flaw in the design of the experiment – it should have been made clear to participants that the operator was out of reach and that they were solely responsible for making the decision. But the more important point for our purposes is that in real-life dilemmas, the fact that there are only two options is never a given. Rather, it is a conclusion the agent can only come to through the exercise of sound practical judgment. As such, it requires them to consider alternative options, such as calling the operator – the person in charge of the station – or looking for other ways to warn the workers. As Rosalind Hursthouse notes, "it will be the mark of someone lacking in virtue that they too readily see a situation as one in which they are forced to choose between great evils" (1999, 86). Thus, by specifying, from the outset, that the agent only has two options, trolley experiments rule out some of the ways a virtuous person could distinguish themselves from the non-virtuous.

A second, closely related reason why virtue ethicists are not particularly interested in trolley experiments is that they are designed to remove the kinds of uncertainty that we have to deal with in real-life situations. Yet one of the ways in which virtuous people distinguish themselves lies precisely in how well they deal with the uncertainties and risks that are typical features of moral decision-making. In more realistic versions of *Bystander*, the agent cannot be sure that the brakes have (definitely and completely) failed, that workmen cannot get out of the way in time, and that they will definitely die if the trolley crashes into them. The consequences of the actions available to us are never specified ahead of time. Again, rather than it being a fact of the matter that one person will die if they divert the trolley and that five will die if they do not, it is a judgment or prediction that the agent must make on their own. And making a good judgment in these circumstances requires knowledge and experience, as well as the ability to stay calm in an emergency. A virtue ethicist would be interested in how well the participant deals with uncertainty: Are they too quick to assume the worst? Do they remain foolishly optimistic, refusing to see the obvious? But, of course, these kinds of questions fall outside the scope of the Trolley Problem.

Interestingly, the degree of certainty appears to have played an important role in how the participants in Stevens' experiment behaved. Only two participants pulled the switch, and both of them appeared to be convinced that they were choosing between five casualties and one. The other participants were much less certain about the choice they had to make. Some of them thought there was a good chance that the workmen will move out of the way in time (because at least one of them will look up, or the train will sound an alarm). Another was unsure what would happen if she did pull the switch – "I had better not touch anything because I don't know if I'll screw something up." It would therefore be a mistake to say of these participants that they decided to let the five workmen die rather than kill the one. They simply failed to make a decision, and part of the reason is that they were unsure what would happen if they did or did not pull the switch.

Thus, an important question for the virtue ethicist is whether any of the participants exercised sound practical judgment: Would a reasonable person conclude, based on the information available to them, that one (and only one) person will die if they pulled the switch, and that five will die if they don't? It could be the case that a bystander who diverts a fast-moving train onto a different track is acting wisely and courageously, that is, if they have good reason to believe it will prevent an even bigger disaster. But it could also be foolish or arrogant to assume they know enough to make the decision to interfere in this way. The important thing to note, then, is that in any realistic version of the bystander's dilemma there will be more than two ways of responding. The agent might decide to sacrifice one to save five, or decide to let the five die rather than kill the one. But they could also fail to make a decision, or make a decision and find themselves unable to execute it, or decide not to interfere. Thus, by forcing a choice between two options, and presenting the likely consequences of each option as a given, trolley thought experiments eliminate many of the ways in which a virtuous person would distinguish themselves from the non-virtuous.

The third feature of real-life moral dilemmas that is missing from trolley thought experiments is that they elicit strong emotional reactions. Any moderately virtuous or empathetic person in a bystander's dilemma would feel afraid for the workmen whose lives are in danger. All seven participants in Stevens' experiment reported being scared or terrified.[6] Some of them exhibited the "freeze response," with one reporting afterwards that he thought about switching (suggesting that he saw it as the right thing to do) but that he found himself unable to do anything. Others appeared confused and bewildered. Only two of the participants stayed sufficiently calm and focused to make a decision and also execute that decision. What this demonstrates,

---

[6] Indeed, Stevens expected subjects to find the experience emotionally challenging and even traumatizing, and took various steps to try to mitigate this.

I think, is that the question "What should you do in this situation?" is a very different question from "What would you do in this situation?" Acting well in a bystander's dilemma requires much more than merely making the right decision. It also requires strength and courage – the ability to overcome or set aside fear and uncertainty for the sake of a noble end.

In summary, then, and in response to the question, "What would a virtuous person do in *Bystander?*" the virtue ethicist will begin by noting that a virtuous person would never find themselves in such a situation, that is, one where (1) they are presented with a choice between two terrible options such that there is no need or opportunity to look for or consider a third option, and (2) they have a high degree of certainty about the consequences of the available actions, and (3) the situation does not evoke strong emotions in them.

7.4 Acting in character in trolley cases

We can side-step the realism problem by fleshing out the description of trolley thought experiments and specifying that the bystander is wise, even-tempered, and virtuous, that he has already figured out that there are only two options, that he is reasonably certain about the outcomes of each, and so on, and then repeat the question: What would a virtuous person do in this situation? Or, more precisely, what would a virtuous person do if they were acting in character? But this presents a further problem, namely, that it is questionable whether it is possible to act in character in trolley dilemmas.

Arguably, cases like *Driver* and *Bystander* are examples of situations that "overstrain human nature," as Aristotle puts it (*NE* 1110a19–26). To begin with, the virtuous agent will only have a few seconds to make a decision. It is true, of course, that virtuous people often impress us with their ability to act well in an emergency. There are many examples of courageous people who, in the space of a few seconds, are able to make a decision to, say, risk their own lives to save someone from drowning, while also figuring out exactly how to go about it. So I don't want to suggest that it is never possible to act in character in a situation where one is forced to make a quick decision. But there are two further features of trolley cases which, in combination with the time constraint, make it difficult – perhaps even impossible – to act well. The first has to do with the novelty of these cases. Virtues are character traits that require knowledge and skill, and thus can only be acquired through practice and experience. Yet very few people would have had the opportunity to learn how to act well in a trolley dilemma. As Julia Annas (2011, 16ff) explains, we learn to become virtuous within the circumstances of our lives. So, for example, the shy academic learns to become courageous by having to address large audiences and ruthless colleagues. But this kind of courage will be of little use in a trolley scenario, which calls for a different kind of courage. We can expect members of some professions – for example, police officers, rescue workers, soldiers, etc. – to have the kind of experience and training that is necessary to act well in emergency situations, but the same is not true of most of us, including people who are genuinely virtuous (courageous, benevolent, just, etc.). It would therefore be a mistake to conclude that the participants who "froze" and failed to make and/or execute a decision in Stevens' experiment were lacking in courage.

The second feature of trolley dilemmas which, in combination with the time constraint, can prevent a virtuous person from acting in character has to do with the nature of the conflict. In some situations, what makes it hard for someone to act well is that they have to fight desires that tempt them in the wrong direction. For instance, if we were to replace the sole workman with the bystander's new (and let us say, uninsured) car, a materialistic person might need a few seconds to overcome the temptation not to do anything. A virtuous person, by contrast, will find it easy to do the right thing. But in *Bystander*, the virtuous agent will find themselves torn between competing *virtuous* desires or dispositions. They will want to rescue the five workmen. And they will also have a strong aversion to doing anything that would harm the workman on the sidetrack. Both these desires are characteristic of virtue, and thus not something that we can expect a virtuous person to set aside or overcome, in the same way we might expect someone to set aside their love of fast cars to save lives. In short, then, trolley dilemmas force the virtuous person into a state of inner conflict that is very different from the inner conflict experienced by the typical rescuer, who has to overcome their fear for their own safety, or by the materialistic bystander, who has to overcome their love of material goods. Whatever the virtuous person decides to do in a trolley dilemma, they will have to find the strength to do (or allow) something that goes against their very nature as a virtuous person.

It will be in the nature of a virtuous person who finds themselves in a dilemma where they are forced to choose between virtuous dispositions to take the time to make a carefully reasoned decision. Unlike the non-virtuous person, who might be over-confident and have a tendency to act impulsively or carelessly – a virtuous agent will want to gather relevant information, consider alternative viewpoints, think through their options, and so on. But of course, this is impossible in trolley dilemmas. The virtuous agent will thus be *forced* to make an impulsive decision, and thus to behave in a way that is *out of character*.[7] Further, it is possible, even likely, that their spur-of-the-moment decision will not match the more reasoned decision they would come to if given the benefit of time, and that they will come to regret their decision later.

7.5 The virtuous agent in *Bystander*

A virtue ethicist might want to end their participation in the Trolley Debate at this point, but I think we can push ahead by asking: If they were to reflect on their actions afterward, would a virtuous person conclude that they made the right decision in the circumstances? Consider the following descriptions of how a virtuous agent might act in *Bystander*:

> Abel sees the trolley racing toward five people on the track ahead. He can see that the trolley is out of control, that it cannot be stopped, that it would be impossible for the five people to get out of the way, and that they will most probably be killed if the trolley crashes into them. He also sees that there is someone on the sidetrack, and realizes that this person will most probably die if he diverts the trolley. Abel is terrified. The thought that crosses his mind is: *the death of five people is worse than the death of one.* Abel pulls the lever.
>
> Brutus sees the trolley racing toward five people on the track ahead. He can see that the trolley is out of control, that it cannot be stopped, that it would be impossible for the five people to get out of the way, and that they will most probably be killed if the trolley crashes into them. He gets ready to steer the trolley onto a sidetrack. But then he notices that there is someone on the sidetrack, and with great alarm realizes that this person will most probably die if he diverts the trolley. Brutus is terrified. The thought that crosses his mind is: *I will kill that man if I pull this lever.* Brutus does not pull the lever.

Although they don't choose the same action, neither Abel nor Brutus behaves in a way that is characteristic of a vicious person. They have not been negligent or careless, they don't show a flippant or casual attitude to human life, and they certainly don't act in a way that can be described as cruel or

---

[7] Aristotle notes, in this regard, that "acts done on the spur of the moment we describe as voluntary, but not as chosen," in the sense that it does not involve rational deliberation (*NE* 1111b5–10).

malicious.[8] Their strong emotional response is entirely appropriate, as it shows that they empathize with the workmen and recognize what is at stake. Yet despite feeling terrified they manage to stay sufficiently calm to make a decision and to execute it, and this shows courage and strength of character.[9] We can add to this that neither Abel nor Brutus will emerge from the dilemma with their lives unmarred, as Hursthouse (1999, 63–90) puts it in her discussion of tragic dilemmas, for they played a role in the horrific death of the workman/men. And finally, their motives are not characteristic of vice. Abel is focused on minimizing harm, and Brutus is motivated by the thought that diverting the trolley will cause the death of the workman. They don't consider the reasons for taking the opposite course of action. This is due to constraints of time rather than arrogance or impulsivity, but it does mean that they won't come away feeling confident that they did the right thing. The question, then, is whether they will conclude, after some reflection, that they made the right decision by turning (or not turning) the trolley.

I think it is unlikely that a virtuous person, having witnessed the death of the workman/men, will describe their options in terms of a distinction between doing and allowing harm (e.g., "I killed the man, but my only other option was to let five people die"). The deontologist's explanations, in terms of actions and omissions, positive and negative duties, intended and merely foreseen effects, etc. will likely come across as hopelessly abstract and detached. As benevolent agents, their focus will be on whether they could have avoided the terrible outcome. The main consideration for Abel will be that five rather than one person would have died if he acted otherwise, and for Brutus, that one rather than five would have died. In both cases, their conclusion will be that diverting the trolley was (or would have been) the right decision.

If pressed to comment – as I am here – on the distinction between killing and letting die, a virtue ethicist can support this conclusion by arguing as follows. We can begin by accepting that, as a general rule (where this rule is

---

[8] We might contrast these two agents with their vicious alter egos: Bad Abel, who happily pulls the lever because he worries about being sued by five families instead of just one, and Bad Brutus, who decides not to pull the lever because he wants to maximize death and suffering. From a virtue-ethical perspective, both act wrongly, that is, in a manner characteristic of a vicious person. However, and as I argue below, it is plausible to claim that Bad Abel makes the right decision.

[9] Though as noted earlier, given the novelty of the situation and the fact that very few people would have had the opportunity to learn how to deal with this kind of situation, even the virtuous person might freeze in this situation and find themselves unable to make or execute a decision. This would amount to be a failure to act courageously in this situation, but it does not necessarily reveal a lack of courage.

based on past experience), killing someone is worse than letting them die. In most instances where someone willingly and knowingly kills another human being they will manifest one or more of the worst forms of vice, such as maliciousness (a desire to harm others), callousness (an insensitivity or indifference toward others' suffering), and cruelty (experiencing pleasure in causing or witnessing suffering). By contrast, most wrongful instances of failing to prevent someone's death are not the result of vice but rather of character flaws or imperfections that are all too common, such as a lack of courage (being too afraid to confront the threat), inattentiveness (not noticing the threat), errors in judgment (mistakenly assuming others will help), and inexperience or ignorance (not knowing how to prevent the death). Any minimally decent person will therefore have a stronger aversion to killing someone than to letting them die, and this would explain Brutus's reaction in *Bystander*. But the virtue ethicist can also note that there are many exceptions to the general rule that killing is worse than letting die. Occasionally, actively ending someone's life can be more humane or compassionate than letting them die (e.g., in some cases of active euthanasia). In other cases, letting someone die can be just as cruel and callous as killing them. And so the virtue ethicist would have no trouble supporting the widely held view that the best thing to do in *Bystander* is to turn the trolley.[10] Although it is an example of killing an innocent person, the action doesn't manifest vice but rather a virtuous desire to minimize the amount of harm caused by the trolley.

7.6 The virtuous agent in *Footbridge*

We can now move on to *Footbridge*, and ask whether a virtuous person would push the big man onto the track. Thomson introduces the *Footbridge* scenario in her 1985 paper:

> [Y]ou are standing on a footbridge over the trolley track. You can see a trolley hurtling down the track, out of control. You turn around to see where the trolley is headed, and there are five workmen on the track where it exits from under the footbridge. What to do? Being an expert on trolleys, you know of one certain way to stop an out-of-control trolley: Drop a really heavy weight in its path. But where to find one? It just so happens that standing next to you on the footbridge is a fat man, a really fat man. He is

[10] Thomson herself supports this view in her 1976 paper, but changes her mind in her 2008 paper, where she argues that it is wrong to turn the trolley and hence that the Trolley Problem is a "non-problem."

leaning over the railing, watching the trolley; all you have to do is to give him a little shove, and over the railing he will go, onto the track in the path of the trolley. Would it be permissible for you to do this? (1985, 1409)

In a more recent paper she notes that the agent has two options:

(i) do nothing, letting five die, or
(ii) shove the fat man off the footbridge down onto the track, thereby killing him, but also, since he's very big, stopping the tram and saving the five. (Thomson 2008, 362)

As noted earlier, thought experiments differ from real-life dilemmas insofar as the available options are presented to us at the outset. In most cases this is a convenient heuristic, as it draws our attention to the issue under discussion. As I often explain to students, cases like *Bystander* and *Footbridge* should not be seen as presenting a problem in Practical Ethics, where the aim is to come up with creative solutions to everyday moral problems. Rather, the aim is to consider a particular problem in Normative Ethics, in this case, the Trolley Problem: Why is it acceptable to kill the workman in *Bystander* but not the big man in *Footbridge*? However, to consider the Trolley Problem from a virtue-ethical perspective, we have to ask how a virtuous person would act in the situation, and to do this we have to imagine them actually being in that situation. An open-ended version of *Footbridge* is therefore more useful:

Caleb is standing on a footbridge over the trolley track. Next to him, leaning over the railing, is a big man. Caleb can see a trolley hurtling down the track, out of control. He turns around to see where the trolley is headed, and there are five workmen on the track where it exits from under the footbridge. Being an expert on trolleys, Caleb knows of one certain way to stop an out-of-control trolley: Drop a really heavy weight in its path. But he can't see any heavy objects near him. What should Caleb do?

Whenever I present this case to students they come up with the standard suggestions: Caleb (and the other man) should yell out, blow a whistle, wave their arms, run toward the workmen, look for a heavy object further down the track, etc. So far, none of them have proposed that Caleb should consider pushing the big man onto the track. When I offer this to them as a possibility, they typically confess that they hadn't thought of it. One explanation for this is that they lack a kind of cleverness, the ability to "think outside the box" displayed, for instance, by the rescuer who sees that she can use a ballpoint pen to save someone's life. A more plausible explanation is that seeing (ii) as an option requires viewing the big man in a way that is entirely uncharacteristic of a virtuous (or, indeed, any moderately decent) person: as a *heavy object*.

As we've seen in *Bystander*, it is easy to imagine how two people – Abel and Brutus – might choose different courses of action without either of them behaving (i.e., reasoning, feeling and acting) in a way that is consistent with vice (or, indeed, inconsistent with virtue). Deciding whether to divert the trolley doesn't involve seeing the sole workman as an object. But the same is not true in *Footbridge*, as the following narrative demonstrates:

> Caleb is standing on a footbridge. He notices the big man standing nearby, enjoying the fresh air and the view of the country. Caleb sees the runaway trolley and alerts the big man of the situation. Together, they face the question: "How can we save the workmen?" They look around, but can't see any heavy objects nearby. But then Caleb 'realizes that the big man's' body can be used as a trolleystop. He now has to decide whether to go through with it.

Regardless of whether Caleb decides to push the big man, he has already failed to respond in a way that is characteristic of a virtuous person. Caleb has made a shift from seeing the big man as a fellow human being, someone who shared with him experiences like enjoying the fresh air and looking for heavy objects to stop a runaway trolley, to viewing him as a trolleystop. If we were to replace the Caleb with a virtuous person, the narrative would go something like this:

> Daniel is standing on the footbridge. He notices the big man standing nearby, enjoying the fresh air and the view of the country. Daniel sees the runaway trolley and alerts the big man of the situation. Together, they face the question: "How can we save the workmen?" They can't see any heavy objects nearby. Daniel starts running toward the workmen, in the hope that he can help them in some way. The big man, who is no great athlete, stays on the bridge, waving and yelling as best he can.

In short, then, I think a virtuous person would not push the big man onto the track to save five others, because it would simply not occur to them to do so. If someone were to suggest this to them as an option (perhaps yelling out from a distance, "Push the big man! Quick!"), they will find it impossible to do so. Using someone as a trolleystop is simply not the kind of thing a benevolent person could do.[11]

One could challenge this point by noting that virtuous people are sometimes called upon to do things that go against their moral instincts. That is,

---

[11] Arguably, it is an example of what Bernard Williams (1993) calls a "moral incapacity."

their virtuousness can be the very thing that leads them astray. Consider, for example, the good doctor who comes across a gunshot victim, sees that he will surely die unless the bullet is swiftly removed, but finds herself in the middle of nowhere, with no medical supplies, and no means of getting help. It doesn't occur to her to use an old pocketknife to remove the bullet, or, alternatively, it occurs to her but she dismisses it as a viable option. After all, she has been trained to perform such procedures in a sterile environment, and has a strong aversion to causing pain and risking infection. We might forgive the good doctor, but still say that removing the bullet is – or would have been – the right thing to do, even if doing so goes against her nature as a good doctor. Reflecting on her actions afterward, she is bound to think: "I couldn't find it in myself to remove the bullet with a pocketknife, with nothing to relieve pain and prevent infection. But I should have done it; I could have saved his life." In this case, then, the doctor's benevolent nature appears to prevent her from acting in a truly benevolent manner, which suggests that virtue is an unreliable guide to right action. Arguably, something similar can be said in *Footbridge*: If virtuous Daniel failed to push the big man onto the tracks, he will regret this later and think, "I could have saved five people by sacrificing only one."

A virtue ethicist can respond to this objection by noting that there is an important difference between the two cases. In the doctor's case, her failure to remove the bullet is not due to her possessing benevolence as a virtue. We learn to become benevolent through practice, by actually helping people, and in the overwhelming majority of cases this does not involve causing extreme pain or risking serious harm. It is for this reason that we might be inclined to forgive the good doctor for her failure to remove the bullet. However, in some cases, risking harm and causing pain – even extreme pain – is consistent with benevolence, and this is one of the reasons why it is difficult to acquire benevolence as a virtue or excellence. Thus, what prevents the good doctor from removing the bullet is that she is not yet fully benevolent. As a virtue, benevolence requires more than just a desire to help someone or even the ability to succeed in doing so in everyday situations. It also requires skill or practical wisdom (in this case, recognizing that the bullet can be removed with a pocketknife, and judging that it is a risk worth taking) as well as courage – the ability to overcome fear (in this case, of causing pain) for the sake of a noble end. It would therefore be entirely appropriate for the good doctor to reflect on her actions, to notice her flaws or weaknesses, and to make an effort to become more benevolent and courageous, that is, to become the kind of person who could remove a bullet with a pocketknife to save someone's life.

By contrast, in *Footbridge*, seeing someone as an object is inconsistent with the virtue of benevolence. Benevolence is an example of what Christine Swanton (2003, 47–48) refers to as a flourishing-based virtue, which she usefully distinguishes from value-based virtues. Value-based virtues have as their aim producing, protecting, or preserving valuable objects such as works of art and rock formations. By contrast, flourishing-based virtues, such as benevolence, generosity, charity, kindness, and compassion, are aimed at the good of sentient beings, and thus require seeing them as beings that have needs and interests and are capable of flourishing. Daniel's inability to see and use the big man as a trolleystop is not something that he can overcome or set aside in order to meet the (actual, though unusual) demands of benevolence. Unlike the good doctor, Daniel will not reflect on his actions and think, "If only I weren't so sensitive and squeamish, I could have saved five people by sacrificing one." Becoming the kind of person who is capable of seeing and using others as objects is not something any moderately decent person would aspire to.

7.7 The loop challenge

We have arrived at a solution to the Trolley Problem that is very similar to the Kantian one, namely, that pushing the big man onto the track involves using him as a mere means to an end, whereas diverting the trolley toward the one does not. Thomson (1985, 1401–1403) uses "the loop variant" (or *Loop*) to reject this solution, so it is worth considering whether the same objection applies to the virtue ethicist's solution.

Loop is identical to *Bystander*, except that the sidetrack loops back onto the main track in such a way that, were the bystander to redirect the trolley, the sole workman's body will stop the trolley, thereby preventing it from looping back around and killing the five. Thus, the bystander in *Loop* needs the sole workman to achieve his goal of saving the five, just as the thin man in *Footbridge* needs the big man to achieve his goal. And yet, according to Thomson, it is permissible to redirect the trolley, for "we cannot really suppose that the presence or absence of that extra bit of track makes a major moral difference" (1985, 1403). Her conclusion is that the Kantian idea, that it is wrong to use someone as a mere means to an end, doesn't explain the difference between *Footbridge* and *Bystander*.

The question, then, is whether a similar objection can be made to the virtue ethicist's solution: The bystander in *Loop* must treat the sole workman as an object in order to save the five, in the same way that the thin man in

Footbridge must treat the big man as an object to save his five. So if we think a virtuous person would not treat others as objects, then we must conclude that the agent in *Loop* should not redirect the trolley, even though the agent in *Bystander* should. In doing so, however, we allow a trivial bit of detail – the extra piece of track – to make an important moral difference.

The virtue ethicist would respond to this objection by denying that the bystander in *Loop* will use the sole workman as an object (or mere means) if he chooses to divert the trolley. Thomson thinks otherwise, because she follows the standard Kantian (deontological) practice of describing an action from an impartial or external point of view, thereby ignoring the agent's own perspective, their reasons, attitudes, and motives. For instance, she gives the following criterion to determine whether the agent uses the one to save the five: "If the agent chooses to engage in the course of action, then he uses the one to save the five only if, had the one gone out of existence just before the agent started, the agent would have been unable to save the five" (1985, 1402). By contrast, the virtue ethicist is interested in whether the agent behaves (reasons, feels, reacts, etc.) in a manner that is characteristic of a virtuous person. She will (or indeed, must) describe their actions from the agent's perspective: What are their reasons, motives, and aims, and what attitudes and feelings do they express by acting in this way? And the bystander in *Loop* can decide to divert the trolley without viewing or treating the sole workman as an object or mere means:

> Ethan sees the trolley racing toward five people on the track ahead. He realizes that they will be killed unless he diverts the trolley onto a sidetrack, where there is only one person. He diverts the trolley, because he reasons: *The death of five people is worse than the death of one.*

Ethan doesn't view the sole workman as an object or trolleystop. He might well notice that the sidetrack loops back onto the main track, and that the five will be killed if the workman is able to get out of the way, but this fact need not figure in his reasoning at all. His reason for diverting the trolley, as well as his attitude to the sole workman, is identical to Abel's, and therefore consistent with virtue. Like Abel, he will be able to reflect on his actions afterward and conclude that he made the right decision, given that the alternative would have been even worse. From a virtue-ethical perspective the only difference between the cases is that it is possible for the bystander in *Loop* to treat the workman as an object:

> Frank sees the trolley racing toward five people on the track ahead. He can see that they will be killed unless he diverts the trolley onto a sidetrack,

where there is only one person. He sees that the sidetrack loops back onto the main track, toward the five. He diverts the trolley toward the one workman on the sidetrack, because he reasons: *His big body will stop the trolley from reaching and killing the five.*

In this case, a virtue ethicist might argue that Frank makes the right decision (because he decides to do what a virtuous person would do in the situation), but he doesn't behave in a way that is virtuous or praiseworthy, given that his attitude and reasoning are inconsistent with virtue.[12]

7.8 Conclusion

In this chapter I discussed some of the reasons why virtue ethicists may not be interested in discussing the Trolley Problem. While these might be good reasons for focusing their efforts on other, perhaps more interesting or pressing issues, they don't prevent the virtue ethicist from discussing (suitably modified) trolley cases and asking: What would a virtuous person do in these situations, if they were acting in character? Following this approach I have argued that there is an important difference between the two central cases. In *Bystander*, a virtuous agent's chief concern would be to minimize harm, and so they would choose to divert the trolley (or, in retrospect, think that they should have diverted the trolley). By contrast, a virtuous agent in *Footbridge* would not push the big man onto the track to save five workmen, because doing so involves viewing and using him as an object. I've tried to show that the virtue ethicist can meet Thomson's loop challenge by noting that diverting the trolley does not necessarily involve viewing the sole workman as an object or means to an end.[13]

---

[12] Deontologists like Frances Kamm (2000) and Pauline Kleingeld (2020) have responded to the loop challenge by distinguishing between different cases where the one person's death is a condition of saving the five.

[13] I would like to thank Hallvard Lillehammer, Stephanie Gibbons, Daniel Weijers, Way Ming Chan, and Joseph Ulatowski for helpful feedback on an earlier version of this chapter.

8   Trolley dilemmas from the philosopher's armchair to the psychologist's lab

Guy Kahane and Jim A. C. Everett

8.1 Introduction

We suspect that Philippa Foot would have been surprised to hear that she is today most widely known for being the originator of the first trolley dilemma. She would be even more surprised that much of the interest in her gruesome thought experiment has come not from moral philosophers trying, as she did, to use it to answer foundational questions in ethics, but from an army of psychologists, neuroscientists, and even driverless car engineers. Foot would be positively startled to hear that these scientists – we will refer to them as "moral psychologists" – assume that trolley dilemmas are the paradigmatic illustration of the conflict between deontological and utilitarian approaches to ethics.

In this chapter, we will look at how Foot's philosophical thought experiment became a key method in the moral psychologist's toolkit – there are by now many hundreds of experiments employing trolley dilemmas and their variants. We will contrast the aims of moral philosophers like Foot with the way trolley dilemmas are usually interpreted in the psychological literature, and raise questions about the benefits, and dangers, of transforming philosophical thought experiments into experimental materials.

Trolley dilemmas have their enemies. Some philosophers think that ethics should avoid speculation about such far-fetched cases; some psychologists raise similar doubts about using trolley dilemmas to empirically investigate human morality. But we are not trolley skeptics. We think that, properly used, trolley dilemmas can shed light on the way people form judgments about certain kinds of moral problems. But we will also argue that many moral psychologists misinterpret what we can learn from trolley dilemmas. Once this misunderstanding is cleared up, the central role that trolley dilemmas have played in moral psychology over the past two decades will seem overblown.

8.2 Runaway trolleys in moral philosophy

Let us begin by briefly introducing the core trolley dilemmas. In Foot's original case, it is the driver of the runaway trolley who must decide whether it's permissible to switch to a sidetrack where only one would die rather than let the trolley run over and kill five. But in a more common variant, it is a bystander who can divert the trolley in this way. We will call this *the Bystander case*. In Judith Thomson's famous variant, *the Footbridge case*, a bystander can again prevent the five from being run over by sacrificing another innocent person, but here one needs to push that person off a footbridge to achieve that goal. Many moral philosophers (and as we now know, the vast majority of lay people; see Greene, 2013; Greene et al., 2001) judge that it's permissible to switch but not permissible to push. The puzzle, the "trolley problem," is to explain *why*.

Foot and Thomson, and those moral philosophers who have followed in their footsteps, typically approach this puzzle not by applying to it some sweeping ethical theory but in a bottom-up manner. The goal is to map a complex local moral terrain without artificially imposing on it any rigid, overarching theoretical structure. The assumption is that each moral domain needs to be explored separately, often using distinctive thought experiments that bring out what might be puzzling in *that* moral context. It may turn out, at the end of the inquiry, that a small set of moral principles can explain morality as a whole. But this is certainly not assumed in advance and, from the point of view of such a bottom-up approach, this seems improbable. The moral principles that explain trolley cases are unlikely to tell us much about, say, the requirements of justice or the limits of beneficence.

We can describe this approach to ethics as an attempt to map what we can call commonsense morality (henceforth CSM) – the complex and seemingly messy set of moral intuitions and convictions that govern everyday moral thought. The background assumption is that CSM is right about the basics more often than not, and that there is no better starting point for moral reflection. This is not to say that CSM does not get some things wrong, even deeply wrong, and some common moral convictions may not survive critical reflection. CSM may be the first word but certainly needn't be the last.

There is a sense in which this approach to ethics can be described as deontological, but only in the minimal sense that it is not (act) consequentialist, rather than because it assumes any overarching Kantian (or other) theoretical framework. Foot and Thomson just take it for granted that, at least sometimes, we are *not* required to act in the way that would lead to the best outcome – and that in some cases acting in this way is simply forbidden. CSM is obviously deontological in that broad sense. This is not to say that the attempt to understand some moral domain cannot nondogmatically draw on Kantian ideas – say, that it's wrong to treat persons merely as means – just as it is open to the idea that, at least in some cases, what matters are the consequences of our acts (saving five lives rather than one in the Bystander case).

Other chapters in this volume will say more about the substance of this philosophical project's attempt to solve the trolley problem. But we wish to highlight one thing that it *doesn't* aim to do. It should already be clear that it doesn't aim to support Kantian ethics or some similar grand theory. But neither does it aim to show that utilitarianism is mistaken.[1] Utilitarianism isn't even on the table – it is no accident that utilitarianism and consequentialism are not even mentioned in Foot's (1967) article introducing the first trolley case – nor, for that matter, is Kant.[2] As we said, this philosophical inquiry simply *assumes* that utilitarianism is false – and that it is wrong to sacrifice the one in Footbridge. That act utilitarians say otherwise is just a background given that is external to the project. The number of lives at stake is held fixed across cases not to keep in view some utilitarian alternative but to hold constant one morally relevant factor to better enable us to disentangle another (which is presumably to do with the *way* one achieves the identical outcome in Bystander and Footbridge). The trolley problem is also not of much interest to utilitarian philosophers – there's nothing philosophically puzzling or significant here for them (though we'll later mention utilitarians who think that *empirical* research into the psychological roots of the trolley problem can support utilitarianism).

So despite the way they are presented in moral psychology, trolley cases were not designed to bring out the key tension between utilitarianism and deontology. Nor are they even particularly central to the long-standing debate between utilitarians and their opponents. A wide range of cases is invoked in that debate – relating, for example, to whether utilitarians can properly account for the value of personal relationships, the tension between utilitarianism and a noninstrumental concern with justice, or the way utilitarianism seems to imply that

---

[1] We will follow the psychological literature in identifying utilitarianism with the maximizing act utilitarianism associated with Bentham, Mill, and more recently Peter Singer. Other types of utilitarianism – for example, rule consequentialism – would not necessarily endorse sacrificing one to save five.

[2] Thomson's (1985) paper does briefly mention Kant – but only to dismiss the idea of using people merely as means as being particularly helpful in solving the trolley problem (p. 1401). Utilitarianism isn't mentioned, though Thomson briefly refers to "utility" – but only in order to assert that the idea that rights can trump utility "must be correct" (p. 1404).

most people in affluent countries must make extremely demanding sacrifices to assist distant strangers in need.[3] There is one famous anti-utilitarian argument that *is* structurally somewhat similar to the Footbridge case, however: Bernard Williams' (1973) "Jim and the Indians" scenario. In that case, the eponymous Jim has to decide whether to shoot and kill one of twenty captives in order for the other nineteen to be freed by their captor. However, Williams, a philosopher who vehemently rejected utilitarianism, actually thought that shooting the one was probably the *right* thing to do in this case; his focus was on the mistaken way that, in his view, utilitarians arrive at this conclusion. We will return to this example, but for now it just serves as a reminder that even if those engaged in the project of trying to solve the trolley problem ended up concluding that it is morally permissible to save the five in *both* the Bystander and Footbridge case, this needn't mean that they have come to endorse utilitarianism or even taken a significant step in its direction.

8.3 Runaway trolleys in psychology

Psychologists and neuroscientists are interested not in the normative question of whether (and why) it is wrong to sacrifice the one in Footbridge, but in the descriptive question of what it is that makes people judge it is wrong to do so. There is, however, at least a degree of surface overlap between the two projects. We said that the philosophers who are engaged in the project of trying to solve the trolley problem can be seen as attempting to map a sector of CSM, at least as a first stage in the inquiry. They want to uncover potentially morally relevant factors that are present in Footbridge but not in Bystander, factors that could explain why it's permitted to sacrifice the one in the former but not in the latter. At least some psychologists are also interested in the descriptive question of which perceived factors in these structurally similar scenarios *causally* explain why people respond to them so differently. Moral psychologists, then, are also interested in mapping CSM, in the trolley context and elsewhere, but such mapping of CSM is also just a first step for psychologists as well. While moral philosophers hope to go on to elaborate a network of consistent explicit principles that will capture at least the core of CSM (though may depart from it in certain respects), moral psychologists

---

[3] Foot's own critique of utilitarianism appealed both to its inability to capture the moral distinctions between doing and allowing, and foreseen and intended – which bear some connection to trolley cases – and to her rejection of the utilitarian assumption that there is such a thing as a "best state of affairs" that acts can bring about. See, e.g., Foot (1985a).

ultimately want to look "under the hood," so to speak, and uncover the underlying psychological and neural mechanisms, as well as the developmental, social, and evolutionary pathways that shape CSM.

There is another important way in which how psychologists interpret trolley dilemmas differs markedly from how philosophers see them. As we mentioned above, psychologists do not usually present trolley dilemmas as a tool for investigating the specific domain of permissible harm – what we will call "instrumental harm." Rather, they see these dilemmas as ways of distilling the key contrast between deontological and utilitarian approaches to morality – they are presented as capturing the core of the long-standing debate between utilitarians such as Bentham and Mill, on the one hand, and Kant on the other. Accordingly, psychologists are *just* as interested in judgments to the effect that it *is* permissible to sacrifice the one in Footbridge as in judgments to the contrary. And, unsurprisingly, they describe such judgments as "utilitarian" and "deontological," respectively. Moreover, when psychologists look "under the hood" when these opposing judgments are made, they often take themselves to uncover the psychological bases for deontological and utilitarian decision-making. And by this, psychologists don't just mean deontological and utilitarian forms of decision-making *in the context of instrumental harm*. Rather, they regularly write as if what they find out in the trolley context tells us something quite general about how these forms of moral decision-making operate *across* moral contexts – and, in this way, informs us about the key psychological processes that shape human morality. In their more ambitious moments, psychologists even think that the psychology of trolley dilemmas can tell us something about the sources of these philosophical theories and explain why the debate between them is so hard to resolve.

We started by saying that Foot would be surprised not just by the centrality of trolley dilemmas for current moral psychology but by the way such dilemmas are interpreted. Given what we've said above about how moral philosophers typically use trolley dilemmas, this framing of their import *should* seem surprising. But it is fairly easy to explain *why* this framing has become so dominant: This was how trolley dilemmas were introduced in the series of seminal studies that launched "trolleyology" in psychology – and which helped launch the broader project of empirical moral psychology as it is currently practised.[4]

---

[4] Though Petrinovich and O'Neill had earlier used trolley dilemmas in two psychological studies that did not receive much attention at the time (Petrinovich et al., 1993; Petrinovich and O'Neill, 1996).

The studies we have in mind are those of Greene and his colleagues. In their 2001 *Science* article, Greene et al. sought to explain why CSM treats Bystander and Footbridge so differently by applying dual-process models of cognition to moral judgments. Dual-process (or dual-system) models conceptualize cognition as resulting from the competition between quick, intuitive, and automatic processes, and slow, deliberative, and controlled processes (e.g., Chaiken & Trope, 1999). Greene et al. (2001) devised a battery of dilemmas that included Bystander and Footbridge but also many new dilemmas that share the same broad structure, where to save the greater number of lives one must sacrifice some innocent person. We shall call dilemmas of this sort "sacrificial dilemmas." Greene et al. distinguished between dilemmas such as Footbridge where saving lives required harming an innocent person in an up close and personal way ("personal" sacrificial dilemmas) from dilemmas like the Bystander one where the sacrifice was done only indirectly ("impersonal" sacrificial dilemmas). Using functional MRI and reaction time data, Greene et al. tried to explain the contrast between Bystander and Footbridge as reflecting that between opposing kinds of processes. In Push, the prospect of directly harming someone evokes an automatic pre-potent emotional reaction that shuts down this option for most people. By contrast, there is no such emotional response in Bystander, when the harm is "impersonal," and therefore there is no affective obstacle to using more controlled, effortful cognitive processes to engage in a "utilitarian" cost–benefit analysis favoring the sacrifice. In later work, Greene et al. reported that when people do endorse the "utilitarian" option in personal dilemmas (a fairly small minority), this decision was associated with increased activation in the DLPFC – an area of the brain implicated in explicit and effortful reasoning. And Greene went on to use these findings to mount much discussed arguments in favor of utilitarianism (Greene, 2007, 2014) – as did Peter Singer (2005). If these arguments are correct, then the philosophical project launched by Foot and Thomson – the project of trying to solve the trolley problem – has been a complete waste of time. Scientific evidence doesn't help us solve the problem but simply dissolves it since, if Greene is right, empirical evidence reveals there is no morally relevant difference between Bystander and Footbridge.

This dual-process model of moral judgment (henceforth, DPM) – on which "deontological" judgments are based in emotion-laden intuitive responses and "utilitarian" ones in effortful reasoning – remains an influential, perhaps the dominant, general model of moral decision-making in current moral psychology. The DPM has also evolved in a number of ways, both conceptual and empirical, that we will describe below. Not all of the very many psychologists who employ trolley dilemmas in their studies endorse this model, and few of them would want to wade, as Greene did, into philosophical questions about the ethical upshots of this scientific research. But many of these psychologists share (whether explicitly or implicitly) the basic framework of interpreting the different ways of responding to moral dilemmas – especially in the case of "personal" dilemmas such as Footbridge – as reflecting opposing deonto-logical and utilitarian modes of moral decision-making.

In what follows, we will focus on this framing of empirical research using trolley (and trolley-like) dilemmas. We will raise questions – both conceptual and empirical – about this influential research framework. We will primarily focus on the aspect of it that most dramatically diverges from the philosoph-ical project we described above – the study of pro-sacrificial "utilitarian" judgments in trolley dilemmas and what, if anything, they can tell us. But we will also say something about "deontological" judgments toward the end.

8.4 Why trolleys?

Trolley-inspired sacrificial dilemmas are by far the most popular experimental paradigm in moral psychology – and seem set to continue to dominate the field. There are, as we said, many hundreds of psychological studies employing variants of these dilemmas. Many of these manipulate aspects of either the dilemmas and their presentation or the contexts in which participants face them to see if this has any effect on the resulting moral judgments – whether by describing the trolley's potential victims in terms that suggest a racial or class background, presenting the dilemmas in a difficult to read font or foreign language, or giving them to people who have alcohol or an antidepressant in their blood, or have been sleep-deprived – and these are just a handful of examples out of very many. But it seems odd that such complex and far-fetched thought experiments, originally devised for a specific philosophical purpose, have become the key way to study the psychological building blocks of moral decision-making. No doubt, some researchers use sacrificial dilemmas simply because they are so dominant in the field – not to mention rather easy to add to an experiment. But that's obviously not much of a justification. And many researchers clearly do assume that by studying sacrificial dilemmas they are learning something quite general about moral decision-making and, moreover, that these dilemmas are uniquely placed to answer such questions. What underlies this is the assumption that sacrificial dilemmas (which psychologists often call "classical moral dilemmas") are the key way to capture the contrast between utilitarian and deontological approaches to morality.

While this rationale is not always made fully explicit, a recent article authored by some leading researchers in the area nicely spells it out. Patil et al. (2021) start by pointing out the ubiquity of moral dilemmas only to go on, in that very sentence, to write as if moral dilemmas *just are* cases where we must decide whether to "prevent a large harm by committing a smaller one." They then tell us that such dilemmas admit of

> two basic solutions, each associated with a broad school of philosophical thought: the utilitarian response that favors maximizing welfare by any means (Mill, 1998) and the deontological response that often forbids causing harm, especially instrumentally (Kant, 2005).

It is this basic moral opposition that they then present as the focus of much recent work in moral psychology, writing that

> Over the last two decades, psychologists have devoted intense theoretical and empirical effort to understanding the processes underlying these competing motives, as well as the process that adjudicates between them.

And they tell us next that to study this opposition, psychologists "typically use hypothetical vignettes that pose a dilemma between harming a few people to save a larger number of individuals from harm" – that is to say, trolley scenarios or sacrificial dilemmas inspired by them.

In other words, sacrificial dilemmas are of interest because by studying them psychologically, we can learn something general about two key ways of approaching ethics. And Patil et al. present the DPM – which, echoing Greene and others, they sometimes describe as the dual-process model of *morality* – as the key example of what we have learned in this way. The model is presented as making entirely general claims about two opposing ways of making moral judgments – deontological and utilitarian – that happen to conflict in "the specific case of sacrificial dilemmas."[5]

So let us look more closely at the DPM. It says that moral decision-making is driven by two systems: The first system is automatic and emotionally based and favors deontological decisions; the second is an effortful, deliberative reasoning system that favors utilitarian decisions. These two systems conflict in emotional scenarios like Footbridge, and this is why it is experienced as a moral dilemma.

---

[5] Noting in passing our past criticism of such claims, Patil et al. later qualify this by saying that their findings tell us about other aspects of utilitarianism only "indirectly," though they offer no support for that claim and ignore considerable evidence to the contrary that we discuss below.

Since it was first introduced in 2001, numerous studies have tried to test the DPM. A wide range of findings has been taken to support it. For example, participants typically take longer to make pro-sacrificial decisions (Greene et al., 2001) and the implementation of cognitive load reduces utilitarian judgments (Trémolière & Bonnefon, 2014); pro-sacrificial judgments are associated with stronger activation in brain regions that support controlled, deliberative processes, such as the dorsolateral prefrontal cortex (Cushman et al., 2012; Greene et al., 2004); and pro-sacrificial judgments are higher in those with damage to the ventromedial pre-frontal cortex, an area of the brain that underlies integrating affect into decision-making (e.g., Koenigs et al., 2007). But other studies have reported findings that are harder to square with the DPM (e.g., Bago & De Neys, 2019; Gawronski et al., 2017; Gürçay Baron, 2017) and some have challenged the model on methodological grounds – both highlighting the far-fetched character of typical trolley-like dilemmas (Bauman et al., 2014) and the apparent gap between hypothetical judgment about trolley cases and actual behavior (Bostyn et al., 2018).

8.5 Two questions

In this chapter, we largely side-step these live empirical debates, focusing instead on broader conceptual questions about what "trolleyology" tells us about the nature of moral cognition generally, and about utilitarianism and (to a lesser extent) deontology specifically.

When people judge that it is morally acceptable to push the one off the footbridge to save five others in Footbridge, researchers routinely describe such responses as "utilitarian judgments," and often assume that the factors and processes that drive or favor such judgments tell us something about "utilitarian decision-making," when this is often understood (or presented) in quite general terms – and in some cases, as in Greene's own work, to even explain the psychological, or even neural, sources of the historical debate between deontologists such as Kant and utilitarians such as Bentham and Mill (Greene, 2007; Greene et al., 2004). But what does it mean, exactly to describe these judgments as "utilitarian," and can studying them really tell us anything useful about utilitarian decision-making or even the foundational ethical debate between utilitarians and their critics? This is not just a terminological question but a question that gets at the very heart of the trolleyology enterprise in psychology – since, as we saw, the key rationale for the extraordinary amount of attention that sacrificial dilemmas have received in psychology is precisely the supposed link to that grand ethical debate.

We have already highlighted the fact that trolley dilemmas weren't designed to bring out this theoretical contrast. This doesn't automatically mean that they cannot be re-deployed for that different purpose – after all, utilitarians do differ from most deontologists in how they respond to these dilemmas (Conway et al., 2018). But this does raise two worries. One is that even if utilitarianism offers distinctive answers to trolley dilemmas, this is just one of many ways in which utilitarianism clashes with CSM. For example, another key way in which utilitarianism conflicts with CSM, and with many alternative ethical approaches, is its radical impartiality. Those who reject utilitarianism often complain that it is too demanding because it asks us to treat ourselves and those closest to us as having equal weight to all other people in the utilitarian calculus, arguably meaning, for example, that we would be required to give up much of our income to charities aiding strangers in developing countries. Is it really plausible that we can learn much about this clash between utilitarianism and less demanding ethical views by studying responses to the trolley problems (Kamm, 2009)? A second worry is whether complex thought experiments that were developed within a (broadly) deontological project are the best way to study the opposition between utilitarianism and deontology even *within* the specific moral domain of instrumental harm.

Since we are asking whether it even makes sense to describe lay responses to trolley dilemmas as "utilitarian" and "deontological," we will use the more neutral label "pro-sacrificial" judgment for conclusions that favor sacrificing some to save a greater number, and "anti-sacrificial' for the opposing conclusion (c.f. Everett & Kahane, 2020). We can now frame our two worries more precisely:

> **The Internal Content Question**: *Do pro-sacrificial judgments reflect processes that can be described as utilitarian in a meaningful way or are they merely judgments that happen to accidentally overlap with this specific verdict of utilitarian theory?*

> **The Generality Question:** *Is there a significant similarity between the factors and processes that drive pro- and anti-sacrificial judgments and those that drive moral judgments in other moral domains where utilitarianism conflicts with deontology?*

8.5.1 The internal content question: Is willingness to sacrifice few to save a greater number really utilitarian?

We mentioned that some studies report findings that seem inconsistent with the DPM. But one especially pressing empirical challenge to the DPM relates to the heavily supported association of pro-sacrificial judgments with mark-edly antisocial personality traits and moral beliefs (Bartels & Pizarro, 2011). It has been found, for example, that pro-sacrificial judgments are associated with reduced aversion to harm (Cushman et al., 2012), psychopathy at both clinical (Koenigs et al., 2012) and subclinical levels (e.g., Bartels & Pizarro, 2011; Kahane et al., 2015), and even with endorsement of rational and ethical egoism: The idea that, contrary to a utilitarian focus on impartial welfare maximization, an action is rational or moral only if it maximizes one's *own* self-interest (Kahane et al., 2015).

These findings are not directly inconsistent with the DPM if it is understood as no more than an account of why people make pro- and anti-sacrificial judgments: The view actually predicts that a reduction in emotional response to harming others would increase pro-sacrificial judgments. The problem they raise is at a deeper level: These findings cast doubt on the assumption that pro-sacrificial judgments actually have much to do with utilitarianism. In short, they raise what we call the Internal Content question by suggesting that the pro-sacrificial judgments of ordinary folk merely accidentally overlap with the prescriptions of utilitarianism (Kahane & Shackel, 2010). People with antisocial personality traits are endorsing pro-sacrificial judgments, but for the "wrong" reasons: because they lack the commonsense, deontological intuition against causing harm, not because they give greater weight to utilitarian considerations.

We can also present the problem in methodological terms: The association with antisocial traits suggests that most work using sacrificial dilemmas has failed to distinguish between (a) those who make pro-sacrificial judgments because they overcome commonsense intuitions and recognize that the sacrifice is a necessary evil needed to save more lives, and (b) those who have a very weak aversion to causing harm in the first place, regardless of the benefit (see Wiech et al., 2013). We cannot tell which of these routes was operative just by knowing whether someone has made a pro-sacrificial judgment.

It's important not to misunderstand this challenge. It is *not* about whether individuals make pro-sacrificial decisions due to a conscious application of utilitarian principles. Few, if any, lay people are likely to do so. Rather, the concern is whether there is at least some meaningful relation – a sufficient similarity – between what would make a card-carrying utilitarian endorse the sacrifice and what makes (at least some) ordinary lay people do so.

8.5.1.1 Different senses of "Utilitarian"?
Proponents of the DPM have offered two responses to this challenge (Conway et al., 2018). The first response is that it assumes an overly demanding

understanding of what is required to describe a judgment as "utilitarian." Now despite all the work in moral psychology describing judgments in trolley-style moral dilemmas as "utilitarian" or "deontological" there has been little-to-no attempt to actually formalize what these labels are supposed to mean.[6] In a much-needed attempt to bring some clarity here, Conway et al. (2018) have proposed a five-level taxonomy of different senses in which a judgment might qualify as "utilitarian":

Level 1: A judgment is utilitarian just if it coincides with the answer that utilitarianism would give

Level 2: A judgment is utilitarian if it arises through aggregate cost–benefit reasoning

Level 3: A judgment is utilitarian if it arises through a concern for the greater good in that specific context

Level 4: A judgment is utilitarian if it arises from a general commitment to utilitarian theory/principles

Level 5: A judgment is utilitarian if it arises from an explicit application of utilitarian theory/principles.[7]

Using this taxonomy, Conway et al. (2018) provide a terminological response to the internal content question by denying the problem exists. According to their suggestion, there is no need for "utilitarian" judgments to arise from meaningfully utilitarian processes or reflect more than a superficial overlap with utilitarian principles because the dual-process framework uses the term "utilitarian" simply in a Level 1 (and sometimes Level 2) way. A judgment can be described as utilitarian simply in virtue of superficially conforming with what utilitarian philosophers say, and researchers needn't make any assumptions regarding "the mindset, intentions, or philosophical commitments of the judge" (p. 242) making that judgment. Since there never was any assumption that pro-sacrificial judgments reflect concern for the greater good, the fact that indifference to harm can drive pro-sacrificial choices is either by-the-by or predicted by the DPM (since it suggests that reduced aversion to harm

---

[6] In earlier work, Greene (2007) suggested that we classify lay judgments as "utilitarian" and "deontological" if they overlap with "characteristic" verdicts of utilitarian and opposing deontological theories; this would correspond to "Level 1" judgments in the taxonomy below.

[7] Like most other moral psychologists, Conway et al. assume that utilitarians directly apply their theory in making moral decisions, even though from at least as early as Mill, utilitarians have highlighted the point that while their criterion of rightness is utilitarian, the best way to maximize utility over time may often be to follow nonutilitarian rules and sentiments. Woodcock (2017) argues that, because of that, it's a mistake to just assume that a genuine utilitarian will sacrifice the one in Footbridge.

should lead to increase in pro-sacrificial judgments). The internal content question, they suggest, simply misses the point.

We are unconvinced. We can, of course, define our terms to mean whatever we want. But some terminologies are more useful and some are positively misleading. Suppose it turned out that the vast majority of pro-sacrificial judgments are "utilitarian" *only* in the superficial Level 1 sense. This would entirely undermine the current rationale for giving such a central role to sacrificial dilemmas in current moral psychology, since, by assumption, there won't be any useful sense in which these judgments reflect "utilitarian decision-making," let alone reveal something about the debate between utilitarians and deontologists. And as the quotes above from Patil et al. clearly show, many researchers in the field clearly *do* assume that pro-sacrificial judgments are often aligned with utilitarianism in a more demanding, and illuminating sense (why else would they assume that such findings can speak, for example, to the moral status of utilitarianism?). Of course, no one in this debate expects ordinary people to be card-carrying utilitarians in the "Level 5" sense, so the critical issue isn't which terminology to adopt, but whether what drives at least some pro-sacrificial judgments bears a meaningful resemblance to the kind of considerations that would drive full-blown ("Level 5") utilitarian judgments about such cases.[8]

8.5.1.2 Process dissociation

The second, more compelling, response to the Internal Content Question implicitly accepts this point. It claims that there *is* a meaningful overlap in the processes underlying at least *some* pro-sacrificial judgments and a concern for the greater good, but that the standard way of using and analyzing sacrificial dilemmas like the trolley problem has simply obscured this.

Conway and Gawronski (2013) have argued that the conventional dilemma methodology fails to distinguish a "utilitarian" tendency to maximize good outcomes from the absence of "deontological" concerns about causing direct harm. Instead, they argue, support for the DPM is better provided by using the technique of process dissociation (PD): Giving participants a battery of multiple dilemmas in which some, like the trolley problem, involve harming for the greater good and others, unlike the trolley problem, involve the same harm but without the good consequences (e.g., pushing someone off a footbridge just for fun). The PD technique measures two parameters.

---

[8] Though we won't frame our discussion below in terms of Levels 2–4 of the Conway et al. framework since these definitions don't really map well onto the points we'll be raising.

The first parameter reflects those with relatively stronger harm-rejection tendencies (the "D-parameter" indicating "deontological" inclinations to avoid causing harm), who consistently reject causing harm, whether or not it leads to overall positive consequences. The second parameter (the "U-parameter") reflects outcome-maximization tendencies – aiming for the best possible consequences regardless of whether doing so requires causing harm or not (i.e., endorsing harm only when it maximizes overall welfare). Conway and Gawronski (2013) argue that using PD, they are able to provide new support for the DPM. They reported that while deontological harm-minimizing tendencies are associated with greater empathic concern, utilitarian outcome-maximizing tendencies are associated with a motivation to engage in effortful cognition. And they found that implementation of cognitive load influenced only the U-parameter. Finally, they found that both parameters were positively associated with participants' self-report ratings of their own internalized moral identity. They therefore argue that "utilitarian inclinations [in sacrificial dilemmas] are at least partially driven by a genuine moral concern rather than indifference to suffering" (Conway & Gawronski, 2013, p. 228). Building on this work, Patil et al. (2021) combine the PD approach with a variety of outcome measures including self-report, performance, computational, and neural assessments of reasoning, claiming that, in line with the DPM, their work shows "a consistent relationship between reasoning and utilitarian moral judgments." Based on such findings from sacrificial dilemmas, they conclude that utilitarian decision-making in general is preferentially supported by reasoning and speculate that this may offer support for utilitarianism.

This empirical work goes some way to suggesting that *at least some* people who make pro-sacrificial judgments are doing so because of a moral concern for saving more lives. This is therefore taken by Greene (see Conway et al. 2018) and others (see Patil et al., 2021) to fully address what we have called the Internal Content Question. Even if this were so, it will of course remain the case that the findings of a great deal of research using sacrificial dilemmas over the past twenty years cannot be taken at face value, and needs to be redone using PD.[9] Another worry is that while PD suggests that *some* people make pro-sacrificial judgments due to utilitarian cost–benefit reasoning, this may

---

[9] Or the more recent "CNI model," which distinguishes not only preferences for consequences and (deontological) norms, but also for inaction (vs. action) (see Gawronski et al. 2017). Of course, one key disagreement between utilitarians and deontologists is precisely over whether we should accept the act–omission distinction – a central deontological norm. That it is treated as psychologically distinct by this model is in line with our argument below for the disunity of "utilitarian psychology."

be a minority given that the correlation between pro-sacrificial judgments and the D-parameter is typically stronger than with the U-parameter (Conway & Gawronski, 2013).

Critically, however, there remains a significant gap between what the U-parameter measures and what is distinctive about a utilitarian approach to ethics. First, to give more weight to saving more lives isn't the same as engaging in the demanding form of aggregate cost–benefit reasoning distinctive of utilitarianism. Classical utilitarianism is a maximizing view, yet there is little evidence that the same people who endorse the sacrifice of one to save five would sacrifice, say, one to save two – yet this is precisely what utilitarianism requires. Second, while utilitarianism says that we are *required* to sacrifice one to save five, most people making pro-sacrificial judgments merely think that doing so is morally permitted (and there is no evidence that people high on the U-parameter see this differently). The U-parameter, then, seems to merely measure the degree to which people give moral weight to saving more lives in "sacrificial" contexts, something considerably vaguer, and weaker, than the maximizing consequentialism of utilitarianism. We will see below that this concern for saving lives isn't even impartial in the sense distinctive of utilitarianism. Given this, the U-parameter really seems to measure the weight that people give to what moral philosophers call the duty of beneficence – a duty that is accepted by most ethical theorists, including Kant!

There is a more fundamental issue with the PD approach. The DPM claims that there are two competing systems – an automatic, emotional "deontological" one and an effortful, deliberative "utilitarian" one. These systems are meant to be causally distinct: The strength of someone's "deontological" aversion to harming people is independent of the degree to which that person gives weight to saving the greater number. This is why the D and U-parameters are presented as distinct: How high you are on one leaves it open how high you are on the other.[10] Conway and Gawronski's criticism of prior research is that they treat the utilitarian and deontological factors that determine one's overall judgment as inversely related when they are actually independent according to the DPM.

This may well be so psychologically, but when we turn to the relation between the so-called D- and U-parameters and the ethical theories from which these labels derive, this is puzzling. Utilitarianism and deontology *are* "inversely related" or, more precisely, logically incompatible: If one is true

---

[10] Though it should be noted that the scoring of the D-parameter requires division by scores on the U-parameter.

then the other is false, and vice versa. This is again, we suggest, a case of psychologists using philosophical concepts in ways that significantly depart from their original meaning. We already suggested that the U-parameter measures something less demanding than a maximizing utilitarian cost–benefit calculation. But the gap from utilitarianism is greater. Utilitarianism doesn't just say that, among our various duties, we have a duty to maximize utility (let alone the looser duty of beneficence). The core claim of utilitarianism is that morality is *just* about maximizing utility, *and nothing else*. There is a great difference between someone who sees the deontological aversion to harming people in certain ways, independently of the consequences, as merely illusory (or as a misfiring heuristic), and someone who thinks there really is a strong moral reason not to harm people in this way (call this "non-maleficence"), but that in some cases this reason may outweighed by considerations of beneficence – which may themselves be sometimes outweighed by, say, considerations of justice or partiality. The first scenario closely mimics how a utilitarian approaches trolley cases (or indeed all moral choices), but the second is merely how CSM typically works: CSM accepts a plurality of non-absolute moral reasons that can conflict with each other and different ones win the day in different contexts. Since there is no strict recipe for weighing these reasons against each other, different people will weigh them somewhat differently. Thus, those who endorse pro-sacrificial judgments because they give more weight to saving lives (as opposed to due to indifference to violence) needn't be engaging in a different *kind* of moral deliberation than those who reject such conclusions, let alone echoing an opposing utilitarian approach. They may just set the weighting of the very same moral reasons differently than others (and a large majority would join them in sacrificing the few if the numbers saved are large enough). *This* is a critical distinction that sacrificial dilemma research, even when supplemented by PD, has so far overlooked.[11]

We can return here to Williams' anti-utilitarian scenario of "Jim and the Indians." Williams' point was precisely this: that utilitarianism is wrong even when it's right – that even when it correctly identifies the right thing to do (sacrifice one to save a greater number), it misrepresents what is involved in making such a difficult, tragic decision and, indeed, *why* it is so difficult and tragic – it is tragic because one is forced to violate what one recognizes as a weighty moral norm. If we did not recognize the alternative moral force, it

---

[11] Talk about aversion to harm obscures this distinction since it's ambiguous between acceptance of a genuine moral reason that is locally defeated and a mere affective force that needs to be overcome.

would simply not be such a difficult decision, nor experienced as a moral dilemma. We don't need to accept Williams' criticism to see that his portrayal of what goes in such dilemmas is psychologically more plausible.[12]

So what, given all that, should we make of the association between the U-parameter and various measures of reasoning capacity and motivation? The Internal Content Question asks whether there's a meaningful relation between what drives pro-sacrificial judgments and utilitarianism *qua* ethical theory. This question also applies to such findings. As Patil et al. (2021) concede, we still lack a detailed account of what such reasoning actually involves. One worry is that such reasoning is merely generic. It most certainly doesn't reflect greater engagement *in* cost–benefit analysis. Surely all participants effortlessly judge that saving five lives is better than saving just one (Kahane, 2012). Yet if the reasoning involved merely reflects the effort of overcoming some strong intuition pointing in a contrary direction, then there is nothing particularly surprising about such an association – making a moral judgment that you find counterintuitive is bound to be harder. But it will be similarly harder to make a counterintuitive deontological judgment or even an egoist one (see Kahane et al., 2012). And if the effort relates to deliberation about the respective weight of beneficence and non-maleficence then it reflects a form of moral reasoning that makes *no sense* on a utilitarian approach (Kahane, 2014).

8.5.1.3 Trolley dilemmas and the psychological roots of instrumental harm

Current evidence, then, suggests that many instances of pro-sacrificial judgments are merely superficially consistent with utilitarianism, and describing such judgments as "utilitarian" seems unhelpful. While the PD approach offers a tool for distinguishing such judgments from those reflecting genuine concern for saving more lives, important gaps remain. This is perhaps why some proponents of PD have recently explained the U-parameter as tracking "outcome maximising" tendencies and the D-parameter as tracking "harm rejection" rather than link them to ethical theories (Reynolds &Conway, 2018; though see Byrd and Conway, 2019).

---

[12] So are we saying that to closely resemble a utilitarian approach one has to be high on the U-parameter and *low* on the D-parameter? No: To care only about consequences is still to be strongly averse to pointless harm; it's just that deontologists have *two* reasons not to cause such harm and utilitarians only one.

A distinctive implication of utilitarianism is that it permits, and in certain cases requires, engaging in highly harmful acts for instrumental reasons – such acceptance of what we call "instrumental harm" is one key way in which utilitarianism departs from CSM. We do not rule out that sacrificial dilemmas can shed light on the psychological roots of this aspect of utilitarianism. But it seems to us that sacrificial dilemma research is still not sufficiently conceptually precise to allow us to make this link, and we suspect that the subgroup of lay people who approach trolley dilemmas in a way that meaningfully echoes utilitarianism is incredibly small. Of course, understanding why a minority of people have a more permissive view of instrumental harm is of psychological and practical interest even if the underlying reasons have nothing to do with utilitarianism. But this wouldn't justify moral psychologists' obsession with trolley dilemmas: There are many other moral domains, and "moral outliers," that are equally worthy of psychological investigation.

8.5.2 The generality question: From trolleys to duties to distant stranger

But let's suppose – just for argument's sake – that the PD approach does allow us to identify a subclass of pro-sacrificial judgments that meaningfully echo a utilitarian approach, or that future research manages to identify such a subclass. Our second question remains: Would this tell us anything *general* about the psychology of utilitarianism – the DPM purports to make entirely general claims about the sources of "utilitarian decision-making" (see Conway et al., 2018; Greene, 2007; and more cautiously, Patil et al., 2021), as opposed to merely uncovering the sources of *utilitarian judgments about instrumental harm* (or even: utilitarian judgments *in the unusual context of trolley-like dilemmas*). But there are many other contexts in which utilitarianism clashes with CSM, and with many deontological views. The context we will consider in depth is that relating to utilitarianism's radical *impartiality*. The kind of moral causes historically most closely associated with utilitarianism haven't been that of pushing large men off footbridges (or even permitting the use of torture in interrogation), but those of, say, equality for discriminated groups, and, more recently, arguing that people in affluent countries should make demanding sacrifices to alleviate poverty, and fighting speciesism. In the background is the utilitarian view that we should aim to impartiality maximize well-being of all sentient beings on the planet without privileging compatriots, family members, or ourselves over strangers – or even non-human animals (Everett & Kahane, 2020; Kahane et al., 2018).

We can ask several questions about the generalizability of findings about trolley dilemmas. To begin with, we can ask whether a tendency to make "characteristically utilitarian" (pro-sacrificial) judgments in the context of instrumental harm is associated with a tendency to make characteristic utilitarian judgments in other contexts. If pro-sacrificial judgments merely reflected indifference to harm, there would, of course, be little reason to expect them to be associated with the judgment that, say, we should generously aid distant strangers rather than spend on ourselves. But if some pro-sacrificial judgments really do reflect a "genuine concern for the greater good," why shouldn't that concern for the greater good express itself in other moral contexts as well? And even if there is no correlation between different kinds of characteristic utilitarian judgments, the DPM – understood as making general claims about utilitarian and deontological decision-making – predicts that at least the processes involved in utilitarian judgments should be similar across contexts.

8.5.2.1 The psychological disunity of "Utilitarian" tendencies

The evidence so far strongly suggests that the answer to both questions is negative. To begin with, there seems to be no tie between judgments relating to instrumental harm and judgments about impartial beneficence. Even after controlling for the antisocial element in pro-sacrificial decisions, either through partial correlations (Kahane et al., 2015) or PD (Conway et al., 2018), there was either no relationship or a negative relationship between the endorsement of the "utilitarian" choice in trolley-style dilemmas and the "utilitarian" choice in dilemmas about impartial beneficence (e.g., whether someone should donate to a less effective local charity or a more effective one supporting distant strangers; eat meat or adopt a vegetarian lifestyle; or spend time volunteering instead of with one's family).[13]

Consonant with that, support for instrumental harm and for impartial beneficence is associated with rather different psychological profiles. For example, Kahane and Everett et al. (2018) showed that while empathic concern, identification with all of humanity, and concern for future generations were positively associated with impartial beneficence, these were negatively correlated with instrumental harm. And while instrumental harm is associated with psychopathy, impartial beneficence is positively correlated with religiosity.

---

[13] An important exception is, of course, trained moral philosophers, a group for whom there is a tight association between instrumental harm and impartial beneficence (Kahane et al. 2018).

The key assumption of the DPM is that deliberation favors "utilitarian" judgments whereas intuition favors "deontological" judgments. We saw that there is evidence supporting that picture in the context of sacrificial dilemmas. What about impartial beneficence?

Capraro et al. (2020) tested this across three studies in which they manipulated participants' cognitive process by priming intuition or deliberation (Levine et al., 2018; Shenhav et al., 2012) and had participants answer a series of statements assessing the endorsement of trolley-style instrumental harm or impartial beneficence. In line with past research, participants who were encouraged to rely on intuition endorsed utilitarian statements about instrumental harm significantly less than those who were encouraged to make their decisions through careful deliberation. Critically, however, this wasn't so for impartial beneficence, where conceptual priming had no impact on participants' endorsements.

Such results provide evidence that impartial beneficence and instrumental harm are not just distinct in terms of trait measurement and their associated individual differences but also in terms of cognitive processing: Conceptual priming of intuition selectively affects endorsement of instrumental harm but not impartial beneficence.[14]

8.5.2.2 Differences in social consequences

The DPM claims that in dilemmas like Footbridge, participants' intuitive judgments oppose instrumental harm. But *why* would moral intuitions align with deontology in this way? One hypothesis is that relying on encoded heuristic rules is simply cognitively cheaper, requiring less computational effort (Crockett, 2013). Another, not mutually exclusive possibility, is that rejecting instrumental harm serves a social function by signaling suitability as a social partner (Everett et al., 2016, 2018).

There is now robust evidence that people who endorse instrumental harm in sacrificial dilemmas are seen as less moral and trustworthy, chosen less frequently as social partners, and trusted less in economic exchanges than those who reject it (Bostyn & Roets, 2017; Everett et al., 2016, 2018; Rom et al., 2017; Sacco et al., 2017; Uhlmann et al., 2013). For example, Everett et al. (2016) investigated individuals' perceptions of agents who either endorsed or rejected the sacrifice in the footbridge dilemma, presenting participants with information about an agent who read this dilemma and either endorsed ("it is better

---

[14] This also seems to be the case in other domains: Rehren et al. (forthcoming) similarly found that contrary to the DPM, greater deliberation wasn't associated with greater endorsement of non-retributive (instrumental) judgments about punishment.

to save five lives than one") or rejected the sacrifice ("killing people is just wrong, even if it has good consequences"). Across a series of studies, Everett et al. found that participants perceived those who gave deontological responses to a sacrificial moral dilemma as more trustworthy than those who gave utilitarian responses. These results have been replicated in multiple studies (Brown & Sacco, 2017; Rom et al., 2017; Sacco et al., 2017) and pre-registered replication projects (Everett et al., 2018).

While endorsing instrumental harm reduces trust, the same is not true for impartial beneficence. Everett et al. (2018) conducted four studies in which they investigated perceptions of people who endorsed either utilitarian or deontological solutions to dilemmas involving either instrumental harm or impartial beneficence. Should, for example, someone spend their weekend cheering up their lonely mother or instead help rebuild houses for families who have lost their homes in a flood? As in the original work on instrumental harm, Everett et al. again presented participants with an agent who made either a characteristically deontological decision that honored special obligations (i.e., spend time with the mother and give money to the grandson) or a characteristically utilitarian decision that focused on impartially maximizing overall outcomes (i.e., spend time rebuilding the strangers' damaged homes, or give the money to charity). Their results suggested that while someone who endorsed impartial beneficence was thought to be a *worse* friend, they were thought to make a *better* political leader. In recent work, Everett et al. (2021) explored this further in an experiment spanning twenty-two countries over six continents. Over 23,000 participants completed self-reported and behavioral measures of trust in leaders who endorsed utilitarian or nonutilitarian principles about instrumental harm or impartial beneficence in dilemmas concerning the COVID-19 pandemic. Confirming previous work, results showed that across both the self-reported and behavioral measures, endorsement of instrumental harm decreased trust, while endorsement of impartial beneficence increased trust. To the extent that such social perceptions play a role in shaping people's moral judgments, these findings suggest that people's support for (or opposition to) instrumental harm and to impartial beneficence have rather different sources.

8.6 Trolleys and deontology

We have raised questions about the relationship between so-called utilitarian judgments in trolley-like dilemmas and a utilitarian approach to ethics. We will end by briefly commenting on the other side of the divide. As we saw, moral psychologists typically present pro- and anti-sacrificial choices as distilling the opposition between Bentham and Mill, on one side, and Kant, on the other side. And because they associate deontology with Kant in this way, psychologists often describe deontological judgments as reflecting rigid, absolute rules. To be willing to break these rules is therefore, they assume, to give up deontology – to go over to the utilitarian side. But we already saw that this is an implausible picture of what many people do when they form pro-sacrificial judgments. Just like utilitarianism, the Kantian view departs from CSM, and as such isn't a helpful conceptual framework for understanding lay moral psychology. We already mentioned that the philosophical project of solving the trolley problem isn't wedded to a Kantian framework, even if it is open to deploying and reinterpreting broadly Kantian ethical ideas. And many prominent Kantians either dismiss the trolley problem (see, e.g., Wood, 2011) or just ignore it.

But deontology isn't synonymous with Kant. The deontological frameworks that are closest to CSM don't appeal to a grand Categorical Imperative but to a plurality of more specific, defeasible moral duties (c.f. Ross, 1930). And we saw that such a picture of potentially competing moral reasons is more likely to capture how ordinary folk think about trolley dilemmas (Kahane, 2014). So while describing anti-sacrificial judgments as "deontological" isn't as problematic as describing pro-sacrificial ones as "utilitarian," even here moral psychologists need to exercise more care in how they draw on philosophical concepts. Still, CSM is obviously deontological in the minimal sense of being non-consequentialist. The DPM claims that the deontological refusal to sacrifice the one to save five in Footbridge reflects an emotional response, and none of the things we said about the contrary pro-sacrificial judgments challenges that. Now few deontologists would be surprised that nonutilitarian views are based in intuition – this isn't news but an explicit assumption of the philosophical project to solve the trolley problem (the focus on Kant again gets in the way here). The link between such intuitions and emotion might be more surprising to some, but it is also emphasized, even celebrated, by nonutilitarians such as Williams (though he wouldn't have liked the label "deontologist"). In any event, one thing that twenty years of psychological research into trolley dilemmas clearly shows is that the intuitive aversion to throw the large man off the footbridge is based on complex unconscious computations, and responsive to multiple factors, even if it has an affective dimension. Even Greene's own later work, for example, found that anti-sacrificial judgments don't merely reflect the "up close and personal" nature of the way the sacrifice has to be done in

Footbridge, but are also responsive to what the sacrifice is intended to achieve (Greene et al. 2009). Tracing deontological judgments to intuition or even emotion thus doesn't, in itself, present any challenge to the philosophical project of trying to solve the trolley problem.

Now Greene and others do put forward arguments that attempt to use empirical findings to undermine such deontological judgments (see, e.g., Greene 2007). We do not have space here to assess these arguments. But we want to end by pointing out that the role of moral psychology needn't be negative in this way. We mustn't think that empirical findings can either undermine the philosophical project of solving the trolley problem, or is irrelevant to it. Another possibility is that it can positively contribute to this project. We already pointed out that there is at least a partial overlap between the aims of moral philosophers and moral psychologists: They both aim to map the underlying structure of CSM, at least in the first instance. And here there is good reason to think that psychological methods can help uncover the factors (whether morally relevant or irrelevant) that underlie our judgments about trolley cases in ways that go beyond what can be achieved in the armchair. In this way, psychological evidence can support, or raise doubts, about possible solutions to the trolley problem (see Kahane, 2013).

8.7 Conclusion

Philosophers have been puzzling about the trolley problem for half a century, moral psychologists, for two decades. In this chapter, we have tried to clarify some aspects of the relationship between these two projects. There is, of course, the obvious contrast between normative and descriptive aims – between trying to figure out what's the *right* thing to do in trolley scenarios, and why, and trying to understand the psychological processes that underlie why some people *think* that certain responses to these scenarios are right – or wrong. But we've highlighted a further contrast, a contrast in what philosophers and psychologists think trolley dilemmas are *about*. Within moral psychology, trolley dilemmas are widely approached as distilling the foundational ethical debate between utilitarianism and deontology – between Bentham and Kant. We raised doubts about the usefulness of framing empirical research into moral dilemmas in these grand terms. We are far from thinking that ethical theories, concepts, and thought experiments – including trolley dilemmas – cannot usefully inform psychological research. But psychologists should take care when they transplant philosophical notions from their original armchair habitat into the very different context of empirical research focusing on moral decision-making in ordinary folk. We have argued that the way many psychologists have linked trolley dilemmas to Kantian deontology and, especially, utilitarianism is problematic and that recent attempts by psychologists to address this worry have only been partly successful. Trolley dilemmas can be a useful tool for studying a particular sector of commonsense morality. But once its assumed tie to grand philosophical debates is put in question, it is hard to justify the extraordinarily central role that trolley dilemmas have so far played in moral psychology.

9 Trolleyology

What it is, why it matters, what it's taught us, and how it's been misunderstood

9.1 What is the "Trolley Problem"? What are "Trolley Dilemmas"? and what do you mean by "Trolleyology"?

The "Trolley Problem" is two related problems. Both concern the moral acceptability of causing harm for the sake of a greater good.

The original Trolley Problem, as defined in classic papers by Philippa Foot (1967) and Judith Jarvis Thomson (1976, 1985), is a *normative* problem, a set of questions about what one *ought* to do when it's possible to sacrifice one life for a larger number of others.

Latent within the original normative problem is a *descriptive* problem, a set of empirical questions about how we think (and feel) about these normative questions.

I believe that solving the normative problem (if it can be solved) requires a better understanding of how we think, that is, a better understanding of the descriptive problem. The idea that understanding moral thinking might be important for ethics seems unremarkable to most people (in my experience) and is not new in philosophy. Many philosophers, from Aristotle on down have taken the time describe how, in their view, moral thinking works. Elizabeth Anscombe (1958, 1) once wrote "It is not profitable for us at present to do moral philosophy; that should be laid aside at any rate until we have an adequate philosophy of psychology, in which we are conspicuously lacking." I wouldn't go that far. But philosophers are taught early on (and rightly, in my opinion) to avoid casually sliding from descriptive "is" claims into normative "ought" claims (Hume, 1751/1975). With Hume's warning in mind, one might believe that normative moral questions can be effectively insulated from questions about moral psychology, just as mathematical problems can be solved without attention to the psychology of mathematics. I think this view of moral psychology is mistaken. The idea that decision-making can be improved through psychological self-knowledge has been enormously influential (Kahneman, 2003, 2011), and for good reason. Why, then, should we think that moral decision-making is somehow immune to this benefit? (More on this below.)

The "Trolley Problem" gets its name from the "trolley dilemmas" originally constructed by Foot, Thomson, and many others since (Fischer and Ravizza, 1992; Kamm 1993, 2007). There are many trolley variants, but the core problem is nicely distilled by contrasting two well-known cases.

In the standard *switch* (or *bystander*) case, a runaway trolley is headed toward five people who will be killed if nothing is done. But you can hit a switch that will divert the trolley onto a sidetrack, where it will run over a single person. Here, most people say that it's morally acceptable for you to turn the trolley so that it kills only one person instead of five.

In the standard *footbridge* case, a runaway trolley is again headed for five people. You are on a footbridge over the tracks, in between the oncoming trolley and the five. Next to you on the footbridge is a large person or (to forestall prejudicial influence) a person wearing a large backpack. The only way to save the five is to push this other person off the footbridge and onto the tracks. This person will block the trolley, thus saving the five, but this person will die in the process.

People often describe moral dilemmas involving such trade-offs as "trolley problems." But the original "Trolley Problem" is not a single moral dilemma. Rather, it's a more abstract dilemma, a meta-trolley problem, arising from our tendency to respond differently to different trolley dilemmas without a clear understanding of why we should. For example, in both the *switch* and *footbridge* cases one can save five lives by sacrificing one life, and yet most people say that it's morally acceptable to turn the trolley in the *switch* case, but that it's wrong (or, at least, *more* wrong; Awad et al., 2021) to push the person in the *footbridge* case.

The normative trolley problem begins with the assumption that these differential responses are probably morally right: It probably *is* morally acceptable to turn the trolley in the *switch* case, and probably *isn't* morally acceptable in the *footbridge* case. The normative challenge is to explain *why* this pattern of response is justified. Of course, one might conclude that it's not justified, as Thomson (2008) did late in her career. But if we didn't feel the pull of saying "yes" to *switch* and "no" to *footbridge*, there would be no Trolley Problem.

The descriptive Trolley Problem, the scientific problem, is to explain why we tend to respond differently to these two cases (among others). What is it about the *switch* case that makes us approve of that five-for-one sacrifice? And what is it about the *footbridge* case that makes us disapprove? And what is it about *us* that makes us respond so differently to these two cases? Over the last two decades, I and hundreds of other researchers have attempted to answer these questions.

I and some others use "trolleyology" as an affectionate term for this scientific enterprise. I'm happy to extend this term to include the original philosophical enterprise – pioneered by Foot and Thomson – of using trolley dilemmas as tools for normative ethical theory.

9.2 Why should philosophers care about the trolley problem?

Philosophers should care about the Trolley Problem because it's inescapable for any philosopher who is serious about resolving real-world moral disagreements. This is not to say that all serious, practical ethics must focus on trolley-type dilemmas. However, the kinds of moral *principles* that could resolve real-world moral disagreements inevitably have implications for trolley-type dilemmas, and those principles cannot be adequately evaluated if those implications are ignored.

The simplest way to dodge the Trolley Problem is to give up on practically relevant normative ethics. Many philosophers make general abstract claims about the nature of ethics while making no attempt to answer practical moral questions. I have no objection to this activity, much as I have no objection to playing chess and writing poetry. But if moral philosophy can't aspire to give the world answers to challenging, real-world moral questions, then it is, in my view, greatly diminished. One of the things that I admire most about the original philosophical trolleyologists – such as Philippa Foot (1967), Judith Jarvis Thomson (1976, 1985), and Frances Kamm (1998, 2008) – is that they are serious about trying to answer real-world moral questions. They study trolley dilemmas to gain clarity in the formulation of moral principles that have important practical implications.

Why is the Trolley Problem inescapable for practically relevant normative ethics? Why can't we just ignore these cartoonish hypotheticals? Nearly all significant real-world moral disagreements involve trade-offs. No matter what, some will be better off and some worse. To take real-world problems seriously is to seek resolutions of these trade-offs. If such recommendations are to have any force, they can't be arbitrary. Nor can they be based on naked intuition, which is effectively arbitrary to anyone whose intuitions differ. Serious answers must be backed up with *reasons*. And to give a reason is to appeal to something more general than one's present opinion – that is, to a *principle*. Even if one reasons by analogy, attempting to resolve a controversial case by comparing it to a less controversial one, one is implicitly appealing to a governing principle, one that deems the two cases similar in relevant respects, however else they may differ (Campbell & Kumar, 2012). And principles, in virtue of their generality, have implications across a range of cases. To evaluate a principle, one must understand its implications. And to understand the implications of a principle more fully, one must consider what it says about cases that have not arisen, including ones that may never arise. The goal is not to get a head start on unlikely future events. The goal is to understand the principle as it exists today, tomorrow, and for all time.

Any principle offering guidance about trade-offs involving human lives and well-being will have implications for trolley dilemmas (which need not involve literal trolleys). That's what makes trolley problems, and the Trolley Problem, inescapable. We don't know what our moral principles really mean until we've put them through the trolley wringer.

If the implications of your preferred principles all seem fine to you and everyone else, then you're in luck. But you're not in luck. No serious moral theorist is so lucky. Given that everyone's preferred principles have counter-intuitive implications in hypothetical cases, there are three options: (A) Blame the principles, and try to improve them. (B) Blame the intuitions – and try to move beyond them. (C) Deny that one needs to do anything because these are just hypothetical cases, and who cares.

Classic trolleyologists such as Foot, Thomson, and Kamm have mostly gone with Option A – urging philosophers, including themselves, to formulate moral principles that give more apparently right answers and fewer apparently wrong answers about real and hypothetical cases. This leads to some very "intricate ethics" (Kamm, 2008).

In my work as a scientifically informed moral philosopher, I've emphasized Option B, arguing that the moral appearances we call intuitions can be systematically misleading, just as intuitions can be systematically misleading in other domains (Kahneman, 2003, 2011).

But many people – both philosophers and others – are tempted by option C: Can't we just ignore these artificial, hypothetical dilemmas?

A common complaint about trolley dilemmas is that they are *hypothetical*, accompanied by the suggestion that hypothetical questions are inherently unimportant. But is that true? Would you marry someone who said that they would cheat on you if, hypothetically, an appealing and willing dalliance partner came along? Would you vote for a politician who said that they would nuclear-bomb millions of foreigners if, hypothetically, this could save one co-national's life? Why not? The truth is that we care a lot about hypotheticals. Indeed, as we look toward an unknown future, *everything* we care about is hypothetical.

This brings us to a related complaint, which is that trolley dilemmas are *unrealistic*. Your spouse really could cheat on you. The President really could start a genocidal nuclear war. But will you ever be faced with a runaway trolley?

You want more realistic cases? Let's call that bluff. When dismissing trolley dilemmas as unrealistic, people invariably point to the greater uncertainty and complexity of real-world problems. In a typical trolley dilemma, it's assumed that there are only two options and that each option comes with a known set of consequences: Under Option A, five live and one dies. Under Option B, five die and one lives. And all the people involved are effectively interchangeable. It's all very pat. The real world isn't like that, don't you know?

Ok. Let's get real. Suppose that it's not a runaway trolley, but something more realistic, such as healthcare decisions in which the allocation of limited resources determines who lives or dies (Mounk, 2020). Instead of considering only two options, let's consider seven options (A–F), each with nine sub-options (A_1, A_2, ... F_8, F_9). Instead of assuming known consequences for each option, let's assume a statistical distribution of possible outcomes for each of these 63 sub-options. However, it's not a single distribution of outcomes, but rather a distinct distribution for each of, say, 58 people who might be affected. But each of these person-specific distributions depends on features of the people affected that we've not yet specified. Old vs. young? Historically marginalized vs. not? Let's suppose there are 120 kinds of people who might be affected. So far, we're up to 438,480 different statistical distributions of possible outcomes that we need to consider, but, really, we're just getting warmed up.

Are we doing better normative ethics now? When people complain that trolley dilemmas are artificially constrained and overly simplified, they are not really asking for fewer constraints and greater complexity. They're rationalizing. They're grasping at reasons to ignore the difficult hypothetical. They are imagining that they can somehow avoid the big questions – *what general factors ought to matter in a moral decision?* – by focusing on details of cause and effect. This is like avoiding the difficult problem of deciding whom to marry by jumping right into wedding planning.

If you're facing a complex, real-world dilemma you can, and should, thoroughly consider your options and their likely consequences. But to assume that there's nothing *else* to do is to assume a form of consequential-ism – with the implication that it's justified to push the man off the footbridge, among other things. If you want to assume that consequentialism is correct, well, I'm sympathetic. But this doesn't address the underlying normative question. It merely assumes an answer.

Trolleyologists study simplified, hypothetical dilemmas not because they've failed to understand that the real world is complicated and uncertain. Rather, they've succeeded in understanding that morality is even more complicated and puzzling than many people realize. Even if one limits one's attention to cases with exactly two options and with guaranteed outcomes, it's still very complicated. To get serious about practical normative ethics, it helps to put aside the more mundane forms of complexity and focus on the stuff that's truly puzzling.

In sum: Serious moral answers are backed by reasons, and reasons follow from general principles. General principles have implications for a wide range of cases, including ones that haven't (yet) happened. Whether such cases literally involve trolleys is incidental. You can freely substitute other causal mechanisms for trolleys. But you can't be serious about answering practical moral questions involving difficult trade-offs and escape the Trolley Problem.

9.3 Why should scientists care about the trolley problem?

I'll be brief here because I've addressed this question many times elsewhere (Cushman & Greene, 2012; Greene, 2013, 2014, Conway et al. 2018; Plunkett & Greene, 2018).

The classic research strategy in social psychology is to study a real-world phenomenon by "operationalizing" it, that is, by creating a version of that phenomenon in the lab. Stanley Milgram (1974), for example, wanted to understand how seemingly ordinary people could be induced to murder innocent people, as they did in Nazi Germany. He therefore engineered a situation in which ordinary people were pressured to deliver what they believed to be potentially lethal electric shocks to innocent people. This strategy has been wonderfully productive, but it's not the strategy of scientific trolleyology. This has been a source of much confusion.

Cognitive psychologists, by contrast, often use probes with unusual properties to better understand the structure of the mind. Chomsky (1957) famously used the weird sentence "Colorless green ideas sleep furiously" to demonstrate the cognitive dissociation between syntax and semantics. To take a more recent example, in 2015, the Internet was ablaze over "the dress," a cropped image of a dress that some people saw very clearly as depicting a black and blue dress, while others saw it as very clearly as showing a white and gold dress. (Many people could see the dress both ways, but not at the same time. The dress is in fact black and blue.) As a visual object, the dress image is exceedingly atypical. But that doesn't make it irrelevant to human vision. On the contrary, it's exceedingly interesting because of what it reveals about how our brains create the experience of color (Lafer-Sousa & Conway, 2017; Wallisch, 2017).

Scientifically, trolley dilemmas are more like the dress (and other visual illusions) and less like Milgram's laboratory ordeal. They were never intended to serve as stand-ins for real-life transportation emergencies. They are, instead, unusual cognitive probes that are interesting because they elicit competing responses in our brains, and consequently reveal interesting things about the cognitive structure of moral judgment (Cushman & Greene, 2012).

9.4 What have we learned from trolley dilemmas? (Part I: The dual-process theory)

Scientifically speaking, the most fundamental thing that we've learned from trolley dilemmas is that moral judgment is not the product of a single process or processing stream. There is no unified "moral sense" or "moral faculty." Moral judgment is not dominated by moral *reasoning*, as developmental moral psychologists believed for many years (Kohlberg, 1969). Nor is moral judgment so overwhelmingly intuitive that reasoning is just a side show (Haidt, 2001). Instead, our moral judgments are importantly influenced by at least two dissociable processes: (1) intuitive and relatively automatic emotional responses to certain kinds of harmful actions; (2) explicit cost–benefit reasoning, along with the control processes needed to apply this reasoning. The dissociation between these two processes is seen most clearly within the *footbridge* case, and in the contrast between the *switch* and *footbridge* cases. This cognitive dissociation is the essence of the *dual-process* theory of moral judgment (Greene et al., 2001, 2004; Greene, 2013; Shenhav & Greene, 2014).

In response to the *switch* case most people give the *utilitarian* judgment, approving of hitting the switch that turns the trolley. (The claim here is that the *judgment* is utilitarian, not that the person making it is a utilitarian. More on this below.) This judgment reflects simple cost–benefit reasoning (Cushman, Young, & Hauser, 2006).

In response to the *footbridge* case, most people say that it's morally unacceptable to save five lives at the expense of one. (For reasons that are unclear, the majority opposing pushing appears to be shrinking; Hannikainen, Machery, & Cushman, 2018.) Here, cost–benefit reasoning applies as well, but there is another major force at work: Most people have an automatic negative emotional response to the action in the *footbridge* case. And this inclines people toward the *deontological* judgment that it's wrong to push, even though it would save more lives. (Here, too, the claim is not that these people are adherents of a deontological philosophy, but rather that they are giving a characteristically deontological *judgment*.) In the *footbridge* case, this emotional response competes with impartial cost–benefit reasoning, whereas in the *switch* case, the cost–benefit reasoning runs mostly unopposed.

The first evidence for this theory came from a functional neuroimaging (fMRI) experiment (Greene et al., 2001). This experiment contrasted "impersonal" dilemmas such as the *switch* case with "personal" dilemmas such as the *footbridge* case. This paper has many limitations, which I've discussed elsewhere (Greene, 2014; Greene & Young, 2020) and is best regarded as a preliminary effort. A subsequent fMRI study (Greene et al., 2004) provided more direct evidence for the implication of cognitive control in utilitarian judgment. And a study published a decade later (Shenhav & Greene, 2014) helped refine the dual-process theory while shoring up evidence for its core tenets. This paper linked deontological responses to activity in the amygdala, utilitarian responses to activity in the dorsolateral prefrontal cortex (DLPFC), and the integration of these responses to activity in the ventromedial prefrontal cortex (VMPFC). (See also Hutcherson et al., 2015, on the VMPFC as a decision integrator and Glenn et al., 2009, on the amygdala and deontological judgment.)

Some of the most compelling results supporting the dual-process theory come from studies of patients with emotional deficits. The VMPFC is one of the key regions damaged in the famous case of Phineas Gage (Damasio, 1994). Patients with VMPFC damage have intact general reasoning capacities (often scoring very well on standard IQ tests), but they are unable to generate or integrate intuitive emotional responses into their decisions (Damasio, 1994), leading to abnormal social behavior. The dual-process theory predicts that patients with VMPFC damage will give typical utilitarian responses to cases like *switch*, thanks to their intact basic reasoning skills. But, critically, it predicts that these patients, due to their emotional deficits, will also give utilitarian responses to cases like *footbridge*. This is precisely what was found by two different research groups, one in the United States (Iowa), and one in Italy (Koenigs et al., 2007; Ciaramelli et al., 2007; Moretto et al., 2010). In the Iowa study, patients with VMPFC damage (compared to healthy controls) made up to five times as many utilitarian judgments (as compared to healthy and brain-damaged control participants) in response to dilemmas like the *footbridge* case, which the authors refer to as "high-conflict" dilemmas. The Iowa patients showed a similar effect with dilemmas involving close relatives ("Kill a sister to save five strangers?") (Thomas et al., 2011).

Previously, Mendez et al. (2005) showed that patients with frontotemporal dementia (also known for their blunted emotional responses) showed a similar pattern, and likewise for patients with social-emotional deficits due to traumatic brain injury (Martins et al., 2012). We see the same pattern in patients with low-anxiety psychopathy (Koenigs et al., 2012) and people with alexithymia (Koven, 2011, Patil & Silani, 2014). Consistent with this, a drug that increases short-term emotional reactivity produced more deontological responses (Crockett et al., 2010), while drugs used to reduce anxiety produced more utilitarian responses (Perkins et al., 2013; Terbeck et al., 2013), as does the administration of testosterone (Chen et al., 2016). Linking the fMRI data with lesion data, Darby et al. (2018) found that the neural regions and networks identified in the aforementioned fMRI studies using sacrificial dilemmas (specifically for deontological judgment) converge on the brain regions that, when lesioned, most reliably lead to criminal behavior.

Studies using patient populations and pharmacological interventions are especially powerful because they involve dramatic changes in traits and states that go beyond ordinary experience. However, these studies are resource-intensive, making them relatively rare. In the Trolleyological literature, there are far more studies using simple behavioral methods and convenience samples of healthy adults. These studies typically fall into two categories: (1) studies of individual differences correlating dilemma judgments with other judgments, behaviors, or traits; and (2) experimental studies in which laboratory manipulations (e.g., time pressure) may influence moral judgments. As explained below, the study of individual differences using moral dilemmas has been revolutionized by process dissociation (Conway & Gawronski, 2013; Conway et al., 2018; Patil et al., 2021). Attempts to experimentally manipulate the moral judgments of healthy adults has been more of a mixed bag, with many studies showing effects consistent with the dual-process theory (e.g., Greene et. al., 2008; Greene 2013; Paxton et. al., 2012; Suter & Hertwig, 2011; Tremoliere et al., 2012; Feinberg et al., 2012; Li et al., 2018; Huang et al. 2019, 2020), some not (e.g., Tinghog et al., 2016; Cova et al., 2021), and some suggesting the need for revisions/refinements of the dual-process theory (e.g., Bago & DeNeys, 2019).

9.5 What have we learned from trolley dilemmas? (Part II: The descriptive trolley problem)

The dual-process theory explains why trolley dilemmas are so dilemmatic: They elicit distinct, and sometimes contradictory, responses from dissociable neural pathways, one that produces intuitive emotional responses and one that implements cost–benefit reasoning. But this doesn't tell us which features of trolley dilemmas are responsible for eliciting these responses. For example, what is it about the *footbridge* case that makes so many people say that it's wrong to sacrifice one life for five lives? And why don't people say the same thing about the *switch* case?

In a landmark study, Cushman, Young, and Hauser (2006) tested a wide range of sacrificial dilemmas and found evidence for three psychological principles operating across cases. First, they found that people are more likely to judge against a sacrificial action if the harm is produced actively rather than passively (by omission). For example, it's worse to push someone off a footbridge than to fail to stop them from falling (see also Spranca, Minsk, & Baron, 1991). Second, they found that people are more likely to condemn the action if the harmful event is intended as a means to an end, rather than its being a foreseen side effect. In the *footbridge* case, the harm is caused as a means, using the person as a trolley-stopper, while in the *switch* case the victim on the sidetrack is harmed as "collateral damage," a side effect of turning the trolley. Third, they found that people are more likely to judge against a harmful action if it's physically direct, for example, pushing vs. hitting a switch (see also Rozyman & Baron, 2002).

A subsequent study (Greene et al., 2009) refined this notion of physical directness, showing that it's the use of "personal force," rather than direct contact, that matters. For example, pushing with one's hands or with a pole applies "personal force," and the application of personal force (as opposed to something like hitting a switch) leads to more negative judgments. This study also showed that effects of intention (means vs. side effect) and the effects of personal force interact, such that their combined effect is especially large. For example, in the standard *footbridge* case the action is both intended as a means and uses personal force. If the harm is caused by incidentally knocking someone off a footbridge as one rushes to hit a switch (a side effect produced through personal force) the effect is much weaker (this is what appears to be going on in Kamm's *Lazy Susan* case; Kamm, 2009). Likewise, in the loop case (Thomson, 1985), where the harm is intended as a means, but not delivered through personal force, the effect is much weaker (see also the *collision alarm* case in Greene, 2013; for a meta-analysis highlighting the aforementioned interaction see Feltz & May, 2017). These effects were recently replicated (with some cross-cultural nuances) in a massive study of participants from forty-five nations representing all inhabited continents (Bago et al., 2022; see below).

9.6 Some have claimed that trolley dilemmas have given us a distorted picture of utilitarianism: Is there any merit to this critique?

There is much merit to this critique. But the presentation of this critique (Kahane, 2015; Kahane et al., 2015, 2018, Everett & Kahane, 2020) has been a source of much confusion. It has misrepresented the dual-process theory and focused the field's attention on a (mostly) empty empirical controversy.

I'll start with what I think this critique gets right. One of my regrets about my trolleyological research is that it's led many people to associate utilitarianism with pushing people off footbridges. This is sad to me because I am a utilitarian, although I prefer to call myself a "deep pragmatist" (Greene, 2013) because "utilitarian" reliably gives people the wrong idea. Being a utilitarian in practice has pretty much nothing to do with killing innocent people, but has a lot to do with working to alleviate global poverty, opposing oppressive social systems, alleviating animal suffering, and attempting to safeguard the long-term future of humanity. In other words, utilitarianism, in practice, is about Effective Altruism (Singer, 1972, 1975, 1981, 2010, 2015; MacAskill, 2015; Ord, 2020).

Why, then, did I choose to focus on moral dilemmas in which the utilitarian response is to kill an innocent person? There are two reasons. The first is scientific. As explained above, these dilemmas have proven useful for illuminating the structure of moral cognition. The second reason is philosophical, and less obvious.

As a philosopher, I have been interested in defending utilitarianism (Greene, 2007, 2013, 2014, 2017). An honest defense of any philosophical view requires focusing on its least appealing implications. Trolley dilemmas such as the *footbridge* case are putative counterexamples to utilitarianism, cases where utilitarianism seems to get things wrong. My goal, then, as a scientifically minded philosopher has been to understand the psychology behind the most potent *objections* to utilitarianism. And, ultimately, my goal has been to explain how these objections arise as overgeneralizations of otherwise useful emotional responses. The upshot of this argument is that we should not be swayed by these objections to utilitarianism, however emotionally compelling they may be. This strategy makes perfect philosophical sense, but it is, unfortunately, not a very good public relations strategy for utilitarian philosophy.

Kahane and colleagues have likewise observed that trolley dilemmas present a highly distorted picture of utilitarianism. They have therefore focused on characterizing the more positive aspects of utilitarianism. More specifically, they have developed a psychometric scale that measures utilitarian tendencies (Kahane et al., 2018). This scale has two factors, one capturing the more centrally utilitarian commitment to "impartial beneficence" (wanting to produce good outcomes for all sentient beings, in a way that's free from bias) and the other capturing the more trolleyological commitment to imposing sacrifices on others when necessary to promote the greater good. Kahane and colleagues could have simply observed that trolley dilemmas present a distorted picture of utilitarianism (by focusing on its least appealing implications) and then moved on to remedying this problem with new research on the more positive aspects of utilitarianism. But, instead, they misrepresented the dual-process theory and consequently focused the field's attention on a controversy that is almost entirely empty.

The misrepresentation begins with the term "utilitarian judgment." I and others have used the term "utilitarian" to label the *judgments* that are required by utilitarianism. For example, utilitarianism requires sacrificing one life to save five in both the *switch* case and the *footbridge* case because this action (*ceteris paribus*) saves more lives and therefore promotes the greater good. Neither I nor anyone else, to my knowledge, has ever claimed that the ordinary people who make such judgments are *utilitarians*. On the contrary, I've made it very clear that this is *not* what I mean. I've claimed that ordinary people make utilitarian judgments by applying simple cost–benefit reasoning, but I've never claimed that such people are in any general way committed to utilitarianism (Greene, 2007, p. 39; Greene, 2013; pp. 113–124; Greene, 2014, pp. 699–700). To say that making a utilitarian judgment makes one a utilitarian is like saying that making an Italian meal makes one an Italian.

Not only is this idea wildly implausible, it's inconsistent with the dual-process theory. According to the dual-process theory, there are two (hence "dual") reasons why one might give a utilitarian response to a case like the footbridge dilemma: One might be especially concerned about the greater good, or one might be especially *unconcerned* about pushing people off footbridges, etc. This is why I and many others predicted that patients with emotional deficits (e.g., due to VMPFC damage, frontotemporal dementia, traumatic brain injury, psychopathy, or alexithymia) would make more utilitarian judgments. No one has claimed that such individuals are *utilitarians* – that they are suffused with a spirit of impartial beneficence. Rather, the dual-process theory predicts that these patients' emotional deficits would make them more likely to rely on simple cost–benefit reasoning, and thus make them more likely to approve of utilitarian sacrifices. It's about the absence of an emotional response that conflicts with simple cost–benefit reasoning, not about a general commitment to utilitarianism.

Nevertheless, Kahane and colleagues presented the dual-process theory as making the wildly implausible claim that those who make utilitarian judgments must be, in some general sense, committed to utilitarian values – that they must also be "impartially beneficent" in general. Kahane et al. then went on to provide evidence against this straw-man theory (Kahane et al., 2015), showing that the people who approve of pushing the man off the footbridge (etc.) are not generally committed to impartial beneficence. They also showed a correlation between utilitarian judgment and antisocial tendencies. They presented these findings as a surprising discovery about trolley dilemmas, even though these findings are perfectly compatible with the dual-process theory and specifically predicted by prior work examining moral judgments in patients with emotional deficits leading to antisocial behavior (Mendez et al., 2005; Koenigs et al., 2007, 2012; Ciaramelli et al., 2007; Moretto et al., 2010; Thomas et al, 2011). (And, to be clear, this prior work was correctly presented as *supporting* the dual-process theory. For similar confusion about the dual-process theory, see Bartels & Pizarro, 2011.) Thus, Kahane and colleagues portrayed trolley dilemmas as poorly designed moral personality tests – aimed at detecting utilitarians, but finding only antisocial personalities. Neither I nor anyone else, to my knowledge, ever used trolley dilemmas as a way to identify utilitarians.

Above I said that this controversy about misidentifying utilitarians is *mostly* empty. I say "mostly" because Kahane et al. did make at least one empirical claim that is at odds with the dual-process theory. They claimed that utilitarian responses to trolley dilemmas "merely express a calculating yet selfish mindset" (Kahane et al., 2015, p. 197). I'm not sure that Kahane and colleagues actually believed this sweeping claim. You would think that at least *some* people who approve of saving more lives do so because they care about saving more lives. But whether Kahane et al. actually believed it or were just being provocative, that's what they said.

In contrast to Kahane's claim that these judgments merely reflect antisocial tendencies, the dual-process theory makes the more moderate prediction that different people approve of utilitarian sacrifices for different reasons: Some are especially concerned with saving more lives, while others are especially unconcerned about harming people. Paul Conway and colleagues have used a method called *process dissociation* to distinguish people who are high in the U factor (more concerned with promoting the greater good) from people who are low in the D factor (less concerned with causing harm)

(Conway & Gawronsky, 2013). (The "*D*" is for "deontological" – reflecting their characteristically deontological objection to utilitarian sacrifices.) Conway and I (along with Jacob Goldstein-Greenwood and David Polacek) repeated all of Kahane et al.'s (2015) experiments using process dissociation measures and showed that sacrificial utilitarian judgments often do reflect concern for the greater good, just as the dual-process theory predicts (Conway et al., 2018).

It is unfortunate that Kahane and colleagues have sown so much confusion with their misrepresentation of the dual-process theory and their promotion of an empty debate about whether ordinary people who make utilitarian judgments are really utilitarians. However, Kahane and colleagues were right to draw more attention to the positive side of utilitarianism, and I hope that in the future students of moral cognition will come to associate utilitarianism more with "impartial beneficence" than with "sacrificial harm."

9.7 Do hypothetical trolley judgments predict real decisions? and does it matter if they don't?

As explained above, trolley dilemmas were never intended to serve as cheap substitutes for real transportation emergencies. The goal is not to "operationalize" typical real-life moral decisions so that people's real-world decisions can be predicted. Instead, trolley dilemmas are best understood as specialized probes that are useful for revealing cognitive structure, much like weird sentences and visual illusions. More specifically – and consistent with the dual-process theory – trolley dilemmas are useful for dissociating cognitive processes *within* people, and are not especially useful for predicting behavioral differences *between* people. Once again, this is because different people can, according to the dual-process theory, give the same response for very different reasons (Conway & Gawronksi, 2013; Conway et al., 2018).

Despite all this, Bostyn et al. (2018) caused a stir with a study in which they attempted to use people's hypothetical sacrificial judgments to predict real-life sacrificial decisions involving captive mice. They reported that trolley judgments do not predict the real-life mouse-killing decisions. There are several problems with this study. One is that it lacks adequate statistical power to compare predictions of real judgments to predictions of hypothetical judgments (Evans & Brandt, 2019). Another is that Bostyn et al. ignored half of their data – the half that provides evidence undermining their main conclusion (Plunkett & Greene, 2019). Instead of following standard practice and having participants give a single response to each dilemma, reflecting an all-things-considered evaluation of both options, they had participants separately evaluate the utilitarian option and the deontological option. Ratings of the utilitarian option were not predictive of the mouse decisions, but the ratings of the deontological options were predictive of those decisions (with a directional significance test). This is consistent with the finding that most of the variance in trolley dilemma responses are accounted for by the "D" factor (Conway et al., 2018). Nevertheless, Bostyn et al. drew their negative conclusions entirely from ratings of the utilitarian option and ignored the ratings of the deontological option. Subtracting the two ratings for each participant – reflecting the need to *contrast* the two options – yielded difference scores that were also predictive of the mouse decisions.

In a follow-up study, Bostyn et al. (2019) compared responses to standard trolley dilemmas with responses to economic dilemmas modeled after trolley cases. Here, participants could direct money away from one participant, with the result that five participants would each receive that amount, thus promoting the greater good. Aggregating across four studies, they found that utilitarian responses to the traditional trolley dilemmas predicted utilitarian responses to the economic dilemmas. The researchers ultimately gave all participants the full bonus amount, but the participants were led to believe that they were making real economic decisions with effects on other participants. Thus, in this set of studies, the hypothetical dilemma judgments predicted what were (from the participants' perspectives) real decisions.

It's interesting to see trolley dilemma judgments directly predicting (subjectively) real decisions in ordinary people. Nevertheless, it's a mistake to think of trolley dilemmas as personality tests designed for predicting individual differences in behavior. As noted above, trolley dilemmas were introduced into psychology to dissociate cognitive processes *within* people. The real-world consequences of these processes are most clearly observed, not in individual differences among healthy people, but in the contrast between healthy people and people with deficits related to one of these dissociable processes. Once again, patients with frontotemporal dementia (Mendez et al., 2005), VMPFC damage (Koenigs et al., 2007; Ciaramelli et al., 2007), traumatic brain injury (Martins et al., 2012), alexithymia (Koven, 2011, Patil & Silani, 2014), and low-affect psychopathy (Koenigs et al., 2012) give more utilitarian judgments to standard trolley cases, as predicted by the dual-process theory. And these patients have readily observable real-world moral deficits. Likewise, the neural systems that are implicated in responses to trolley dilemmas (Shenhav & Greene, 2014) are those that are most often implicated in antisocial behavior (Darby et al., 2018). How the tension between emotional aversion to harm and cost–benefit reasoning will play out for any given individual is complicated by both internal dynamics (the U and D factors) and situational factors that have not been well characterized. But what's constant in healthy people (and missing in various types of psychopathology) is the robust operation of both processes. It's difficult to predict what individuals will do, but recent research shows that, at a national level, trolley dilemma judgments can predict broad cultural features such as how socially mobile a society is (Awad et al., 2020; see below). They also predict important real-world attitudes, such as attitudes toward mandatory vaccinations (Clarkson & Jasper, 2022).

9.8 What about the relationship between the descriptive trolley problem and the normative trolley problem? Can science really tell us anything about what's right or wrong?

I've covered this topic at length elsewhere (Greene, 2007, 2013, 2014, 2017), and so I will, again, keep it short here.

As noted above, philosophers are rightly wary of moving from descriptive claims about what "is" to normative moral claims about what "ought" to be (Hume, 1751/1975). And thus, one might assume that science is irrelevant for the purposes of normative ethics because science can only tell us what "is," while normative ethics is concerned with what "ought" to be. But this is a mistake. It's true that science can't tell us what's right or wrong *all by itself*. But if we're willing to make some normative "ought" assumptions, we can combine those with scientific knowledge in a way that yields new "ought" conclusions.

In some cases, this is not especially interesting or surprising. For example, if we believe that we "ought" not to poison people, and science tells us that a certain plant "is" poisonous, then we might conclude that we "ought" not to put that plant in someone's salad. (Duh.) But science can do more than inform about cause and effect out in the world. Science can tell us about our own minds, and when it does that, it can challenge our values in more fundamental ways.

The fulcrum on which the "is"–"ought" lever turns is moral intuition. Any time we rely on moral intuition, we are making a jump from "is" to "ought." We are starting with a psychological fact ("this seems wrong to me") and using it as the basis for a normative conclusion ("therefore it's probably wrong"). When philosophers balk at the action in the *footbridge* case and conclude that utilitarianism (which endorses that action) must be wrong, they are jumping from a rather small psychological "is" to a rather large normative "ought."

This might be avoided if philosophers could logically derive substantive moral conclusions from self-evident first principles, as Kant (1785/1959) aspired to do. But no one has done that successfully. And so we're all forced to draw conclusions about how things ought to be based on how it *seems* to us that they ought to be.

The question, then, is not whether we will move from psychological "is" claims to moral "ought" claims. This is unavoidable, whether we acknowledge it or not. The question, instead, is whether we will make our "is"–"ought" moves with or without the benefit of scientific self-knowledge. Will we trust our intuitions blindly? Or will we draw on science to gain a better understanding of how our moral intuitions work, and perhaps shift our moral allegiances as a result?

In the *footbridge* case, it seems wrong to kill one to save five. In the *switch* case, it seems morally acceptable. There are three competing hypotheses about the relationship between these moral intuitions and the moral truth:

(A) Things are just as they seem. It's wrong to push, but it's ok to hit the switch.
(B) We're getting things wrong in the *switch* case: It seems ok to turn the trolley, but it's not.
(C) We're getting things wrong in the *footbridge* case: It seems wrong to push, but it's not.

For many people, A and B seem more plausible than C. But with the benefit of scientific self-knowledge, I'd say that option C is the most plausible.

The psychological research casts doubt on option A. As noted above, part of what's going on in the *footbridge* case is that we're sensitive to "personal force," to the difference between pushing vs. hitting a switch. No one thinks that this is an important normative moral distinction – that whether there's a switch involved should determine who lives and who dies. What's more, this distinction is entangled with another distinction that many philosophers do take seriously, namely, the distinction between harm as a means and harm as a side effect, enshrined in the "doctrine of double effect" (Aquinas, unknown/ 2006). Harm as means seems more acceptable if it doesn't involve the use of personal force, and that makes little sense, too. So, the science gives us good reason to doubt option A. All is not well with our intuitions.

What about option C? Could our negative feeling about the *footbridge* case be leading us astray? Indeed, there is a perfectly natural scientific explanation for how this might be so. A scientific understanding of our *footbridge* intuition makes it very likely that it's an overgeneralization of an otherwise good emotional response (Greene, 2013, 2014, 2017). When we think about harmful actions like pushing the man off the footbridge, we see a response in the amygdala (Shenhav & Greene, 2014; Glenn, Raine, & Schug, 2009), a part of the brain responsible for attaching negative feelings to candidate actions. It's what we see in a human or a rat that has learned not to touch something that will deliver an electric shock (Blair, 2007; Phelps, 2006). Why would we feel bad about the idea of pushing the man off the footbridge?

One possibility is that our amygdalae have somehow encoded a complex moral principle that explains why it's wrong to push in the *footbridge* case but not in the *switch* case, perhaps something like the doctrine of double effect. That's not impossible, but it's not at all clear how or why that would be the case. Fortunately, there is a much simpler explanation for why our amygdalae would respond so negatively to the action in the *footbridge* case: Because it's a basic act of physical violence – active, intentional, and direct – precisely the kind of thing that we're taught as toddlers not to do, sometimes with stern negative reinforcement. And it's good that we receive this negative reinforcement as toddlers because basic acts of physical violence nearly always do more harm than good.

The *footbridge* case, however, is very weird. It's a case in which a basic act of physical violence is stipulated to promote the greater good. Now, how should we expect our amygdalae to respond to such a weird case? Based on how this learning system works – attaching values directly to actions, independent of consequences (Cushman, 2013; Crockett, 2013) – we would not expect this system to account for the fact that this unusual act of violence will do more good than harm. In other words, we would expect this emotional response to be *myopic*, to ignore some the important facts about consequences. In other words, it seems likely that the *footbridge* case is analogous to a visual illusion. It's a weird case in which a kind of action that normally leads to net harm produces net good. In short, there is a highly plausible scientific explanation for why our intuitive response to the *footbridge* case would be misleading.

What about option B? Could we be wrong in thinking that it's ok to hit the switch? This would require turning the argument around, such that the saving of more lives is just a misleading cue and not something that ought to matter very much. But how can saving more lives be mistakenly overvalued? The reason we feel that pushing is wrong, it seems, is because of the *usual consequences* of pushing. Thus, consequences play a key role in our best scientific explanation for why it feels wrong to push. And yet consequences are the reason *to* push. In other words, science is telling us that this is a dilemma between actual current consequences and feelings based on past consequences. Put that way, it's pretty clear which should guide our judgment.

An analogy: Imagine that you're standing on the second-floor balcony of a burning building. If you jump, you'll survive. As a conscious reasoner (with a DLPFC, etc.), you understand that you need to jump. But your amygdala is telling you not to jump. Why? Because in the past falling from high up has been painful, and not especially conducive to your survival.

Your intuition that it's wrong to push in the *footbridge* case is very much like your intuition that it's a mistake to jump. It's essentially the same neural circuits operating according to the same principles for learning and decision-making, setting up a conflict between what you know to be true in the present and what you feel to be true based on the past.

Science cannot, by itself, give us the moral answers. But as the foregoing discussion suggests, science can give us a valuable perspective on our moral intuitions, letting us know when our moral intuitions are especially likely to lead us astray. To be clear, I do not think that the scientific evidence presented here provides a general argument in favor of utilitarianism. These data do not tell us that we ought to value the interests of sentient beings impartially, or that it makes sense to aggregate such interests in our decision-making. In other words, these findings have little to say about the *axioms* of utilitarianism. However, these results do tell us something about *objections* to utilitarianism. They support debunking explanations, arguing against the validity of deontological constraints on promoting the greater good.

Before closing on this topic, I'd like to emphasize a couple of points that I've made elsewhere (Greene, 2014) in response to Berker (2009).

First, there is nothing essentially *neuroscientific* about this argument. I think it's helpful to describe these processes in terms of the physical structures that implement them because it implicitly reminds us that our moral intuitions are generated by mechanical processes, not whispers from Heaven. It also helps connect psychological processes across domains and to connect human psychology to that of other creatures such as rats and monkeys (Greene, 2017). But everything that I'm saying here can be cashed out in purely psychological terms without reference to the brain. And to the extent that brain imaging studies provide relevant evidence, they do so by telling us something about the underlying psychology.

Second, this is not a deductive proof. I am not claiming that science – and certainly not neuroscience – *proves* that our intuitions about the *footbridge* case or anything else are wrong. My claim is that scientific self-knowledge makes it more likely that some of our moral judgments are based on unreliable intuitions. And, as I've argued elsewhere, I think that improved scientific self-knowledge has the overall effect of deflating and debunking objections to utilitarianism (Greene, 2007, 2013, 2014, 2017).

Finally, I'll take this opportunity to emphasize that utilitarianism is not primarily about pushing people in front of trolleys. Sacrificial dilemmas such as the *footbridge* case generate *objections* to utilitarianism, and psychology can help us address these objections. But there are limits to how much we should dwell on them. From a utilitarian perspective, there are more important things to do, such as figuring out how to overcome the psychological obstacles to effective altruism (Caviola, Schubert, & Greene, 2021; Caviola & Greene, under review; Jaeger & van Vugt, 2021).

9.9 What's going on in trolleyology these days?

A lot. Much more than I can describe in this limited space. But I'll mention a few of the most important developments from the second decade of scientific Trolleyology.

As noted above, one of the big advances in the field is the application of *process dissociation* (PD) to moral judgment, pioneered by Paul Conway and Bertram Gawronski (2013). PD has turned trolley dilemmas into a useful tool for studying individual differences. As noted above, one can approve of harmful sacrifices, such as pushing the man in the *footbridge* case, for two general reasons: increased concern about the greater good or decreased concern about causing harm. PD separates these two motivational tendencies by having people respond to a set of dilemmas that vary in the extent to which harmful actions produce good consequences. This yields two independent factors for each respondent, a U factor that tracks with sensitivity to the greater good, and a D factor that tracks with an *unwillingness* to cause harm regardless of whether it promotes the greater good. If one is low in both U and D, approving of harmful actions regardless of the extent to which they promote the greater good, is indicative of antisocial tendencies.

As noted above, this technique has provided evidence that sacrificial utilitarian judgments are not merely reflective of antisocial tendencies (Conway et al., 2018). It's also provided more nuanced views of the relationship between logical reasoning and moral judgment (Byrd & Conway, 2019) and of the relationship between moral judgment and gender (Friesdorf, Conway, & Gawronski, 2015). As explained below, PD has also been used to make sense of the foreign language effect in moral judgment (Costa et al., 2014) and to provide linchpin evidence for the link between model-based decision-making and utilitarian judgment (Patil et al., 2021). PD has become an exceptionally useful tool for studying individual differences in moral judgment.

Another major development is the reconceptualization of the dual-process theory of moral judgment – and dual-process theories more generally – in terms of the distinction between model-based and model-free systems for learning and decision-making (Cushman, 2013; Crockett, 2013). It's difficult to overstate how fundamental this development is, not only for the science of moral judgment, but also for its normative implications. For a detailed and lucid presentation of this idea, I refer readers to Cushman's 2013 masterpiece: "Action, Outcome, and Value: A Dual-System Framework for Morality" (Cushman 2013). For a discussion of this idea's normative implications, I refer readers to my 2017 paper, "The rat-a-gorical imperative: Moral intuition and the limits of affective learning" (Greene 2017).

But here's the gist: Machine learning researchers realized that there are two general ways of attaching values to actions (Sutton & Barto, 1998). One is to rely on a *model*, an understanding of cause–effect relationships. We see this in humans and other animals. For example, rats rely on cognitive maps to navigate (Tolman, 1948). (A map is one type of causal model, indicating the expected outcomes of different navigational actions in different contexts.) One might make a series of specific left and right turns because one understands that this will lead one to one's desired goal. This is called *model-based* decision-making, and it relies, of course, on learning a model. One can think of this as *planning*.

The alternative mode of attaching values to actions is to do so directly, without relying on a causal model of the world. This is called *model-free* learning, which produces its own more intuitive form of decision-making. For example, one can learn a navigational route simply by *habit*, turning left at the post office and then right at the park (etc.), without having a map of the territory in one's head. One simply has a sense for what one should do given certain contextual cues. Both humans and other mammals use this strategy as well as model-based strategies (Dickinson et al., 1995; Moser, Kropff, & Moser, 2008; Balleine & O'Doherty, 2010).

The deontological response to moral dilemmas such as the *footbridge* case seems to be the product of model-free learning, associating a negative value directly with an action. By contrast, utilitarian judgments seem to be driven by model-based learning and decision-making, an explicit understanding of the consequences likely to follow from one's behavioral options. This is beautifully demonstrated by Patil et al. (2021) who combined process dissociation measures of the U and D factors with general measures of the tendency to rely on model-based vs. model-free learning in a context that has nothing to do with morality. Consistent with this, patients with damage to the hippocampus, which is essential for making cognitive maps, tend to give more emotion-based deontological responses to sacrificial dilemmas (McCormick et al, 2016; Verfaelle, Hunsberger, & Keane, 2021; but see Craver et al., 2016).

Scientifically, this mapping of model-free and model-based learning onto deontological and utilitarian judgment turns the dual-process theory (which describes only static response tendencies) into a dynamic computational theory that explains how these tendencies arise. And, most importantly for present purposes, this work is pregnant with normative implications, as discussed in the previous section. Model-free learning is a "quick and dirty" way to make decisions with limited computational resources. Model-based learning is the gold standard, provided that one has the resources to execute it well. It's the difference between relying on a hunch and relying on an explicit understanding of one's circumstances. (Think, again, of the case of jumping from a burning building.) Understanding dual-process moral psychology in terms of model-based and model-free learning underscores a key point made above: that anti-utilitarian intuitions are best understood as overgeneralizations of otherwise good emotional heuristics (Greene, 2007, 2013, 2014, 2017; see also Baron, 1994).

Another notable development is research on the Foreign Language Effect (FLE) in moral judgment. You may have noticed that swear words spoken in a foreign language (that you understand) don't pack the same emotional punch as the swear words spoken in your native language (Dewaele, 2004). If deontological responses to dilemmas such as the *footbridge* case are driven by emotional responses, then one might expect one's responses to be less deontological and more utilitarian when the dilemmas are presented in a foreign language. That is exactly what Costa et al. (2014) found, giving rise to a new line of research working out the mechanics of this effect. This includes a study using process dissociation to show that the FLE is due to reducing the D factor, not increasing the U factor (Hayakawa et al., 2017; see also Muda et al., 2018 and Geipel et al. 2015, who observed the effect but attribute it to different causes).

Yet another important development is the emergence of big data trolleyology, beginning with two landmark studies using trolley-type dilemmas to examine cross-cultural variation in judgments about self-driving cars (Bonnefon, Sharif, and Rahwan, 2016; Awad et al., 2018). A recent study by the same group examined responses to the *switch*, *footbridge*, and *loop* dilemmas across 70,000 people in forty-two nations (Awad et al., 2021). In every nation studied, people judged the sacrificial action to be most acceptable in the *switch* dilemma, followed by the *loop* dilemma, and least acceptable in the *footbridge* dilemma. There was, however, significant variation in the overall level of utilitarian judgment, especially for the *footbridge* dilemma. Awad and colleagues also found that people in nations with higher relational mobility (where alienating current social partners is less of a concern) were more likely to give utilitarian responses across all three dilemmas. This finding speaks to the question raised above about whether trolley dilemma judgments can predict real-world phenomena (Bostyn et al., 2018). As noted above, a more recent study of thousands of people from forty-five nations (Bago et al., 2022) found that people around the world distinguish among these dilemmas for the same reasons, responding to whether the harm is intentional (rather than a side effect) and whether the harm is caused through the application of personal force. These studies provide the most compelling evidence to date that trolley dilemmas tap into universal features of human morality.

While variation in trolley judgments can be explained partially by culture, there is also evidence for genetic influences. Responses to sacrificial dilemmas are much more similar between monozygotic twins (MZ) than dizygotic twins (DZ), indicating a strong genetic influence (Smith & Hatemi, 2020). It's also been found (in a discovery sample and a replication sample) that variation in the oxytocin receptor gene (OXTR) predicts responses to sacrificial dilemmas (Bernhard et al., 2016).

Finally, my collaborators and I have applied Rawls' (1971) and Harsanyi's (1955) idea of reasoning from behind a veil of ignorance to trolley dilemmas (Huang, Greene, & Bazerman, 2019). For example, we asked participants to imagine having an equal probability of being each of the six people in the *footbridge* dilemma (the one who could be pushed and the five on the tracks). What, then, would they want the decision-maker to do? If she pushes, you have 5/6 chance of living and a 1/6 chance of dying. If she doesn't push, you have a 1/6 chance of living and 5/6 chance of dying. Here, most people say that they would want the decision-maker to push. We then presented people with the standard *footbridge* dilemma. We found that working through the veil-of-ignorance version prompted people to make more utilitarian judgments about the original *footbridge* dilemma. Likewise, we found that engaging in veil-of-ignorance reasoning makes people more comfortable with utilitarian autonomous vehicles that minimize the loss of life and with decisions to donate to a foreign charity where the funds can do more good. In a second set of studies we found that engaging in veil-of-ignorance reasoning eliminates age-related bias in older participants when considering whether ventilators (for emergency COVID-19 care) should be preferentially allocated to younger patients with more years to live (Huang et al., 2021).

These findings are especially interesting from a normative perspective. The veil of ignorance is a device for encouraging fair, impartial reasoning. It essentially asks, "What would I want if I didn't know who I was going to be?" Rawls believed that veil-of-ignorance reasoning provided an argument against organizing society around utilitarian principles. The economist John Harsanyi, who developed veil-of-ignorance reasoning independently of Rawls (Harsanyi, 1955, 1975), thought the opposite was true. He argued that veil-of-ignorance reasoning provides a foundation for utilitarian social philosophy. The dilemmas we consider here are different from the grand social dilemma debated by Rawls and Harsanyi, both in scale and in structure. Nevertheless, it is interesting that people's judgments, across a range of cases, are more consistent with Harsanyi's vision than with Rawls'. For a discussion of these normative issues see Greene, Huang, and Bazerman (2022).

9.10 Concluding thoughts

For over two decades, trolley dilemmas have helped us understand the mechanics of moral judgment. And, for even longer, they've served as useful tools for ethicists aiming to resolve difficult, real-world moral problems by appeal to more general principles. As scientific tools, trolley dilemmas have connected our understanding of moral psychology to the brain's core networks and to its most general algorithms for learning and deciding. They've also illuminated general features of moral actions that shape our responses to them. Trolley dilemmas have proven useful in combination with every major method used in experimental psychology and cognitive neuroscience. Trolley dilemmas have also forged connections with fields such as law, economics, anthropology, genetics, and computer science/artificial intelligence. Trolley dilemmas do not resemble everyday moral decisions, but to dwell on this is to miss the point. The cognitive processes that are engaged by trolley dilemmas are very much real, explaining broad patterns in behavior across situations and cultures. Trolley dilemmas help us understand the limitations of our moral intuitions, revealing patterns in our moral thinking that are hard to endorse upon reflection. What's more, they connect our moral thinking to broader scientific theories that make sense of these limitations and show us how we might overcome them.

10 Cross-cultural responses to trolley problems and their implications for moral philosophy or

How I learned to stop worrying and love (constructivist) relativism

Natalie Gold

10.1 Introduction

The power of Thomson's (1976) trolley problem lies in the way that the basic cases provoke strong and widely shared intuitions about the correct course of action. These then raise a question for normative ethics: Why may the agent in Bystander turn the trolley whereas the agent in Footbridge must let five die? Answering this question is supposed to help uncover moral principles. For instance, Frances Kamm says that we use trolley problems to discover our intuitive response to cases; we then use them to formulate a set of principles that explain our case judgments and that express morally significant ideas, in order to discover a deeper – potentially universal – structure of morality (Voorhoeve, 2009).

These intuitions were shared amongst the professional philosophers who devised trolley cases. However, professional philosophers are not a particularly diverse bunch. They tend to come from Western, Educated, Industrialized, Rich, and Democratic (WEIRD) societies, mainly the United States and the United Kingdom or – outside of those countries – the anglophone philosophy community. Across numerous domains, ranging from perception through cooperation through self-concepts, WEIRD people respond differently to those from other societies (Henrich, Heine, & Norenzayan, 2010).

Are WEIRD people also outliers in their responses to trolley problems? If so, what are the implications for moral philosophy? These are the questions I will address in this chapter.

First some ground clearing. What would it mean to have a culturally different response to a trolley problem? There are two ways that researchers have looked for cultural differences in trolley problems. The first asks whether the difference in judgments between Bystander and Footbridge replicates in other cultures.

This is done by giving participants from another culture both scenarios and seeing whether they make different judgments in the two cases. The second way is to make a direct comparison between two or more cultures, by taking a single case (Bystander or Footbridge) and comparing responses across cultures to see if they are on average different. I review both of these in Section 10.2.

If there are cultural differences, then we need to think about why there are differences and whether the causes of those differences are problematic for moral philosophy. Do differences in moral judgments represent genuine moral disagreement and, if so, how does that connect to differences in culture and society? I address these questions in Section 10.3. Then in Section 10.4, I turn to the implications of my findings for moral philosophy and, in particular, metaethics.

One thing I will take as given is that trolley problems shed light on our basic moral judgments. Foot (1967) thought that they illustrated a general problem of conflicting rights, nowadays philosophers are probably more likely to see them as illustrating a general problem of the distribution of benefits and harms. However, if you don't think they address core moral beliefs, then you may be less inclined to think they have any lessons for ethics at all (see Gold, forthcoming, for further discussion).

10.2 Cultural differences in judgments in trolley problems

10.2.1 Methods

I collected as many trolley experiments as I could find that investigated the moral judgments of people from non-anglophone or non-WEIRD cultures in Bystander vs Footbridge, or that compared across cultures on either a single Bystander or Footbridge scenario. The scenarios could have been reimagined so that they did not involve trains or trolleys, or so that the outcomes were not deaths, so long as they retained the basic structure of the problems: Bystander typically involves diverting a threat in order to save many, which has the side effect of a single person being harmed; Footbridge typically involves using a single person as a means to save many, with an element of bodily contact. I extracted relevant studies from multi-study papers.

Trolley experiments also vary in how they frame the question. Some studies follow philosophical conventions, by asking about what is "permissible." Others aim for a more colloquial turn of phrase, for instance, asking about what would be "acceptable" or what would be "wrong." Still others ask about what someone "should" do, which is arguably slightly different because people might weigh other normative desiderata against morality. I included any experiment that targeted a normative question, for example, what participants should do, or whether the action was right/permissible/acceptable. I included both rating scales and binary (Y/N) judgments. However, I excluded probes about taking action or asking participants to predict their own action (though I will occasionally comment on the findings from those probes because a pattern does emerge). There are a lot of reasons why actions or predictions of action might differ from judgments, including philosophical reasons such as that an action can be permissible but one need not do it (no obligation to act) or that an action can be morally required but one would not do it (akrasia), and psychological arguments that judgments and actions are generated by two different systems (Tassy et al., 2013).

Trolley experiments also vary in whether the participant in the experiment is being asked to imagine themselves in the scenario (first-person judgment) or asked about what a third-person character should do. There may be differences in judgments depending on whether the participant in the experiment is being asked to make a first-person or a third-person judgment, which may be related to the well-known actor–observer bias in psychology (Nadelhoffer, & Feltz, 2008). Again, first-person and third-person judgments may be the product of different brain systems (Avram et al., 2014). However, I collected both first-person and third-person judgments.

My inclusion and exclusion criteria are summarized in Table 10.1.

I did not search databases, as one would in a formal scientific systematic review (Uman, 2011), but I did a targeted search, making use of a previous search by Machery (2009), searching on Google Scholar, and searching reference lists of papers. I made a list of the papers I found and put a call down Philos-L, the largest Philosophy email list in the world, asking people to send me any papers I had missed. The list currently boasts 13,000 members in over 60 countries, with an additional 11,000 Facebook subscribers and 5,600 twitter followers (https://www.liverpool.ac.uk/philosophy/philos-l). No-one notified me of any papers that were not already on my list, so I am confident that the list is fairly comprehensive.

10.2.2 Results

In order to understand the results in Tables 10.2 and 10.3, it is important to know a little bit about classical null hypothesis testing, which is used to assess the results of experiments. The simple takeaway is that $p < 0.05$ is a conventional standard, which we can use to judge whether there is a difference in moral judgments between the groups being compared in the experiment.

Table 10.1. Inclusion and exclusion criteria

	Inclusion criteria	Exclusion criteria
Participants	Non-WEIRD or non-anglophone participants included in the sample	Only participants from WEIRD anglophone countries (e.g., US, UK, Canada, Australia)
Intervention	At least one of Bystander or Footbridge Scenario, or a study that was designed to preserve the main features of these scenarios but reimagined so that they did not involve trains or trolleys; scenario could be in first person or in third person	Other trolley scenarios or vignettes investigating moral judgments that did not take the form of Bystander or Footbridge
Comparator	Comparing Bystander and Footbridge scenarios within a culture; or comparing at least one of Bystander and Footbridge across two different cultures	Studies without comparators
Outcomes	Moral judgment about taking action (could be "acceptability," "permissibility," "right" or "wrong") or question about whether the agent "should" take the action; both binary Yes–No judgments and rating scales	Decision about taking action or prediction about taking action

The longer explanation is as follows: We test a *null hypothesis,* which in this case is that there is no difference between the two groups being compared (judgments in Bystander vs Footbridge; judgments between cultures), and an *alternative hypothesis,* in this case that different moral judgments are being made in the two groups. The *p-value* is the probability of observing a difference at least as extreme as we see in the experiment, if the null hypothesis is true. So the lower the p value, the less likely it is that the null hypothesis is correct. The scientific community uses a probability of 5%, that is, $p < 0.05$, as a conventional standard to reject the null, and $p < 0.05$ is called a "statistically significant difference."[1] In other words, if $p < 0.05$, then we reject the null hypothesis that the two groups gave the same responses. We

---

[1] Sometimes values between 0.05 and 0.1 are called "marginally significant," though there is an argument that that standard is too permissive and leads to too many false positives. Some scientists have even argued that 0.05 is too permissive (Benjamin et al., 2018). The community standard imposes a binary distinction on a scale that is continuous, so it is not particularly surprising that there is disagreement over where to make the cut.

Table 10.2. Comparison of moral judgments in Bystander and Footbridge within non-Western cultures: all third-person except where stated; scenarios administered in the native language, except where indicated; figures for Y/N judgments represent percentage saying "yes"

Paper	Culture	N*	Question	Notes	Bystander (% Y/ Mean)	Footbridge (% Y/ Mean)	P value**
Arutyunova, Alexandrov, & Hauser, 2016	Russian	327	Pulling the lever is: 1 (Forbidden) – 2 – 3 – 4 (Permissible) – 5 – 6 – 7 (Obligatory)	Speedboat scenario; native language; third-person judgment	3.61	3.08	<0.001
			Pulling the lever is: 1 (Forbidden) – 2 – 3 – 4 (Permissible) – 5 – 6 – 7 (Obligatory)	Burning scenario; native language; third-person judgment	4.87	3.55	<0.001
			Pulling the lever is: 1 (Forbidden) – 2 – 3 – 4 (Permissible) – 5 – 6 – 7 (Obligatory)	Boxcar scenario (the standard trolley scenario); native language; third-person judgment	3.74	2.91	<0.001
			Pulling the lever is: 1 (Forbidden) – 2 – 3 – 4 (Permissible) – 5 – 6 – 7 (Obligatory)	Switch scenario; native language; third-person judgment	3.92	3.66	0.003
			Pulling the lever is: 1 (Forbidden) – 2 – 3 – 4 (Permissible) – 5 – 6 – 7 (Obligatory)	Chemical scenario; native language; third-person judgment	4.31	4.03	0.002
			Pulling the lever is: 1 (Forbidden) – 2 – 3 – 4 (Permissible) – 5 – 6 – 7 (Obligatory)	Shark scenario; native language; third-person judgment	4.39	3.88	<0.001
Abarbanell & Hauser, 2010 Condition 1 and Condition 5	Rural Mayan	30	What did you think of the man's decision (which was always the utilitarian decision)? (5-pt scale: very impermissible–a little impermissible–a little good–regular good–very good)	Condition 1; *Side-effect killing [Truck]*, where agent calls out and the truck swerves (Bystander) vs *Means-contact killing [Truck]*, where agent pushes a man onto the path of the truck (Footbridge); native language; third-person judgment	4.07	1.63	<0.001

Study	Sample	N	Measure/question	Method			
	Less rural and more educated Mayan	30	What did you think of the man's decision (which was always the utilitarian decision)? (5-pt scale: very impermissible–a little impermissible–a little good–regular good–very good)	Condition 5; *Side-effect killing [Truck]*, where agent calls out and the truck swerves (Bystander) vs *Means-contact killing [Truck]*, where agent pushes a man onto the path of the truck (Footbridge); native language; third-person judgment	2.83	2.30	.054
Ahlenius & Tännsjö, 2012	US vs Russian vs Chinese	3,000	Should you flip the switch? (Y/N/don't know)/Should you push the man? (Y/N/don't know)	Phone or face-to-face interviews; language not specified but presumably in native language; first-person judgment	81% USA vs 63% Russia vs 52% China	39% USA vs 36% Russia vs 22% China	n/a, 3000 participants
Awad et al., 2020	42 countries, 10 languages	70,000	What should the man in blue do? (Two images shown side by side show the two possible decisions and their outcomes. The measure is simply the image they click.)	Reports country-level averages of clicking the image of the man taking action; third-person judgment	81%	51%	n/a
Hauser et al., 2007	Australia	5,000	Is it morally permissible for [the agent] to [take the action]? (Y/N)	The subject in the side-effect version is the driver of the train (not a bystander); scenarios were all in English; third-person judgment	90%	15%	<.001
	Brazil				82%	29%	.002
	Canada				84%	12%	<.001
	India				88%	0%	<.001
	US				90%	10%	<.001
	UK				83%	15%	<.001
	American Indian/Alaskan Native				40%	7%	.048
	Asian/Pacific Islander				80%	12%	<.001
	Black Non-Hispanic				90%	26%	<.001
	Hispanic				80%	16%	<.001
	White Non-Hispanic				90%	10%	<.001

Table 10.2. (*cont.*)

Paper	Culture	N*	Question	Notes	Bystander (% Y/ Mean)	Footbridge (% Y/ Mean)	P value**
Moore et al., 2011	US	35	Was the action "morally appropriate"? (Y/N)	Battery of 24 dilemmas, here Bystander is what they call "impersonal other" and Footbridge "personal-other"; all harms are deaths; scenarios translated into Chinese; first-person judgments	45%	44%	< .001
	Chinese	41			40%	31%	
Winking & Koster, 2021 Study 2	Mayangna; 120 participants in total, sample sizes ranged from 59 to 61 for each scenario	120	Acceptability of utilitarian decision (5-pt scale: very bad-bad-neither good nor bad, but in the middle-good-very good)	Standard scenario; scenarios translated into Mayangna; third-person judgment	3.70	3.64	.721
		120	Acceptability of utilitarian decision (5-pt scale: very bad-bad-neither good nor bad, but in the middle-good-very good)	Stampede scenario (cattle), for cultural relevance; scenarios translated into Mayangna; third-person judgment	3.68	3.44	.193

* N = number of participants

** The p value, which tells you the likelihood that the results were observed by chance compared to the initial theory, or "null hypothesis." Generally, in the tests in the table, the null hypothesis is that the responses will be the same in the two scenarios. By convention p < 0.05 is the threshold for statistical significance, the point where we declare that the results are so unlikely that we reject the hypothesis that the responses being compared are the same.

Table 10.3. Cross-cultural comparisons: comparing the same scenario across two or more cultures: all third-person except where stated; scenarios administered in the native language, except where indicated; figures for Y/N judgments represent percentage saying the action is morally acceptable

Paper	Cultures compared (n*)	Scenario	Question	Notes	Results (% Y/ Mean)	P value**
Ahlenius & Tännsjö, 2012	US vs Russian vs Chinese (3,000 total)	Bystander	Should you flip the switch? (Y/N/ don't know)	Phone or face-to-face interviews; language not specified but presumably in native language; first-person judgment	81% USA vs 63% Russian vs 52% Chinese	n/a
		Footbridge	Should you push the man? (Y/N/ don't know)	Phone or face-to-face interviews; language not specified but presumably in native language; first-person judgment	39% USA vs 36% Russian vs 22% Chinese	n/a
Arutyunova, Alexandrov, & Hauser, 2016	Russian (327) vs Western (USA, UK, Canada; 332)	Bystander	Pulling the lever is: 1 (Forbidden) – 2 – 3 – 4 (Permissible) – 5 – 6 – 7 (Obligatory)	Speedboat scenario; native language; third-person judgment	3.80 Western vs 3.61 Russian	.18
		Bystander	Pulling the lever is: 1 (Forbidden) – 2 – 3 – 4 (Permissible) – 5 – 6 – 7 (Obligatory)	Burning scenario; native language; third-person judgment	4.90 Western vs 4.87 Russian	.78
		Bystander	Pulling the lever is: 1 (Forbidden) – 2 – 3 – 4 (Permissible) – 5 – 6 – 7 (Obligatory)	Boxcar scenario (the standard trolley scenario) ; native language; third-person judgment	4.30 Western vs 3.74 Russian	< 0.01
		Bystander	Pulling the lever is: 1 (Forbidden) – 2 – 3 – 4 (Permissible) – 5 – 6 – 7 (Obligatory)	Switch scenario; native language; third-person judgment	4.55 Western vs 3.92 Russian	<0.01
		Bystander	Pulling the lever is: 1 (Forbidden) – 2 – 3 – 4 (Permissible) – 5 – 6 – 7 (Obligatory)	Chemical scenario; native language; third-person judgment	4.95 Western vs 4.31 Russian	<0.01

Table 10.3. (cont.)

Paper	Cultures compared (n*)	Scenario	Question	Notes	Results (% Y/ Mean)	P value**
		Bystander	Pulling the lever is: 1 (Forbidden) – 2 – 3 – 4 (Permissible) – 5 – 6 – 7 (Obligatory)	Shark scenario; native language; third-person judgment	4.60 Western vs 4.39 Russian	.096
		Average Bystander	Pulling the lever is: 1 (Forbidden) – 2 – 3 – 4 (Permissible) – 5 – 6 – 7 (Obligatory)	All six scenarios; native language; third-person judgment	4.51 Western vs 4.12 Russian	<0.01
		Footbridge	Pulling the lever is: 1 (Forbidden) – 2 – 3 – 4 (Permissible) – 5 – 6 – 7 (Obligatory)	Speedboat scenario; native language; third-person judgment	3.50 Western vs 3.08 Russian	.003
		Footbridge	Pulling the lever is: 1 (Forbidden) – 2 – 3 – 4 (Permissible) – 5 – 6 – 7 (Obligatory)	Burning scenario; native language; third-person judgment	3.66 Western vs 3.55 Russian	.48
		Footbridge	Pulling the lever is: 1 (Forbidden) – 2 – 3 – 4 (Permissible) – 5 – 6 – 7 (Obligatory)	Boxcar scenario (the standard trolley scenario); native language; third-person judgment	3.80 Western vs 2.91 Russian	<0.01
		Footbridge	Pulling the lever is: 1 (Forbidden) – 2 – 3 – 4 (Permissible) – 5 – 6 – 7 (Obligatory)	Switch scenario; native language; third-person judgment	4.27 Western vs 3.66 Russian	< 0.01
		Footbridge	Pulling the lever is: 1 (Forbidden) – 2 – 3 – 4 (Permissible) – 5 – 6 – 7 (Obligatory)	Chemical scenario; native language; third-person judgment	4.71 Western vs 4.03 Russian	<0.01

Study	Scenario	Question	Result	p
Footbridge	Shark scenario; native language; third-person judgment	Pulling the lever is: 1 (Forbidden) – 2 – 3 – 4 (Permissible) – 5 – 6 – 7 (Obligatory)	4.30 Western vs 3.88 Russian	.003
Average Footbridge	All six scenarios; native language; third-person judgment	Pulling the lever is: 1 (Forbidden) – 2 – 3 – 4 (Permissible) – 5 – 6 – 7 (Obligatory)	4.04 Western vs 3.52 Russian	<0.01
Gold, Colman, & Pulford, 2014 — British vs Chinese (Real-life orphans: 45 British vs 61 Chinese; hypothetical scenarios: 55 British vs 45 Chinese)				
Bystander	Orphans - judgment given after making a decision about whether or not to click on a switch to divert a threat so that five orphans did not lose a meal; study conducted in English; first-person judgment	How wrong or right was it to switch the lever? (9-point scale from 1 *Definitely wrong* to 9 *Definitely right*; dichotomized so 1–4 = wrong and 6–9 = right)	69.8% British vs 47.6% Chinese	.006
Bystander	Orphans – hypothetical version of study above; translated into simplified Chinese; first-person judgment	Please indicate how wrong or how right you think it would be to switch the lever: (1 *Definitely wrong* to 7 *Definitely right*).	4.89 British vs 4.07 Chinese	.011
Bystander	Train – standard trolley scenario; translated into simplified Chinese; first-person judgment	Please indicate how wrong or how right you think it would be to pull the lever: (1 *Definitely wrong* to 7 *Definitely right*).	4.18 British vs 4.31 Chinese	.736
Bystander	Game show – scenario transposed to a game show, with financial harms; translated into simplified Chinese; first-person judgment	Please indicate how wrong or how right you think it would be to press the button: (1 *Definitely wrong* to 7 *Definitely right*).	4.58 British vs 4.22 Chinese	.292

Table 10.3. (*cont.*)

Paper	Cultures compared (n*)	Scenario	Question	Notes	Results (% Y/ Mean)	P value**
		Bystander	Is it morally wrong for you to switch the lever? (Yes/No) Answers re-coded to represent percentage "not wrong."	Orphans – hypothetical version of study above; translated into simplified Chinese; first-person judgment	69.9% British vs 64.4% Chinese	.623
		Bystander	Is it morally wrong for you to switch the lever? (Yes/No) Answers re-coded to represent percentage "not wrong."	Train – standard trolley scenario; translated into simplified Chinese; first-person judgment	54.6% British vs 64.4% Chinese	.317
		Bystander	Is it morally wrong for you to press the button? (Yes/No) Answers re-coded to represent percentage "not wrong."	Game show – scenario transposed to a game show, with financial harms; translated into simplified Chinese; first-person judgment	85.5% British vs 84.4% of Chinese	.888
Michelin et al., 2010 Experiment 3	Monolingual Italian (50) vs Slovenian-Italian bilingual (36)	Bystander	Should the person pull a cord to save three people? (Y/N)	Harming 3 to save 5; all tested in Italian; third-person judgment	>60% in both groups	ns
		Footbridge	Should the person push one person to save five people? (Y/N)	Harming 3 to save 5; all tested in Italian; third-person judgment	40% monolingual Italians vs >60% Slovenian Italians	.02
Moore et al., 2011; Experiment 1	US (35) vs Chinese (41)	Bystander	Was the action "morally appropriate" or "morally inappropriate"	Battery of 24 dilemmas, here comparing impersonal other (i.e., consequences are visited on other people) and avoidable deaths; first-person judgment	45% US vs 44% Chinese	> .08 for main effect, *ns* interaction effect

Study	Type	Question	Description	Results	p
Sheskin et al., 2018 Bali (30), Costa Rica (18), France (21), Guatemala (20), Japan (14), Madagascar (34), Mongolia (40), Serbia (59), and the USA (27)	Footbridge	Is action was "morally appropriate" or "morally inappropriate"	Battery of 24 dilemmas, here comparing personal-other (i.e., consequences are visited on other people) and avoidable deaths; first-person judgment	40% US vs 31% Chinese	
	Bystander	Should the sailor take the buoy back and throw it toward the group of five? (Y/N)	Buoy 2: sailor can throw a life buoy to save one or five, it lands exactly in the middle, but the waves will push the buoy toward the single person; translated into native language; third-person judgment	70.0% Bali vs 66.7% Costa Rica vs 66.7% France vs 80% Guatemala vs 38.2% Japan vs 92.9% Madagascar vs 55% Mongolia vs 83.1% Serbia vs 74.1% US	<0.01
	Bystander	Rate the strength of the sailor's duty on a scale ranging from 1 "He should throw the buoy again" to 9 "He should not throw the buoy again."	Buoy 2: sailor can throw a life buoy to save one or five, it lands exactly in the middle, but the waves will push the buoy toward the single person; translated into native language; third-person judgment	3.60 Bali vs 3.83 Costa Rica vs 3.83 France vs 3.65 Guatemala vs 5.38 Japan vs 2.8 Madagascar vs 5.46 Mongolia vs 2.8 Serbia vs 4.11 US	< 0.01
	Bystander	Should the take the buoy back and throw it toward the group of five? (Y/N)	Buoy 3: sailor can throw a life buoy to save one or five, it lands directly next to the single person; translated into native language; third-person judgment	50.0% Bali vs 72.2% Costa Rica vs 71.4% France vs 65.0% Guatemala vs 29.4% Japan vs 28.6% Madagascar vs 45.0% Mongolia vs 78.0% Serbia vs 51.9% US	< 0.01
	Bystander	Rate the strength of the sailor's duty on a scale ranging from 1 "He should throw the buoy again" to 9 "He should not throw the buoy again."	Buoy 3: sailor can throw a life buoy to save one or five, it lands directly next to the single person; translated into native language; third-person judgment	4.60 Bali vs 3.28 Costa Rica vs 4.52 France vs 3.95 Guatemala vs 6.15 Japan vs 6.21 Madagascar vs 5.74 Mongolia vs 3.54 Serbia vs 5.04 US	< 0.01

Table 10.3. (cont.)

Paper	Cultures compared (n*)	Scenario	Question	Notes	Results (% Y/ Mean)	P value**
Sorokowski et al., 2020	Canadians (95) vs Yali (109)	Bystander	Is it appropriate for you to push the falling tree to avoid the deaths of the five people?	"Falling tree dilemma," which would be ecologically valid for Yali; translated into Yali; first-person judgment	68% Canadians vs 37% Yali	< 0.01
Winskel & Bhatt, 2020	Hindi–English bilinguals (166) vs English monolinguals (127), all living in Australia	Bystander; trolley	Moral permissibility ratings (1 = *completely wrong*, 7 = *completely right*).	Hindi speakers randomly allocated to Hindi vs English versions; first-person judgment	3.99 English Monolinguals vs 4.14 Hindi-English Bilinguals	> .1
		Bystander; family game show	Moral permissibility ratings (1 = *completely wrong*, 7 = *completely right*).	Financial harms; Hindi speakers randomly allocated to Hindi vs English versions; first-person judgment	3.87 English Monolinguals vs 3.60 Hindi-English Bilinguals	> .1
		Bystander; waterpark gameshow	Moral permissibility ratings (1 = *completely wrong*, 7 = *completely right*).	Financial harms; Hindi speakers randomly allocated to Hindi vs English versions; first-person judgment	4.03 English Monolinguals vs 3.51 Hindi-English Bilinguals	> .1
		Footbridge; trolley	Moral permissibility ratings (1 = *completely wrong*, 7 = *completely right*).	Hindi speakers randomly allocated to Hindi vs English versions; first-person judgment	2.35 English Monolinguals vs 2.16 Hindi-English Bilinguals	> .1
		Footbridge; family game show	Moral permissibility ratings (1 = *completely wrong*, 7 = *completely right*).	Financial harms; Hindi speakers randomly allocated to Hindi vs English versions; first-person judgment	3.40 English Monolinguals vs 2.95 Hindi-English Bilinguals	< .05
		Footbridge; waterpark gameshow	Moral permissibility ratings (1 = *completely wrong*, 7 = *completely right*).	Financial harms; Hindi speakers randomly allocated to Hindi vs English versions; first-person judgment	3.64 English Monolinguals vs 2.57 Hindi-English Bilinguals	< .001

Study	Groups compared (N)	Dilemma	Question	Methodology	Results	Statistics
Xiang, 2014	Tibetan Buddhist monks (48) vs lay Tibetans (40) vs American Christian ministers (27) vs lay Americans (41) vs lay Han Chinese (47)	Footbridge	"Do you think it is morally acceptable for Joe to push the man with the backpack in order to save the five people?"	Questions asked in-person in English for US participants and in Mandarin Chinese for Chinese and Tibetan participants (would be the second language for Tibetans); third-person judgment	83% Tibetan monks vs 64% lay Tibetans vs 33% American Christian ministers vs 15% lay Americans vs 19% lay Han Chinese	Lay Tibetans were different from lay Americans, $p<.001$; Tibetan monks were different from American Christian Ministers $p<.001$; Lay Tibetans differed from lay Han Chinese, $p<0.001$
Yamamoto & Yuki, 2019	US (132) vs Japanese (124)	Bystander	"Do you think pulling the lever in this situation is ethically wrong?" (Y/N)	Runaway train (following Gold, 2014); native language; first-person judgment	71.0% Japanese vs 62.9% US	all n.s. in logistic regression
		Bystander	"Do you think pulling the lever in this situation is ethically wrong?" (Y/N)	Orphan (following Gold, 2014); financial harms; native language; first-person judgment	66.9% Japanese vs 67.4% US	all n.s. in logistic regression
		Bystander	"Do you think pulling the lever in this situation is ethically wrong?" (Y/N)	Runaway train (following Gold, 2014); financial language; first-person judgment	75.8% Japanese vs 72.0% US	all n.s. in logistic regression

* N = number of participants

** The p value, which tells you the likelihood that the results were observed by chance compared to the initial theory, or "null hypothesis." Generally, in the tests in the table, the null hypothesis is that the responses will be the same in the two cultures. By convention $p < 0.05$ is the threshold for statistical significance, the point where we declare that the results are so unlikely that we reject the hypothesis that the responses being compared are the same.

conclude there is evidence that the groups are different (although technically, we don't accept the alternative hypothesis – the test is a test of the null).

However, the value itself says nothing about the size of the effect. The p value is also affected by the number of participants in the experiments: If there are very many participants, then we will be able to detect very small effects (including differences that are so small as to be meaningless), but if there are very few participants then we may fail to detect a large effect. Therefore, if $p > 0.05$, that may be because there is no effect or because the number of participants was too small to detect the effect, given its size. Similarly, with a very large number of participants, even an effect that is so small as not to be meaningful may be statistically significant. Therefore, I have given the sample size for the experiments.

10.2.1.1 Studies comparing bystander to footbridge

I found seven papers that compared judgments in Bystander versus Footbridge. In most cases, the researchers translated the materials into the native language of the participants, avoiding the worry that people give different (more "utilitarian"[2]) responses to trolley problems when they answer in a second language (Costa et al., 2014). Hauser (2007) is the exception. Only two asked for first-person judgments (Ahlenius and Tännsjö, 2012; Moore et al., 2011).

Across virtually all cultures, there was a greater willingness to judge that it is right to take action in Bystander than in Footbridge (see Table 10.2). This includes two papers that report internet surveys with large numbers of participants covering a large range of countries, with Awad et al. (2020) covering forty countries and ten languages, and Hauser et al. (2007) covering six countries and five ethnicities. There were also Bystander–Footbridge differences in Chinese samples (Ahlenius and Tännsjö, 2012; Moore et al., 2011), in a rural Mayan population in Mexico (Abarbanell & Hauser, 2010), and in Russian populations (Ahlenius and Tännsjö, 2012; Arutyunova, Alexandrov, & Hauser, 2016).

There are two exceptions that prove the rule, both of which tested people from small-scale societies. Abarbanell and Hauser (2010) found a marginally significant result among a less rural and more educated Mayan population, with the judgments hovering around the midpoint of the scale, which was

---

[2] I use scare quotes because although the judgments seem consistent with utilitarianism, understood as an impartial concern with the greater good, arguably they are not expressions of a general utilitarian outlook (Kahane et al., 2015).

labeled "a little good" (Bystander M = 2.83 vs Footbridge M = 2.30, $p < .054$). The Mayangna, a small-scale indigenous population in Nicaragua, showed no differences in moral ratings of Bystander and Footbridge, rating the acceptability of both as good (Wiking & Koster, 2021).

It is worth noting that the differences between Bystander and Footbridge are also replicated across different demographic categories, that is, not just across culture. Hauser et al. (2007) found the difference in all religions and in all age groups they were able to test. Awad et al. (2020) do not provide statistical analysis, but visual inspection suggests that demographics do not impact responses, apart from college education, which makes people less likely to agree that the correct action is to push the man in Footbridge. In a whole battery of trolley-type scenarios, Banerjee, Huebner, and Hauser (2010) found that gender, education, politics, and religion do not tend to affect the pattern of moral judgments (i.e., the differences when comparing pairs, including Bystander–Footbridge) and that the very few statistically significant differences in judgments have extremely small effect sizes.

10.2.1.2 Studies Comparing Different Cultures on a Single Scenario

I found ten papers that compared the moral judgments of different cultures on a Bystander or Footbridge scenario, many of which presented multiple studies.

Direct comparisons of judgments in the same scenario across cultures reveal some cross-cultural variation (see Table 10.3). Two studies did not use native-language translations (Gold et al. 2014's real-life decision has Chinese answering in English, Xiang's 2014 Tibetans answered in Chinese), but in both cases the authors give reasons to think that this did not have too much impact on results.

Although the vast majority of paired comparisons are of Eastern vs Western cultures, the results are somewhat mixed. I'll first look at the results overall, split by comparisons in the Footbridge scenario and comparisons in Bystander, and then hone in on East–West comparisons.

Differences were more likely to show up in Footbridge than in Bystander. The following studies gave participants both Bystander and Footbridge, finding no difference in Bystander but the following differences in Footbridge: 40% monolingual Italians say the agent should push vs >60% bilingual Slovenian-Italians (Michelin et al., 2010); English monolinguals give higher moral permissibility ratings than Hindi–English bilinguals in two out of three versions of Footbridge – the two that involved financial harms rather than death (Winskel & Bhatt, 2020). Another study that only used Footbridge scenarios, found that

Tibetans (lay people and monks) were more likely to say it was morally acceptable to push than Americans (lay Americans and Christian Ministers) and lay Tibetans were also more likely to say it was morally acceptable to push than lay Han Chinese, but there were no differences between lay Han Chinese and lay Americans (Xiang, 2014). In contrast, Ahlenius and Tännsjö (2012) found that 39% of Americans said they should push the man in Footbridge compared to 36% of Russians and 52% of Chinese. No statistical testing was done, but given the large number of participants it seems likely that their Chinese participants were more permissive.

Other studies that focused on Bystander had more mixed results.

The Yali horticulturists in Papua, Indonesia (a traditional, indigenous, non-Western society inhabiting the remote Yalimo valley) found it less appropriate to take action in Bystander than Canadians, 37% Yali vs 68% Canadians (Sorokowski et al., 2020). Ahlenius and Tännsjö (2012) appeared to find cultural differences in Bystander, with 81% of Americans saying they should take action compared to 63% of Russians and 52% of Chinese. This is consistent with Arutyunova, Alexandrov, and Hauser's (2016) finding that Westerners were more willing than Russians to harm one to save many across a set of dilemmas. Sheskin et al. (2018) found differences across ten countries in both Y/N judgments and rating scales about whether an agent should take action in Bystander versions of the dilemma. They find that Japanese are numerically less likely to think the agent should take action (there are no post hoc tests to ascertain which nationalities drove the overall differences).

This contrasts to Yamamoto and Yuki (2019), who found no differences between US and Japanese participants in one standard scenario with a runaway train and two other scenarios where the harm was financial, rather than death. Their studies were modeled on Gold et al. (2014), who also found no difference in ratings of moral wrongness on three Bystander scenarios, when considered individually. However, the results from the three scenarios in Gold et al. were in the same direction and a regression on a composite measure, which combined the responses from all three scenarios, found that Chinese gave lower ratings. Both nationalities, on average, indicated that taking the action would be right, so the cultural difference represented a small shift along the "right" side of the ratings scale. Further, Chinese were more likely to choose the midpoint of the scale and when the scale was dichotomized into right–wrong judgments, discarding the midpoint, British were more likely to say it was right to switch the lever than Chinese, 69.8% British vs 47.6% Chinese. Moore et al. (2011) found that there were no differences between Chinese and American judgments (though note that the sample size seems small, at 76 participants), though on average across Bystander- and Footbridge-type scenarios, participants were more likely to say that the action was morally appropriate in Bystander.

The cultural difference that is most often discussed in the literature is that between East and West. It is worth noting that the evidence of East–West differences in moral judgments of Bystander and Footbridge is rather mixed. In the Footbridge scenario, one study found differences between US and Chinese participants (Ahlenius and Tännsjö, 2012); another found differences between US and Tibetan participants, but not US and Chinese (Xiang, 2014). In the Bystander scenario, one study found US–Chinese differences (Ahlenius and Tännsjö, 2012), one study with a relatively small sample size found no differences (Moore et al., 2011), and one found small differences that would ideally be corroborated (Gold, 2014). Two studies investigated Japanese–US differences, of which one study finds differences between Japan and UK (Sheskin et al., 2018) but one does not (Yamamoto & Yuki, 2019).

Arguably, there is a clearer East–West difference when it comes to taking action in trolley problems (as opposed to making judgments). A number of the papers had participants take actions or predict what actions they would take, as well as make moral judgments, and the cross-cultural differences in action were more pronounced. Gold et al. (2014) found that 80% of British clicked a switch to move a lever in a Bystander scenario where orphans lost meals, compared to 49.2% of Chinese ($p < .001$), and the differences also showed up in hypothetical scenarios involving trains (76.4% British vs 64.4% Chinese) and material harms (the hypothetical version of the real-life orphans decision, 90.9% British vs 73.3% Chinese, and a scenario that placed the action in a television game show, 76.4% British vs 64.4% Chinese). Rehman and Dzionek-Kozłowska (2020) found 61.4% of Americans said they would push the man in Footbridge, but only 25% of Chinese ($p < .001$).[3] Yamamoto and Yuki (2019) found US participants were more likely to say that they would take action than Japanese: 68.2% US vs 50.8% Japanese in a hypothetical train scenario, and in two hypothetical scenarios involving material harms based on Gold et al.: 79.0% US vs 71.8% Japanese in a scenario where the harms were meals being taken away from orphans and 63.6% US vs 51.6% Japanese in a scenario where the harms were financial losses in a game show.[4]

---

[3] They did not find statistically significant differences in Bystander, indeed the numerical values were not in the direction that would be expected (88.6% US vs 92.3% Chinese), but the sample size of 122 is relatively small.

[4] The runaway train difference was not statistically significant in an unadjusted Chi-2, but was in a regression that controlled for gender and age.

It is also interesting to consider the results in small-scale nonindustrialized societies, though unfortunately there is only a small amount of data. The Mayangna (Winking and Koster, 2021) and the Yali (Sorokowski, 2020) did not show standard patterns of judgments, though rural Mayans did (Abarbanell & Hauser, 2010). Again, there is potentially a difference between judgment and actions. Wiking and Koster's (2021) Mayanga study, which did not find differences in moral judgments between Bystander and Footbridge, still showed the standard pattern when participants were asked to make Y/N judgments about whether they would *take* the necessary action in a version of the trolley problem that was designed to be culturally relevant (a stampede scenario with cattle), with 93.9% saying they would take action in Bystander and 62.1% in Footbridge ($p = 0.003$). So it may just be that there are clearer cross-cultural differences in propensity to act (or self-reports of propensity to act) than in moral judgments.

10.2.1.3 Conclusion

Across cultures, there is generally agreement that acting in Bystander is more morally acceptable than acting in Footbridge. Comparing individual scenarios, there is mixed evidence on cultural differences in Bystander and more consistent (but considerably less) evidence of differences in Footbridge.

There is not enough evidence to draw a strong conclusion about cultural differences in the permissibility of acting in the individual trolley scenarios. However, I suspect the evidence I have presented is a rather conservative estimate of cross-cultural differences for the following reasons. First, there is more data on Bystander than on Footbridge. However, there is quite high agreement that it is permissible to turn the train in Bystander; the disagreements seem to be preponderant in Footbridge. Second, I limited my comparisons to Bystander and Footbridge. I suspect the case for cross-cultural differences could be bolstered by drawing on other trolley scenarios or other types of moral judgment. Third, and related to the focus on Bystander versus Footbridge and the associated distinction between causing harm as a side effect versus as a means, I ignored other moral distinctions that people in the West are wont to make, which also may not be consistent across cultures. For instance, Abarbanell, and Hauser (2010) do not find evidence of actions and omissions being judged differently in a Mayan population. Fourth, the most promising place to look for differing judgments may be among small-scale societies. For instance, the only two populations that did not show a Bystander-Footbridge difference were small-scale societies. But there is least evidence from these cultures.

There seem to be bigger cross-cultural differences in propensity to act than in moral judgments, especially for Bystander. Many of the experiments asked questions like whether the action is permissible or acceptable, which includes the possibility that the alternative action is also permissible or that the action is acceptable but not required. Or these differences between judgments and actions could simply reflect a lower propensity to act on moral judgments. We would need more research to understand their causes.

10.3 Causes of cultural differences in moral judgments

I found that there is a quite cross-culturally consistent difference between judgments in Bystander and Footbridge (though small-scale societies may be an exception), with the action in Bystander rated as more morally acceptable than in Footbridge. However, the moral acceptability of acting in the individual dilemmas varies somewhat across cultures, with there being mixed evidence about the comparison between Western and Eastern cultures, and little evidence on small-scale versus industrialized societies. I will take it that there are cross-cultural differences in moral judgments in individual scenarios, despite the mixed evidence; both for the sake of argument and for the reasons I gave at the end of Section 10.2 about why this body of evidence may underestimate the size of the differences.

That raises the question of why there is a cross-culturally consistent difference in judgments between Bystander and Footbridge (at least in industrialized societies), but variation on some individual scenarios. I suspect that the answer involves the personal contact in the Footbridge scenario and a universal aversion to causing harm by personal force. Feltz and May (2017) conducted a meta-analysis of experiments that tested for differences in the acceptability of causing harm as a means or a side effect. Meta-analysis assesses an entire body of research. They found that, overall, there is a small difference between moral judgments of causing harm as a means or a side effect. However, the effect size was moderated by whether the outcome is brought about by personal contact, typically involving the use of force. In other words, the difference in judgments between Bystander and Footbridge is more due to the personal force involved in Footbridge than to the means–side effect difference. I would need more space than I have to argue the point, but it is plausible that there is a shared psychological aversion to harming people using personal force. This is the simplest explanation of the data, so we should accept it according to Occam's Razor.

It is worth pausing to note that there are also differences between judgments within societies. In some of the experiments I reviewed, there was a roughly 50–50 split *within a culture* about whether or not acting would be morally permissible. Any differences in moral judgments pose some issues for moral philosophy, but cross-cultural differences pose very particular ones because of what they may imply about the causes of the differences.[5]

In order to derive the implications for moral philosophy, we first need to think about why there are differences in judgments. Is there really a moral disagreement? Maybe people from different cultures put a different interpretive spin on the question, which causes them to give different answers due to differing interpretations rather than moral disagreement. Or maybe there is a disagreement that can be explained with reference to nonmoral beliefs, in a way that does not threaten the idea of the existence of universal moral principles (Doris and Plakias, 2008). It looks more worrying if different judgments are explained either by learned aspects of culture or by some sort of interaction between genetics and culture, where we have evolved a universal moral faculty some of whose parameters are set during ontogeny by interaction with the environment – as has been proposed by John Mikhail (2007), following Chomsky's idea of a universal grammar.

This requires me to assess some of the explanations for cultural differences in judgments, to determine if the causes are at base moral disagreements. Putative East–West cultural differences have had most attention, so despite the mixed evidence above, in this section I will take them as given. Of course, East–West is also a narrow view of differences. The evidence I surveyed suggests that there are likely to be differences between industrialized and small-scale societies, which is also borne out by other types of study (Henrich et al., 2005). And there are other potential ways of splitting societies, such as the Global North and South. But I'll start with an East–West explanation and then broaden out.

One type of explanation cites cultural or religious belief systems. For instance, Gold et al. (2014) found that belief in fate and the view that it is best to let events run their course was associated with judging that action in Bystander is morally wrong (as well as a lower propensity by participants to say they would take action). Their Chinese participants tended to believe in fate and nonintervention, but the British participants did not; they suggest that these beliefs explain cultural differences in moral judgments and actions. Should we class the belief in fate as a nonmoral belief or as a moral one?

---

[5] We might also note that there is a tendency to conflate "culture" and "society." Cross-cultural research usually refers to comparison across societies, but there may in fact be more than one culture (in terms of groups with distinct attitudes and practices) living in a single society.

On the one hand, belief in fate as a force beyond human control is not in itself moral. On the other hand, the associated ethical principle of action through nonaction (*wu-wei*) is at the heart of Taoism, which is a religious doctrine (Kirkland, 2004).

This is not the only instance in which it may be difficult to distinguish between moral and nonmoral beliefs, especially if moral beliefs include religious beliefs. In general, it is hard to discriminate between "mere" cultural versus religious differences, since religious differences often correlate with cultural differences and we don't know whether it is religion or culture that is causal. For instance, Awad et al. (2018) discovered three clusters of countries in their data on moral judgments: Western, Eastern, and Southern. Within each of the three clusters, countries have geographical and cultural proximity to each other, but they also have religious commonalities. The Western cluster contains North America as well as many European countries of Protestant, Catholic, and Orthodox Christian cultural groups. The Eastern cluster contains many far eastern countries such as Japan and Taiwan that belong to the Confucianist cultural group, and Islamic countries such as Indonesia, Pakistan, and Saudi Arabia. The Southern cluster consists of the Latin American countries of Central and South America, in addition to some countries that are characterized in part by French influence, which are overwhelmingly Catholic. Should we ascribe the differences in judgments between clusters to differences in nonmoral beliefs, to culture, or to religion? However, we may not need to address problems of causality, since other convincing explanations quite firmly place the emphasis on culture, in a way that looks like a genuine moral disagreement.

A second type of explanation for cross-cultural differences in judgment, which is often used to explain putative East–West differences, is the difference between individualist and collectivist societies. People in individualist societies tend to place more emphasis on individual rights, whereas people in collectivist societies emphasize relationships and their place in the larger whole (Hoefstadeter, 1984). Awad et al. (2018) argue that participants from individualistic cultures and collectivistic cultures show systematic differences in judgments in trolley problems, with those from individualistic cultures showing a stronger preference for acting to save the greater number of people. Further, the individualist–collectivist distinction goes beyond East–West differences. Shweder et al. (1997) argue that, outside of the West in general, there is more likely to be an ethic of community, in which morality derives from the fulfillment of interpersonal obligations that are tied to an individual's role within the social order. Consistent with this, Winking and Koster (2021) present a content analysis of comments that their Mayangna participants spontaneously offered, which suggests that Mayangna moral reasoning relied on community-based moral frames. For example, one participant commented that, "If five die, it is a great cost to the community. It's a lot of work to bury all of them. One is much less." Another reported, "The Mayangna are few in number. If five die, that's a lot. If he calls him, he saves five. It's good because he's thinking of the five." Others discussed the cost to the families, such as, "There's always trouble. If five die, there will be many children who will be abandoned. He was thinking of the five." As an explanation of cross-cultural differences, individualist versus collectivist societies looks particularly problematic for moral philosophy because it seems likely that being from a socially individualist versus a socially collectivist culture has a causal effect on the principles that underpin moral judgments.

A third type of explanation points at differences in social structures. Awad et al. (2020) found that *relational mobility,* or the fluidity with which people can develop new relationships, was positively correlated with the propensity to judge that the protagonist should act in dilemmas. The idea is that, in societies with low relational mobility, people develop lifelong relationships but have few options to develop new ones. As a result, they show greater social cautiousness, in order to avoid conflict in existing relationships. Awad et al.'s effect of relational mobility was mostly driven by Asian countries, which tend to be in the lower half of relational mobility, whereas non-Asian countries tend to be high in both relational mobility and propensity to endorse acting in trolley problems.

Relational mobility looks potentially like a psychological explanation, rather than a moral disagreement. However, there is strong evidence of the influence of social structure from other cross-cultural experiments, in a way that does suggest that the social structures that underpin relational mobility are intertwined with moral principles. For instance, market integration and religion predict higher offers in ultimatum and dictator games, while community size predicts the tendency to turn down inequitable offers (Henrich et al. 2010). The authors suggest that norms and institutions for exchange in ephemeral interactions culturally coevolved with markets and expanding populations, i.e. that social structures are inextricably connected to normative principles. Of course, these are examples of social structure predicting actions and we saw above that there are greater cultural differences in propensity to take action than in moral judgments. However, it seems likely that the actions would also correlate with moral judgments.

We may struggle to make a coherent distinction between culture and institutions, or to attribute differences in judgments to one or the other; the two are probably symbiotic. However, we do not need to adjudicate. If the society you live in affects your moral judgments and moral principles, that is enough to raise issues for moral philosophy.

10.4 Implications for philosophy

The existence of cross-cultural differences in moral judgments raises questions for metaethics, especially about the metaphysics and epistemology of moral practice. In metaphysics we might ask: Are there any moral facts that are independent of human minds? In epistemology, we might ask: If there are moral facts, how would we know them; and how should we understand and resolve ethical disagreement? These two types of question are intertwined.

The position that there are objective moral facts is called *moral realism.* To say that a claim is objective is to say that its truth does not depend on the particular speaker, also sometimes cashed out as being *mind-independent.* It is easiest to illustrate realism by comparison with a natural fact, of the type studied by scientists, about the physical structure of the universe: The Earth orbits the Sun. This is true independently of the existence of or thinking of humans.

The status of facts is also relevant to how we can come to know them and how we resolve disagreements. Again, let us start with natural facts. Prior to the fifteenth century, people thought that the Sun revolved in a circular orbit around the Earth, a model that went back to Ptolemy. However, that could not explain all the evidence about planetary motion. Copernicus presented a heliocentric model, which explained the existing evidence and was verified by appeal to further evidence (the universe as viewed through Galileo's telescopes) and refinements of the model (Kepler's proposal that planets have elliptical orbits). In the light of these developments, we are able to say that the Ptolemaic model is wrong and resolve the disagreement in Copernicus' favor.

The epistemology of moral "facts" (if they exist) has some parallels but also some differences. The doyen of trolley problems is surely Frances Kamm, who gives the following explanation of the methodology: We use trolley problems to discover our intuitive response to cases; we then need to formulate a set of principles that explains our case judgments and that expresses morally significant ideas, in order to discover a deeper – potentially universal – structure of morality (Voorhoeve, 2009). According to this method, there is a sense in which our judgments play the role of evidence, which needs to be explained by our theory, from which we learn facts. However, unlike physical evidence, if our intuitive moral judgments do not fit our best theory, then it may be the judgments that should change. There needs to be a "reflective equilibrium" between judgments and theory, but the movement can be in either direction, which is not the case for scientific facts.

It is clear that this leads to a problem for moral epistemology: If our theory and our intuitions disagree, then how do we know which needs to be revised? And if people from different cultures disagree about judgments, how are we supposed to resolve the disagreement? Most problematically of all: If different cultures reach different reflective equilibria between judgments and theories, and therefore endorse different sets of moral principles, how would we adjudicate between them?

Mackie (1977) claimed that the best explanation of the variation of ethical opinion is that people participate in different ways of life and they tend to approve of those ways of life in which they participate. (See also Sugden, 2004, on the idea that the social system evolves to an equilibrium state, that people expect the equilibrium strategies to be played, and these expectations become normative: They begin to think that others ought to play their part in the equilibrium.) Mackie gave what is sometimes called the "Argument from Disagreement": If cultures disagree, then rather than having to explain why one culture enjoys a privileged access to the moral facts, the best explanation is that there are no facts for them to disagree over. This led Mackie to *error theory*, the idea that all our moral claims are false and no moral facts exist for them to correspond to.

In effect, Mackie was making an argument from the problem of moral epistemology to a particular position in moral metaphysics. One doesn't even need cultural differences to make this argument: If the judgments of reasonable people do not converge, then we might wonder whether there is really anything for them to agree over. Therefore, one way to challenge this argument is to challenge the idea that moral judgments must converge on a single set of moral facts. In order to do that, we need to put aside the analogy to mind-independent natural facts and explore other ways that we could have moral facts, which would be neither wholly mind-independent nor completely subjective.

There may be in between positions where we deny that morality is completely mind-independent *without* denying that there exists some type of moral fact. This will involve denying the parallels between moral facts and natural facts, and revising our idea of what morality is. Here are three different moves that have been made in this direction.

One move starts with the function of morality, as a method of promoting social harmony. This has been cashed out in three slightly different ways.

Two of these were developed in an evolutionary context. Kitcher (2011) argues that the original function of morality was to solve "altruism failures" and resolve social tensions, but that over time it evolved new functions, such as how to contribute to the surrounding society and the flourishing of individuals within it. Alexander (2019) argues that morality is a social technology, which provides guidance on how to behave in interactions where our outcomes are interdependent with those of others: In other words, considering it as a game theoretic problem where people have different preferences and each individual's outcomes depend on the actions of everyone. For both Kitcher and Alexander, an ethical system needs to be internally coherent. However, different societies can have different internally coherent systems of morality, generating different moral judgments. In particular, for Alexander (2019) morality may be different in different times and places because not all societies are attempting to solve exactly the same kinds of problems under the same kinds of constraints. And, even if two societies were trying to solve exactly the same problems under the same constraints, there might be multiple equilibria: different solutions that are functionally equivalent, like whether a country drives on the left or right side of the road.

However, these two views have different implications for the possibility of adjudicating between moralities. Since Kitcher (2011) starts with a notion of the function that a moral system is supposed to fulfill, he can compare societies according to how well they fulfill those functions. He argues that there can be ethical progress, which consists in fulfilling the functions of ethics more thoroughly and more efficiently. In contrast, Alexander (2013) argues that if ethics solves decision problems where our goals interact, then the solution expresses what we currently care about. If the background problem changes substantially, then so will the ethical solutions. He thinks that we have the perception that there is ethical progress because, in the West, the background problem has been relatively stable for hundreds of years, but it is only local progress and is not clearly better than the ethical practices of other societies.

A third view that starts from the premise that the function of morality is to regulate conflicts of interest is that of Wong (2009), who developed his position in the light of differences between individualistic Western cultures that value autonomy and more communitarian Eastern cultures. Wong argues that because morality has a shared function across cultures, it has a common core that is universally valid across all kinds of societies. However, this is not enough to give determinate answers to moral questions, so it will be supplemented by criteria that are local to a given society. (So it might suit his argument that there is more agreement in Bystander than in Footbridge, if we have reason to think that judgments in Bystander stem from core principles and Footbridge from peripheral.) Therefore, Wong concludes that there is no one true morality and he advises that we recognize that moral approaches other than our own may also be valuable. Wong's focus is on moral accommodation between societies, so he does not provide a guide to adjudicating between conflicts or to assessing what would count as progress.

A second move is to argue that moral facts are based on emotional responses that are inculcated by culture. Prinz (2007) argues that the moral right and wrongness of an action consists in the fact that people are disposed to have certain emotions toward it. If people from different cultures have different values based on different emotional responses, then that would be a genuine moral disagreement and would show there is no single correct morality. Prinz draws on the ideas of anthropologist Rick Schweder – that many non-Western cultures involve ideas of purity, sacredness, and authority – and argues that these are constructed from very basic emotions of disgust. Since Prinz thinks that moral facts are constructed from our sentiments, he thinks a society based on these values has an alternative set of moral facts. Prinz argues that we need to be more tolerant of societies with different values. However, he also contends that some moral values are better than others and we can adjudicate somewhat by assessing them against nonmoral standards. According to Prinz, we expect our moral judgments to have virtues such as consistency, coherence with facts, stability, ease of implementation, universality, conformity to biological norms, and promoting welfare and well-being. Prinz thinks these are not moral standards (though that is a tendentious claim about welfare and well-being), so that when we deploy these standards in assessing moral systems we are stepping outside of morality. Of course, these standards themselves embody values that may vary across cultures. So, while they may be standards that promote moral change within societies, it is not clear how we avoid some sort of regress when adjudicating between societies, where we may have cross-cultural disagreement about nonmoral standards leading to intractable disagreements about which morality is better.

A third move is to deny that moral facts are independently existing facts that we discover and, instead, to argue that the moral facts are determined by the outcome of some epistemological procedure: The procedure having the outcomes it does is what determines or constitutes the facts. This is *constructivism.* Normative truths are grounded in what is sometimes called the "practical point of view," the point of view of a deliberating agent, including their motivating states such as desires, and their normative and evaluative judgments (Lenman &

Shemmer, 2012). There are different theories of what this practical point of view consists in. An early theory of constructivism in ethics was Korsgaard's (1996) *Kantian constructivism*, which grounds morality in our practical reason. According to Korsgaard, pure practical reason commits one to particular substantive values and we can characterize rational norms of deliberation; so we can derive universal moral values that should be arrived at from the standpoint of any rational valuer. Therefore, it is not clear that Korsgaard's position allows for moral disagreement, so I will not discuss it here. For our purposes, a form of *Humean constructivism* will be more useful. According to the Humean, the content of the practical point of view is contingently given. In particular, it includes the set of values with which the agent finds herself (Street, 2010). Note that these are not "mere" desires, the practical point of view includes the values that the agent takes herself to have reason to hold. Nevertheless, we must recognize that these are contingent and that the endpoint of practical reasoning may depend on the particular values that the agent started with. Consequently, "truth and falsity in the normative domain must always be relativized to a particular practical point of view" (Street 2008, 224).

Like the idea of morality as a social technology, Humean constructivism aims to produce a coherent web of interlocking values. Like all the other moves that aim to accommodate relativism, it struggles to answer the question of why one internally coherent system of judgments should be considered better than another. In order to adjudicate between moral systems there needs to be some set of commitments or values, concerning what makes one system more worthy of endorsement than another, from which one can reason about which morality is better. However, there is no view from nowhere, where one can coherently step back from the entire set of one's interlocking normative judgments at once and ask whether the entire set is correct or incorrect. We can co-opt an analogy that is sometimes used in the theory of knowledge: It is as though we are on a boat at sea. We cannot pull up every plank of the boat at the same time; some have to be taken as foundational while we pull up the others for examination.

Humean constructivism seems to me to quite clearly depict the epistemology of moral judgments. The idea that all judgments are made relative to some moral framework or other could be called *constructive relativism* (Lillehammer, 2004).

But it also turns the epistemology into a story about the metaphysics of those judgments, in the same way that Mackie moved from epistemology to metaphysics in his Argument from Disagreement. Do we need to make the move from epistemology to metaphysics? Could we accept that there are moral facts in a mind-independent sense but conclude that we will never be able to truly know them? We are caught between constructivist relativism and skepticism about moral facts.

10.5 Conclusion

There is not a great deal of evidence on cross-cultural variation in response to trolley problems and it is rather mixed, but a preliminary inspection suggests that it is plausible that cross-cultural differences in judgments exist. It is also plausible that these differences exist because one's moral judgments are shaped by one's culture. This raises issues for the metaphysics and epistemology of moral judgments. One possibility is that the reason there is disagreement is that there are no moral facts. Alternatively, some cultures may have a better grasp of a set of mind-independent moral facts than others – but that raises questions about how we know which culture is right. A third possibility is that moral facts and moral judgments are intrinsically connected to culture, so that the epistemology and metaphysics are inextricably connected. This idea lends support to some form of constructivism in ethics.

The ideas of morality as fulfilling a social function, moral facts as sentiments, and Humean constructivism reach a compromise where there are moral properties that we can discover, but they are not completely mind-independent. The first of these makes a claim about the function of morality, which permits morality to vary across cultures. The second reinterprets moral facts, so that they can be intrinsically tied to sentiments that are inculcated by culture. The third connects the content of morality to the actual process of making moral judgments and acknowledges that people cannot take a view from nowhere, so their judgments may depend on where they are situated. These are all ways of explaining differences in judgments. But they all leave a problem about how we adjudicate moral disagreements, which requires some core value or nonmoral standards according to which we could judge. Whatever the status of moral facts, maybe the best that we can hope for is that we can have rational debate about those core values and adjudicate moral disagreements by prespecifying the functions or goals of the system, or by privileging some values and ends as axiomatic or prior. It is that, or some form of skepticism about the existence or moral facts or skepticism about whether we could ever come to know them.[6]

[6] Thanks to Edouard Machery for help finding papers; to Karina Arutyunova, Heather Winskel, and Xin Xiang, for giving me data that was not reported in the published version of their papers; to Matthew Chrisman for guiding me through the metaethics; and to Rocky Clanchy, Gabriel Abend, and Hallvard Lillehammer for comments.

11 Ethical accident algorithms for autonomous vehicles and the trolley problem

Three philosophical disputes

Sven Nyholm

In this chapter, I discuss whether it is helpful for those interested in the real-world ethics of crashes involving self-driving cars to compare that set of ethical issues with the trolley problem. What the phrase "the trolley problem" refers to should be clear to readers of this book, but it is something we will have occasion to return to below.[1] The usefulness of comparing real-world ethical issues concerning self-driving cars to the standard cases and philo-sophical issues associated with the trolley problem is controversial among philosophers who have written on this topic (e.g., Nyholm & Smids 2016; JafariNaimi 2017; Himmelreich 2018; Keeling 2019; Kamm 2020a). In this chapter, however, my most general thesis is that it *is* instructive to reflect on the comparison between crashes with self-driving cars and the trolley problem and the examples associated with it. Indeed, as I see things, it is almost impossible for it not to be useful to compare the ethics of crashing self-driving cars with the trolley problem. It is either directly or indirectly useful. It can be directly useful because the trolley problem itself brings up ethical issues that are of immediate importance for the ethics of self-driving cars. Or it is at the very least indirectly useful because the process of highlighting key

---

[1] I follow Judith Thomson (2016) and Frances Kamm (2016) in taking "the trolley problem" to refer, not to any particular dilemma case involving a runaway trolley, but rather to the philosophical question(s) raised by such cases. According to Kamm (2016), the basic philosophical problem is this: Why are certain people, using certain methods, morally permitted to kill a smaller number of people to save a greater number, whereas others, using other methods, are not morally permitted to kill the same smaller number to save the same greater number of people? For example, it is thought to be permissible for the bystander to save five people by sacrificing one person in the standard "switch" trolley case that we will get to below. But why is it not permissible for a medical doctor to save five patients in need of organ-transplants by "harvesting" five organs from a perfectly healthy patient who just came into the hospital for a routine checkup? The transplant case doesn't mention trolleys. But Kamm thinks that it nevertheless falls under the wide umbrella of the trolley problem.

differences between the real-life ethics of self-driving cars and the philosophy of the trolley problem is a good way of clarifying what matters most for the ethics of self-driving cars.

This chapter divides into the following sections. First, I provide some more background and context for my discussion (Section 11.1). Next, I divide up my discussion into three main segments, each of which considers what I will call a particular "philosophical dispute" that one finds in the literature regarding whether it is useful to discuss the trolley problem within the ethics of self-driving cars. The first dispute is about whether there is something flippant, or perhaps even downright immoral, about comparing real-world ethics with the trolley problem (Section 11.2). The second dispute is about whether the dis-analogies between trolley problem cases and crashes involving self-driving cars in the real world are significant enough to make this comparison unhelpful (Section 11.3). The third dispute is about whether the academic literature on the trolley problem has been about rather different issues than those that matter the most in relation to the real-world ethics of crashes involving self-driving cars (Section 11.4). Having introduced these three disputes, I turn to the question of what we should make of all of this (Section 11.5). I argue that it partly depends on whether we think one should be a monist or a pluralist about methodology in ethics: that is, whether one thinks only one method should be used or whether one thinks it is best to combine insights from multiple methods. My view is that we should be pluralists about methodology, and that this is part of why the self-driving cars/trolley problem comparison cannot help but being either directly or indirectly relevant to the real-world ethics of self-driving cars.

The last thing I will mention in this introduction is that whether or not there will ever be many real-life crash scenarios involving self-driving cars that are very similar to the cases associated with the trolley problem, there have already been many real-world crashes involving self-driving cars. And some of these have been fatal, both to people in- and outside of the self-driving cars. Already in 2015, there were about twenty minor crashes involving self-driving cars. Nobody was seriously injured, and what happened was simply that people driving regular cars bumped into self-driving cars (Schoettle & Sivak, 2015). In 2016, however, a crash involving a self-driving car and a bus was clearly caused by an experimental self-driving car operated by Google (LeBeau 2016). Later in that same year, the first person died in a self-driving car when his Tesla car operating in "autopilot" mode crashed into a white truck that the car's sensors did not properly distinguish from the bright sky (Tesla 2016). In 2018, a pedestrian was, for the first time, struck and killed by a self-driving car. Elaine Herzberg was crossing the street in

Tempe, Arizona, when an experimental self-driving car operated by the ride-hailing service company Uber drove into her, leaving her with fatal injuries (Levin & Wong 2018). There have also been other serious accidents involving cars with different levels and kinds of automation. So, in other words, ethical questions about crashes involving self-driving cars are real-world issues. They are very serious issues; human lives are at stake. It can be hard to discuss the trolley problem without discussing comical and absurd scenarios. It can be fun, and also instructive, to do so. But as we do, we should keep in mind that real crashes involving self-driving cars are no joke.

11.1 Background

It is easy to think of examples involving crashing self-driving cars that bear at least a superficial resemblance to the thought experiments commonly associated with the trolley problem. Notably, we can distinguish between (a) examples with crashing self-driving cars that are rather loosely based on or similar to the examples associated with the trolley problem and (b) examples that are closely modeled on the trolley problem examples. The former are more common than the latter. More on this below.

In the most famous trolley problem case,[2] a trolley is about to drive into five people on a train track, and it is possible for a bystander to save the five by pulling a switch and redirecting the trolley onto a sidetrack. On that other track, there is one person, who will be hit and killed if the train is redirected. In the second most well-known variation of the example, there is no sidetrack. But there is a large and heavy person up on a footbridge who could be pushed off the bridge down onto the tracks. His weight is hefty enough to set off the automated brakes of the trolley. This would save the five, but kill the large person (Kamm 2016). Similar to these kinds of trolley examples, we can imagine cases in which, for instance, self-driving cars are about to drive into five people on the road, but where, say, another person would be hit and killed if the self-driving car turned onto a side road. Just as philosophers have imagined numerous forced dilemmas where people are killed by

---

[2] I am using the phrase "trolley problem cases" to refer to the examples discussed in the literature about the trolley problem, such as the cases above. For a review of many of the most relevant cases – and the perhaps most thorough discussion of the trolley problem to date – see Kamm 2016. For the history of the trolley problem, see Edmonds 2013.

out-of-control trolleys, we can also imagine different variations of bad outcomes involving people being hit and killed by self-driving cars facing forced dilemmas (Davnall 2019: 432–433).

This observation has sparked the imagination of academics and non-academics alike. It was picked up by the media around 2015, and has since then often been revisited in mass media headlines and articles. By simply picking some of these headlines, one can tell a sort of "rise and fall" story or discern a "hype cycle" with respect to how publicly accessible debates about this topic have developed in recent years:

Driverless Cars Are Colliding with the Creepy Trolley Problem (Washington Post 2015)

Why Mercedes Plans to Let Its Self-Driving Cars Kill Pedestrians in Dicey Situations (Business Insider 2016)

Google's Chief of Self-Driving Cars Downplays 'The Trolley Problem' (Washington Post 2016)

MIT Study Explores the 'Trolley Problem' and Self-Driving Cars (Venture Beat 2018)

Should a Self-Driving Car Kill the Baby or The Grandma? Depends on Where You're From. The Infamous "Trolley Problem" was Put to Millions of People in A Global Study, Revealing How Much Ethics Diverge Across Cultures (Technology Review 2018)

Trolley Dilemmas Shouldn't Influence Self-Driving Policies, Experts Argue (Robotics Business Review 2019)

A lot of these articles were prompted by the MIT study referred to in two of these just-quoted headlines: the so-called moral machine experiment (Bonnefon et al. 2016; Awad et al. 2018). This was an enormous survey of intuitions about dilemma cases that was run – not by moral philosophers – but by a team of psychologists and behavioral economists. It was a study inspired by the extensive empirical investigations of ordinary people's intuitions about trolley problem cases that had been carried out by psychologists, philosophers, and legal researchers in the previous few years (e.g., Greene 2013). As the authors of the moral machine study put it in one of their first publications on this topic:

... situations of unavoidable harms, as illustrated in [our examples of crashes with self-driving cars], bear a striking resemblance with the flagship dilemmas of experimental ethics – that is, the so-called 'trolley problem'. (Bonnefon et al. 2015: 3)

What Bonnefon and colleagues did was to create a large set of vignettes (basically, cartoon-like images showing two options, where different driving paths of self-driving cars involved killing different people), which were made available on the moral machine website.[3] People were asked to judge what the self-driving cars in the vignettes should do (e.g., kill three grandfathers on the left, or go right and kill four toddlers). The responses were collected and patterns in people's intuitions identified.[4]

One interesting finding of this study – as one of the headlines above indicates – is that there are differences among countries in the patterns of people's intuitions, for example with respect to whether the young should be prioritized over the old, or whether breaking traffic laws should make one more liable to being killed by the self-driving car (Awad et al. 2018). Another striking finding from the same lab is that people have different attitudes regarding how their own self-driving cars should be programmed (they should always save the person riding in the car, even if this does not minimize overall harm) and how other people's cars should be programmed (they should minimize overall harm even if it is detrimental to the person riding in the car) (Bonnefon et al. 2015, 2016). This research team has also offered a normative argument for why they think we should engage in this kind of research. But let us save that until later.

The next thing I will note in this section is that it is not only the mass media and empirical researchers who make this comparison between crashes with self-driving cars and the trolley problem. Perhaps more important for our current purposes – since we are looking at three philosophical disputes about this comparison – is that many philosophers have also made and endorsed this comparison, again in more or less loose ways. Here are two quick quotes to illustrate this. Patrick Lin, in one of the earliest philosophical papers about the ethics of self-driving cars, wrote the following:

> One of the most iconic thought-experiments in ethics is the trolley problem. ... and this is one that may now occur in the real world, if autonomous vehicles come to be. (Lin 2015: 78)

---

[3] www.moralmachine.net

[4] Sütfeld et al. (2017) have pursued a fascinating related line of experimental ethics by examining how people respond to AV collisions presented in virtual reality. Their idea is that we can model people's moral preferences by fitting predictive models for their decisions based on relevant features of the collision, for example, whether it involves a person or a nonhuman animal.

Similarly, when discussing another kind of autonomous vehicles (namely, driverless trains), the authors of *Moral Machines: Teaching Robots Right from Wrong,* Wendell Wallach and Colin Allen write:

> [C]ould trolley cases be one of the first frontiers for artificial morality? Driverless systems put machines in the position of making split-second decisions that could have life or death implications. As the complexity [of the traffic] increases, the likelihood of dilemmas that are similar to the basic trolley case also goes up. (Wallach and Allen 2009: 14)

Geoff Keeling (2019), in turn, has published a powerful article-length defense of this comparison entitled "Why Trolley Problems Matter for the Ethics of Automated Vehicles". So, while most philosophers who make this comparison usually do so in a quick and underdeveloped way, there are also those who have devoted whole articles to defending this idea (see also Wolkenstein 2018).

Moreover, it is perhaps also interesting to note here that going back even further in time, one of the most important contributors to the philosophy of the trolley problem, Frances Kamm (1996), once imagined a self-driving ambulance. This ambulance had to be preprogrammed to either always prioritize getting dying patients to the hospital as quickly as possible, even if this would mean crashing into pedestrians, or to never do so. The question in that example was whether the former kind of programming could ever be justified. As we will see below, Kamm has since then joined the discussion of real self-driving cars and the trolley problem, and she thinks there are important differences between what she was interested in while discussing her ambulance case and the real-world ethics of self-driving cars. But it is nevertheless striking that Kamm already came up with an example in her influential 1996 book *Morality, Mortality* that had some similarity to the topic of this chapter.

In short, the idea of comparing ethical questions regarding crashing self-driving cars with the trolley problem is an idea that has not only fascinated philosophers interested in the ethics of self-driving cars. It is also an idea that has resonated with many people outside of philosophy. And millions of people all over the world have been surveyed about their attitudes regarding these kinds of examples. This makes it important to reflect on whether it is helpful to the ethics of self-driving cars to make this comparison. Let us now turn to the three philosophical disputes about this issue that I want to discuss in this chapter.

11.2 First philosophical dispute: Is making this comparison perhaps morally required, or is there something morally problematic about the trolley problem/self-driving cars comparison?

Bonnefon et al. (2015, 2016) and Awad et al. (2018)[5] argue that their moral machine experiment testing people's intuitions about trolley problem-inspired cases is not only in itself interesting and motivated by the academic interest in studying patterns in ordinary people's intuitions about trolley-like scenarios involving self-driving cars. It might also be morally required. As they see things, given the potential that self-driving cars might (eventually) become much safer than regular cars, it is important that the general public should accept – and be willing to use – self-driving cars. For this goal to be achieved, self-driving cars should be programmed to handle accident scenarios in ways that fit with how the general public finds it acceptable for autonomously operating cars to handle such scenarios. Hence the need for the moral machine experiment and its surveys of people's intuitions about how self-driving cars should crash when crashes are unavoidable. We should not leave this to ethical reflection by academics alone. As they themselves put it:

> [E]ven if ethicists were to agree on how autonomous vehicles should solve moral dilemmas, their work would be useless if citizens were to disagree with their solution, and thus opt out of the future that autonomous vehicles promise in lieu of the status quo. Any attempt to devise artificial intelligence ethics must be at least cognizant of public morality. (Awad et al. 2018: 59)

Some philosophers who have responded to this idea, however, have argued that there is something inherently ethically problematic about this whole approach and the mindset behind it. John Harris (2020), in particular, responds directly to Bonnefon et al. and their "moral machine experiment" in very sharp terms. Nassim JafariNaimi (2018) responds more generally to the idea of considering trolley problem-inspired moral dilemmas in the context of ethical reflection on self-driving cars, reflecting concerns similar to those expressed by Allen Wood (2011) and others in more general critical discussions of trolley problem-like approaches to moral reasoning.

---

[5] To be clear: Bonnefon et al. and Awad et al. are members of the same research team. So, these references refer to work by the same group of researchers, not to two separate teams.

As I understand it, Harris' (2020) response to the way that Bonnefon et al. compare the ethics of self-driving cars to the experimental approach to the trolley problem has two main parts. Firstly, how issues of life and death are handled in society should not be based on people's gut reactions to cartoon-like vignettes, but on careful deliberations and legal processes. Secondly, the idea that self-driving cars should "target" some people rather than others in accident scenarios seems to suggest that they should make judgments about who lives or dies, which Harris finds highly problematic (cf. Purves et al. 2015). Life and death decisions, Harris argues, are serious matters. Decisions about how society should deal with life and death decisions should be the outcomes of slow and careful legal and moral deliberations, which are allowed to take time. And we should not arrive at a situation where the AI in machines like self-driving cars is allowed to "punish" certain people and condemn them to death.

JafariNaimi, in turn, argues that the idea of comparing ethical questions about life and death decisions involving self-driving cars to trolley dilemmas involves an objectionable "utilitarian" framing, reducing all ethical issues to numbers and quantities, whereas in real life, the ethics of self-driving cars is much more complicated (JafariNaimi 2018: 303). She summarizes her overall criticism as follows:

> First, ethical situations are marked by a deep sense of uncertainty and an organic character. Second, our place within ethical situations matters greatly. Third, the impact of our actions in response to ethical situations is not limited to immediate outcomes[;] consequences are broad and long ranging. Therefore ... principles that appear to solve the scenarios of experimental ethics may or may not serve similar ethical situations encountered in real life. (JafariNaimi, 2018: 306)

These criticisms anticipate some of the other disputes about the trolley problem/self-driving cars ethics comparison that we will get to below. But what I in particular want to highlight in this section is the overall message from JafariNaimi that there is something reductive/oversimplifying, and therefore insensitive, about thinking that the ethics of crashes and risks involving self-driving cars could be adequately accounted for if we try to tackle these real-world issues by consulting either our own or the general public's intuitions about stylized dilemmas where self-driving cars have to "choose" whom to crash into.

These worries about there being, potentially, something morally problematic about comparing the ethics of crashing self-driving cars with the trolley problem echo more general ethical worries about the trolley problem that some critics have expressed in more general discussions. Wood, for example, approvingly cites a Tanner Lecture on Human Values from 2001, where a novelist, Dorothy Allison, had commented on the trolley problem, which she said she had heard about from some philosophers she knew. In her lecture, Allison said that her reaction was to reject the problem itself and to refuse to form an opinion about it. She focused on what she called "lifeboat cases" (cf. Gibbard 2008, chapter two). Commenting on choices regarding whether to save five people or one person if there is only one lifeboat and one can only go to the five or to the one, Allison said that there was something immoral about thinking about the problem in this crass way. The only ethically appropriate question was why provision had not been made to make available more lifeboats to begin with. Wood approvingly remarks that this reaction from Allison can be applied to the cases usually discussed in relation to the trolley problem, the novelist's reaction being "far more sensible and right-minded than what we usually get from most of the philosophers who make use of such examples" (Wood 2011: 67).

Wood writes, furthermore, that in relation to many trolley cases, "the right reaction is to regard it as simply indeterminate what the agent should do, and the only real moral issue raised by the problem is … how the situation in question was permitted to arise in the first place" (ibid.: 72). Because "even if some choices do inevitably have the consequence that either one will die or five will die, there is nearly always something wrong with looking at the choice only in that way" (ibid.: 73). Given that this is what Wood has to say about the traditional trolley problem, one can only imagine what he might say about the trolley-problem-inspired moral dilemmas that Bonnefon et al. depict when they present the general public with moral dilemmas involving self-driving cars.

What's at issue here, in other words, is whether there is something frivolous, inherently insensitive, misguided, or perhaps downright immoral about reflecting on these kinds of forced dilemma scenarios – whether they involve crashing self-driving cars or runaway trolleys. Harris and JafariNaimi take this view with respect to the self-driving cars issue. Allison and Wood take this view in relation to trolley cases. This clashes starkly with Bonnefon et al.'s view that it would be morally problematic not to engage in trolley problem-like research about patterns in people's intuitions regarding different cases involving crashing and life-threatening self-driving cars, since making self-driving cars acceptable to people requires programming them in ways that fit with how ordinary people think that self-driving cars should be programmed to handle accident scenarios.

11.3 Second dispute: Are any real-life crashes involving self-driving cars relevantly similar to the examples associated with the trolley problem?

The second and third philosophical disputes regarding the comparison of the ethics of self-driving cars and the philosophy/psychology of the trolley problem are closely related. In fact, back in 2015 when it became very popular to compare crashing self-driving cars with runaway trolleys in what was sometimes fast and loose ways, it struck me and my collaborator Jilles Smids that somebody should write a philosophical article examining skeptically whether the analogy between the ethics of self-driving cars and the trolley problem is as close as many academics and others were making it out to be. We learned shortly thereafter that Noah Goodall had had the same thought, and the year after, we – as well as Goodall – had papers out on this (Nyholm & Smids 2016; Goodall 2016).[6] When we wrote our pieces, we didn't draw a sharp distinction between the issue of whether real-world crashes involving self-driving cars are interestingly similar to trolley problem examples, on the one hand, and the issue of whether the trolley problem literature has treated the ethical issues most relevant to the ethics of crashing self-driving cars, on the other hand. The two issues are clearly closely related. But here I am focusing on the former issue, and in the next section on the latter.

When it comes to whether any real-world crashes involving self-driving cars are sufficiently analogous with the examples associated with the trolley problem for it to be worth making this comparison, there are those both in- and outside of philosophy who deny this. Outside of philosophy, as one might expect, representatives from the car and technology industries have bemoaned philosophers' and psychologists' comparisons between the trolley problem and crashes with self-driving cars, claiming that they are very unlikely to happen, for which reason they say that it is stifling innovation to make such comparisons. (Recall the *"Google Chief of Self-Driving Cars Downplays the 'Trolley Problem'"* headline quoted above!) Inside of philosophy, interventions from Johannes Himmelreich (2018) and Rebecca Davnall (2019) stand out when it comes to what Keeling (2019) calls the "not going to happen" objection to comparing crashing self-driving cars to the trolley problem. According to Himmelreich, if self-driving cars drive so fast that

---

[6] Alexander Hevelke and Julian Nida-Rümelin had already briefly discussed whether we should compare the ethics of self-driving cars to the trolley problem, and expressed skepticism about this, in their 2015 article about who should be held responsible when self-driving cars crash. But they made some brief remarks about this in passing, and the main focus on their article lay elsewhere.

crashes become unavoidable and tragic choices have to be made, then the cars will not be able to make meaningful choices quickly enough that it is possible to program in any particular forms of responses into how the cars function. According to Davnall, if we are considering a self-driving car that is otherwise operating normally (e.g., there is nothing wrong with the brakes or anything like that), and a crash is unavoidable because there are cars or people within the car's breaking distance, then it will always be safest to simply brake very hard rather than to try to veer off in any other direction.

Keeling (2019: 295–296), in contrast, responds to this supposed lack of realism by calling the examples we use when we imagine self-driving cars facing trolley problem-like scenarios theoretical "idealizations." The idea, according to Keeling, is not that trolley problem-like scenarios involving self-driving cars are likely to happen. It is rather that we can think about such cases in order to get clear on what is important to us – in order, in other words, to get clear on what our priorities are. Just like the ideal gas law in physics describes an idealization used for theoretical purposes – and does not describe the behavior of all actual gases in the real world – so do trolley problem cases involving self-driving cars describe idealized scenarios that we consider for theoretical, not practical, purposes, according to Keeling. We can think, in other words, that our moral ideas about what values should guide the programming of self-driving cars could be sharpened by, or benefit from, considering trolley problem cases even if we do not think that these are likely to occur in real life (cf. Goodall 2016). The comparison between imagined cases involving crashing self-driving cars and the cases associated with the trolley problem is not important, on this view, because of the realism of these cases, but because of the role(s) they can play in theorizing about important ethical issues.

Setting aside the realism issue as it relates to the likelihood of real-world instances of trolley problem-like crashes with self-driving cars, though, we can also ask whether there are other important disanalogies between cases involving self-driving cars in traffic and out-of-control trolleys in philosophical thought experiments.[7] One thing that Jilles Smids and I in our above-mentioned article – and also Goodall in his above-mentioned piece – highlighted and presented as a key difference here concerns the distinction between decision-making in the face of uncertainty and on the basis of assessments of risk, on the one hand, and

---

[7] For further apparent disanalogies, see also the discussion in Gogoll and Müller (2017), especially p. 690.

decision-making about certain and known outcomes, on the other hand (Nyholm & Smids 2016; Goodall 2016). This also resonates with JafariNaimi's above-cited claim that real-world ethical choices are often marked by "a deep sense of uncertainty."

In the trolley problem cases, we imagine that we know for certain that the five can be saved if the trolley is redirected to the sidetrack where the one is standing, or if the large and heavy person is pushed onto the track, and so on. So, the question is simply what it is right to do, given those certain and known facts. In stark contrast, when choices are made about how self-driving cars should be programmed to deal with accident-scenarios, we are dealing with the real world, which means dealing with uncertainty and making risk assessments about what might happen with some degree of probability and some unknown magnitude of harm. In a more general discussion of the relevance of the trolley problem, Sven Ove Hansson (2012: 44) complains about the trolley problem as a way of modeling real-world ethical decision-making because it does not involve any uncertainty nor any assessments of risks. If those are aspects of most real-world moral decision-making, and we want our theorizing about the ethics of crashes involving self-driving cars to involve the sort of considerations we have to take into consideration in real-world decision-making, we have an important disanalogy here between the ethics of crashing self-driving cars and the thought experiments associated with the trolley problem (Nyholm & Smids 2016: 1284–1286).

Another thing – Smids and I also argued – that distinguishes the real-world ethics of crashing self-driving cars from the philosophy of the trolley problem concerns issues of moral and legal responsibility (ibid., 1282–1284). Think about how it is when philosophy teachers present the trolley problem to their students during ethics courses. Often, what happens is that one of the students will raise their hand and ask whether it wouldn't be the case that one would go to jail if one pushed a large person off a bridge to his death in order to save five people on the tracks, or even if one redirected a train onto a sidetrack where one person is hit and killed by the trolley. What philosophy teachers usually do when they get this very good question is to tell the student to set any such issues about legal or moral responsibility aside and simply focus on what the right or best choice to make is in the circumstances, here and now – wholly independent of any further consequences or any worries about who is responsible for what. This is another thing that makes the philosophy of the trolley problem very different from real-world cases involving crashes with self-driving cars. When it comes to the latter, issues related to legal and moral responsibility are inescapable.

Just think of the real-world crashes mentioned in the introduction: the Google car that collided with a bus; the Tesla car that crashed into a truck and killed the person in the car; and the experimental Uber car that hit and killed a pedestrian. In all of these cases, questions of responsibility were immediately raised. Google admitted partial responsibility for the crash involving their car (LeBeau 2016). Tesla released a statement denying all responsibility, but expressed their sympathy for the victim (Tesla 2016). Uber tried to evade legal accountability by proposing a financial settlement to the family of the woman who was hit and killed by their self-driving car (Wakabayashi & Conger 2018). In the Tesla and Uber cases, many commentators felt that those companies had not properly been held legally responsible for what happened. The question of how to move forward in a responsible way was raised in all of these cases. Google promised to update the software in their cars to make them better able to predict the behavior of buses. Tesla promised to update their sensors to make them better able to detect white trucks on sunny days. And Uber temporarily ceased their testing of self-driving cars in Tempe, where the deadly accident happened. (For further discussion, see Nyholm 2020, chapter 3.)

The general point here is that in the real world, ethically salient decisions and incidents causing harm and potentially death are always intimately tied to questions of responsibilities, duties of care, and other issues pertaining to how we are related to those around us, not just in the immediate present, but also over time, and as members of a shared society (JafariNaimi 2016). In trolley problem reasoning intended to pump intuitions about moral principles, we are asked to set such contextual considerations and responsibility-related issues aside (Kauppinen 2020). This can be seen as a rather stark contrast. The second philosophical dispute about the self-driving cars/trolley problem comparison is about whether these differences concerning real-world ethical issues related to crashing self-driving cars are stark enough that comparing crashes with self-driving cars with trolley problem cases is perhaps interesting in the abstract, but not obviously and clearly relevant to the real-world ethics of our future with self-driving cars. Here too one could bring up Keeling's (2019) point about idealizations for purely theoretical purposes versus attempts to depict realistic situations lining up perfectly with real-life case studies. But I will set that point aside for now. Let us now instead turn to the third philosophical dispute I want to bring up.

11.4 Third philosophical dispute: Is the literature about the trolley problem relevant to the ethics of crashes involving self-driving cars?

When Smids and I wrote our 2016 article, one of the things we were asking ourselves was whether the philosophical and psychological literature about the trolley problem has been concerned with the sorts of issues that are most relevant to the ethics of crashes with self-driving cars. We wrote:

> [T]he key issues ... of great importance for the ethics of accident-algorithms for self-driving cars are typically not discussed in the main literature on the trolley problem. For example, this literature is not about the risks or the legal and moral responsibilities we face in traffic. On the other hand, the main issues that the literature on the trolley problem does engage directly with have to do with rather different things than those ... most pressing for the ethics of accident-algorithms for self-driving cars... [T]his literature discusses things such as: the ethical differences between positive and negative duties and killing and letting die, and psychological and neuro-scientific theories about how different types of moral judgments are generated by our minds and brains. (Nyholm & Smids 2016: 1276)

Taking those considerations together, we concluded that the literature on the trolley problem is not the best, nor perhaps even a particularly good, place to turn to for source materials and precedents directly useful for the ethics of accident-algorithms for self-driving cars (cf. Cunneen et al. 2019). Others have chimed in with similar conclusions. Antti Kauppinen (2020), for example, argues that an important difference between what is (or is not!) discussed in the trolley problem literature and what we should discuss when we think about how self-driving cars should handle crash scenarios has to do with whether people are liable in relation to risky situations that they are part of.[8] If an accident scenario is caused by the reckless behavior of one party – which can often happen in real traffic – it can seem morally fitting that they bear a greater risk in the resolution of the dangerous situation than somebody who was taking all appropriate precautions in their traffic behavior.

Kamm (2020a) makes virtually the same point in her recent paper about what she calls "uses and abuses of the trolley problem." She notes that in the trolley problem as she and others have discussed it, the people at risk (e.g., the

---

[8] For more general discussions of that type of reasoning concerning risks people are (partly) responsible for and what their responsibility does to their liability to be harmed, see, for example, McMahan (2005, 2009) and Frowe (2015).

five on the tracks or the large and heavy man on the footbridge) are no different from each other in terms of whether their being at risk is their own fault. Kamm, like Kauppinen, thinks that in cases of real-world car crashes, we cannot similarly assume that everyone is equally innocent in this way. We must instead count on its being possible that some are more liable to be harmed than others. In addition, then, to not being about crucial topics such as risk and uncertainty, and legal and moral responsibility – all of which are highly relevant to the ethics of self-driving cars – the trolley problem literature has also not been about the important issue of greater liability to be harmed because one bears more responsibility than others in creating a risky situation.

Kamm also turns this on its head by noting that the kinds of cases some philosophers and psychologists compare to the trolley problem fail to track the philosophical concerns that she and others who have discussed the trolley problem have been particularly interested in (ibid.). The trolley problem, Kamm argues, involves examples that have been very carefully engineered to serve certain illustrative purposes, for example, teasing out certain ethical distinctions. And many of the envisioned cases involving crashing self-driving cars or other forced dilemmas fail to track the sorts of issues that those interested in the philosophy of the trolley problem have been concerned with. For example, consider this question: When different people under immediate threat are all equally innocent, and a bystander could save some of them but not others, but this would involve killing some of those people, what ethical considerations should that bystander take into account? Many self-driving car cases – such as those in the moral machine vignettes – are not about that issue. But it is a central question in the trolley problem literature (Kamm 2016; Thomson 2015). Accordingly, just as we might not learn anything about the ethics of self-driving cars by considering some parts of the literature about the trolley problem, it might also be that we do not learn anything about the key issues engaging those interested in the trolley problem by considering the sorts of cases of crashing self-driving cars that are sometimes compared with the trolley problem in a fast and loose way.

Not everyone agrees that the trolley problem literature has primarily focused on issues that are unhelpful for the ethics of crashes with self-driving cars, however. I have already mentioned Keeling above, but there are others as well. A paper by Dietmar Hübner and Lucie White (2018) makes a strong case in favor of the idea that the trolley problem literature – in particular the early papers by Philippa Foot and Judith Jarvis Thomson – contains important moral distinctions that matter to the issue of how self-driving cars should handle accident scenarios. Hübner and White think that the classic trolley problem discussions about the difference between negative rights and positive rights (Foot 1967) and differences between people's moral claims (Thomson 1976) are useful when we think about how self-driving cars should respond to situations involving unavoidable crashes. Specifically, they argue that various suggestions in the early trolley literature about how to draw the ethical difference between "involved" and "uninvolved" parties are highly relevant to the real-world ethics of self-driving cars (Hübner & White 2018).[9] In short, whether the literature on the trolley problem – be it the early contributions to it or more recent ones – is relevant to the ethics of how people should behave around self-driving cars and how self-driving cars should be made to behave around people is a matter of philosophical dispute.

11.5 What should we make of all of this?

During an auto-show in Paris in 2016, a representative of Mercedes, named Christoph von Hugo, was interviewed about the company's self-driving car prototype that was being showcased at the event. When asked about how their self-driving cars would be programmed to respond to accident scenarios, Mr. von Hugo answered that Mercedes' cars would always prioritize their owners (Taylor, 2016). He even presented some off-the-cuff arguments for why this would be a good policy (which prompted the headline quoted above about "*Why Mercedes Plans to Let Its Self-Driving Cars Kill Pedestrians in Dicey Situations*"[10]).

Given many people's above-discussed attitudes about the moral machine thought experiments suggesting that they would prefer buying a car that would be programmed to always save them, one might have predicted that this would go over well with people. However, there was an outcry. And von Hugo had to later retract his previous statements. He ended up claiming that his previous statements – which included his arguments for why it would be a good idea to always prioritize the owner of the car – were taken out of context.

---

[9] Hübner and White think that going back to the early trolley literature is a way of "clearly transcending the restricted horizon of purely utilitarian optimization, and providing important frameworks for taking people's individual responsibilities and mutual obligations into account" (Hübner, personal correspondence). There is a striking difference here between that view and JafariNaimi's above-cited view that trolley problem-reasoning inevitably leads to a "utilitarian framing" of ethical reflection. Foot and Thomson, it can be noted, used the trolley problem examples to illustrate what they regard as crucial deontological distinctions; and Kamm (2016) also uses the trolley problem in her defense of a "nonconsequentialist" view of ethics.

[10] For example, von Hugo said "Save the one in the car. If all you know for sure is that one death can be prevented, then that's our first priority" (Taylor 2016). For more on this Mercedes controversy and the issue of whether to always put the passenger first, see Katherine Evans's interesting discussion in her contribution to Keeling et al. 2019.

Mercedes had certainly not made up their minds to program their cars to always prioritize their owners (Orlove 2016).

The person who interviewed von Hugo had clearly heard about ethical discussions inspired by the trolley problem about how self-driving cars should be programmed to handle crash scenarios. And Mr. von Hugo seemed to also have heard about this – moreover, he also seemed to potentially have heard about the empirical finding that most people would want to buy or use a car programmed to always save them. Presumably he may even have thought that his answers would appeal to potential buyers and users of self-driving Mercedes cars, but seems to have not predicted the reactions from others, who might not be comfortable with the idea of self-driving Mercedes cars that would drive around and do everything to save their passengers if any crash scenario should arise where different people's lives would be at stake. Safer in the end, then, to take everything back and assure the general public that the company had not made up its mind and that they would leave it to others – for example, regulators or other public officials – to make decisions about these things.

Given all the above-discussed disagreements about whether comparing the ethics of crashes with self-driving cars with the trolley problem is a good idea, one might think that a similar conclusion would be what would make most sense with respect to the three philosophical disputes discussed above as well. In other words, one might think that ethical issues about how self-driving cars should behave in risky situations should not be discussed and argued about by philosophers and other academics interested in the trolley problem. In fact, this is the suggestion that Himmelreich ends up making in his above-mentioned article criticizing the self-driving cars/trolley problem comparison. Himmelreich suggests that people will have so many disagreements that the best thing to do is to treat the issue of how self-driving cars should handle risky situations as a "social choice" issue that should have some sort of political solution.[11] It should not be seen as an ethical problem at all, but a political one (see also Rodríguez-Alcázar et al. 2020). Filippo Santoni de Sio (2017), in turn, suggests something that has some similarity to Himmelreich's approach. Rather than basing reasoning about how self-driving cars should

---

[11] When Himmelreich (2018) suggests that we should take a "social choice" approach, he uses that phrase in a slightly looser sense than it is sometimes otherwise used. Standardly, social choice theory is understood along fairly narrow lines, namely, as the subdiscipline of economics that looks at aggregating individual judgments to determine a collective judgment. But in his article, Himmelreich has in mind a more deliberative democratic approach, like that of John Rawls (1993) in *Political Liberalism*, which aims for an "over-lapping consensus."

handle accident scenarios on ethical theorizing, it might be better, Santoni de Sio thinks, to turn to legal arguments. In particular, the suggestion is to consider legal reasoning related to emergency situations and specifically the so-called doctrine of necessity that is found in Anglo-American jurisprudence and elsewhere. This has something in common with Harris' (2020) suggestion that rather than on ordinary people's gut reactions to the sorts of dilemma scenarios the MIT moral machine experimenters have confronted people with, it is better to base reasoning about the ethics of self-driving cars on precedents from the legal context.

Should we follow the lead of these writers, and conclude that it is best to not make comparing the ethics of self-driving cars to the trolley problem part of the tool box we use for thinking about real-world ethical issues concerning self-driving cars and risky traffic situations? When we think about this issue, it is useful to distinguish among three different methodological approaches we could take. The first would be to approach the ethics of self-driving cars by only considering cases similar to those associated with the trolley problem (while perhaps also consulting the literature about the trolley problem) and doing nothing else than this. A second approach would be to do what I just described as the first approach, but to also do other things when we think about the ethics of self-driving cars – for example, make use of arguments inspired by legal reasoning like Santoni de Sio suggests, or any other type of ethical methodology we might find helpful in this context. This second approach would be what one might call a methodological pluralism approach. The third approach would be not to do anything at all associated with the first approach, and to only use methods wholly divorced from anything resembling the trolley problem when thinking about the ethics of dangerous situations involving self-driving cars.

It seems to me that the sections above have reviewed enough critical arguments raising skeptical worries about comparing the ethics of self-driving cars with the trolley problem that what I call the first approach in the paragraph above does not seem like a very satisfying approach. Clearly, there is potentially something morally suspect about drawing a very close analogy between crashing self-driving cars and the philosophy of the trolley problem (see the first dispute above). There are clearly also important disanalogies between real-life crashes involving self-driving cars and the examples associated with the trolley problem (see the second dispute above). And, lastly, there is clearly a question of whether the literature about the trolley problem has consistently been about issues of crucial importance for the real-world ethics of self-driving cars (see the third dispute). But that there are reasons – encapsulated in these three philosophical disputes – for shying away from ethical theorizing about self-driving cars that is primarily or exclusively about trolley problem-like cases does not mean that the self-driving cars/trolley problem comparison has no value or that we should not pay any attention to it.

After all, by considering reasons for being skeptical about drawing a close analogy between the ethics of self-driving cars and the philosophy of the trolley problem, we are in effect creating an account of what issues are most important for the real-world ethics of crashes involving self-driving cars. In other words, comparing the ethics of self-driving cars with the trolley problem is at the very least indirectly important. It helps us to highlight what is and what is not important for the ethics of self-driving cars. And, furthermore, while many philosophers who have written about the self-driving cars/trolley problem comparison have been highly skeptical, there are also those who see great value in this comparison, such as Keeling, Hübner, and White, and others. They have presented interesting and important arguments for making this comparison. If they are right – and surely some of their arguments are sound – then the self-driving cars/trolley problem comparison is also directly useful to the real-world ethics of self-driving cars.

Accordingly, it seems to me that just as the first methodological approach mentioned a few paragraphs above is problematic, so is the third methodological approach. In other words, we do best to take the second approach. We should neither rely too heavily (or indeed exclusively) on the comparison between the ethics of self-driving cars and the trolley problem, nor wholly ignore and pay no attention to the comparison between the ethics of self-driving cars and the trolley problem. Rather, we do best to make this one – but not the only – thing we do when we think about the ethics of self-driving cars. With what is still a relatively new issue for philosophical ethics to work with, and indeed also regarding older ethical issues that have been around much longer, using a mixed and pluralistic method that approaches the moral issues we are considering from many different angles is surely the best way to go. In this instance, that includes reflecting on – and reflecting critically on – how the ethics of crashes involving self-driving cars is both similar to and different from the philosophy of the trolley problem.

At this point, somebody might say, "[W]hat if I am somebody who really dislikes the self-driving cars/trolley problem comparison, and I would really prefer reflecting on the ethics of self-driving cars without spending any time on thinking about the similarities and differences between the ethics of self-driving cars and the trolley problem?" In other words, should everyone working on the ethics of self-driving cars spend at least some of their time reflecting on the comparison with the trolley problem? Luckily for those who are reluctant to spend any of their time reflecting on the self-driving cars/ trolley problem comparison, there are others who are willing and able to devote at least some of their energies to this comparison.

In general, I think we should view the community that works on the ethics of this issue as being one in which there can be a division of labor, whereby different members of this field can partly focus on different things, and thereby together cover all of the different aspects that are relevant and important to investigate regarding the ethics of self-driving cars. As it happens, there has been a remarkable variety in the methods and approaches people have used to address the ethics of self-driving cars (see Nyholm 2018a, b). So, while it is my own view that anybody who wants to form a complete overview of the ethics of self-driving cars should, among other things, devote some of their time to studying the comparison with the trolley problem, it is ultimately no big problem if not everyone wishes to do so. There are others who have been studying, and who will most likely continue to reflect on, this comparison.[12]

[12] For helpful feedback on this chapter, I am thankful to Geoff Keeling, Lucie White, Dietmar Hübner, and the participants of Fleur Jongepier and my "Moral Theory and Real Life" PhD course. My work on this chapter is part of the research program "Ethics of Socially Disruptive Technologies," which is funded through the Gravitation program of the Dutch Ministry of Education, Culture, and Science and the Netherlands Organization for Scientific Research (NWO grant number 024.004.031).

12   A new trolley problem?

Ezio Di Nucci

12.1 Introduction

Healthcare and the *Trolley Problem* go way back, in fact further than the trolley problem itself, if you trace the latter to Philippa Foot's classic article on abortion (Foot 1967), when we still had "trams" instead of Judy Thomson's "trolleys" (Thomson 1976, 1985).

Since, the Trolley Problem – and its great-grandmother, the *Doctrine of Double Effect*[1] – have been applied to a diverse set of cases and problems in healthcare, including for example, on top of abortion, assisted suicide, embryos, and reproductive technologies (the list would be too long, but here are some representative examples: Andrade 2019, Babaee 2011, Carter 2017, Di Nucci 2013a, 2013b, 2014b, Kolber 2009, Loh 2018, Oftedal et al. 2020, and Swann et al. 2010). Instead of offering an overview of these discussions, this chapter will introduce a new healthcare application of the trolley problem, from our most recent crisis, the COVID-19 pandemic.

This is not only done in order to provide readers with an accessible and representative example of the Trolley Problem within healthcare; it will also make a methodological contribution to debates around trolleys in addressing the following question: everybody agrees that the Trolley Problem is a thought-experiment; in fact, some believe it is the kind of thought-experiment that gives philosophy a bad reputation. But is it also a genuine *problem*, as its name suggests?

If you are at all familiar with the relevant literature, you will have noticed that increasingly people have started to talk about trolley "cases" instead of a "problem" (Kamm 2007, Scanlon 2008, Edmonds 2013): Is that a sign that there is no problem to begin with? That's one of the questions we want to address here through our new healthcare application of the trolley problem, COVID-19 pandemic interventions.

---

[1] If you are interested in the connections between trolleys and double effect, please see Di Nucci (2014a). But to be sure, this connection is at least historically pretty uncontroversial, given that the doctrine even features in Foot's title.

12.2 Pandemic trolleys?

I propose that the difference between pursuing herd immunity and lifting lockdown restrictions during the COVID-19 pandemic is a version of the trolley problem (this suggestion is, as far as I am aware, original and I only previously sketched it myself in a brief blogpost on the *JME* blog[2]).

Before presenting this new case, let us be clear about this chapter's tasks:

1. Introduce a new – and representative – healthcare application of the trolley problem;
2. Establish whether the trolley problem is a genuine problem or just another philosophical thought-experiment or analytical tool;
3. Put forward a new way of thinking about the ethics of herd immunity and pandemic interventions.

Be charitable: Already achieving just one of the three objectives above would be pretty good for a single chapter, but we will aim for all three and by the end you are welcome to hold us to that ambitious target.

Now, here is our new trolley case: Early in the COVID-19 pandemic, there has been a lot of talk of herd immunity and of whether the aim of "achieving herd immunity" was at all ethically justifiable. You might wonder why "immunity" would even be a problem, but if you do you must have spent the early twenties on a faraway planet, because by now everybody is a couch-epidemiologist – even the token philosopher at the local public health department!

So here we go: Immunity itself is a good thing – that's what all the noise around vaccines is about, after all – but immunity early in a pandemic is achieved through infections; and infections by a CFR (case fatality rate – was it a different galaxy altogether that you were on?) of around 1% – and a herd immunity threshold of at least 60%, but more like 80% – are going to kill an awful lot of folks, at least 0.6% of the overall population – more than 2 million people in the United States alone (which at the time of writing had around 500.000 official COVID-19 fatalities).

That was a lot of empirical detail for a philosophy paper, I know, but given that we haven't even made it to Mars yet, I trust you knew most of it already, so let us move on. The ethical problem with trying to achieve herd immunity

---

[2] https://blogs.bmj.com/medical-ethics/2020/06/09/herd-immunity-and-lifting-lockdowns-a-new-trolley-problem/. There is also an interview I gave on the ethics of COVID-19 where this issue came up: www.thelocal.dk/20200506/the-intricate-ethics-of-lifting-coronavirus-lockdowns/

is its price in terms of unnecessary deaths, basically. And that is why apart from a few members of the British ruling classes (for a short time) and Swedish pragmatists (for a bit longer than anybody was comfortable with), nobody took the aim of herd immunity through infection seriously, not in public anyway.

As everybody this side of Alpha Centauri knows, most governments went for a different approach: restrictions and what have become known as "lock-downs." Which approach ultimately leads to fewer excess deaths is beyond the scope here, but if you are into math (and a lot of my public health and philosophy colleagues are!) here you go: 1% CFR + 60/80% herd immunity threshold gives you a sacrifice of 0.6–0.8% of overall population, which is around 500.000 people in the UK, for example, where official COVID-19 fatalities were around 120.000 at the time of writing and estimated COVID-19 excess deaths were nearer to 150.000.

Obviously, the math needs doing at the end and not in the middle of a pandemic. Things are, as always in philosophy even more than mathematics, complicated. Luckily the number of excess deaths is not crucial to our argument, as you will find out below, so please read on.

What we are comparing here isn't trying to achieve herd immunity through infection with restrictions and lockdowns. What we will be comparing through the lenses of the trolley problem is rather trying to achieve herd immunity with *lifting* restrictions and lockdowns, which is what governments around the world started doing both in 2020 and 2021 once the infection curves flattened.

In case you are wondering, the obvious similarity between pursuing herd immunity and lifting lockdowns is that both have the likely consequences that more people will die – in the immediate future if not long term anyway – as a result of the measure. Here we are not interested in the number of these "intentional" deaths but, indeed, in whether this consequence is "foreseen" or "intended." For now it will be enough to hold on to the conceptual difference between "intentional" and "intended" and the falsity of the so-called Simple View of intentional action (Bratman 1984, 1987; Di Nucci 2009, 2010), everything else I will be reminding you of as we go along.

Enter the trolley: there are many – wait for it – *variants* on trolley case-pairs but the basic structure is that the two cases are consequentialistically compar-able but intuitively different, like the infamous kill one to save five where in both cases either one or five die so that's not the difference and then the question is: What is the difference? If you want to think in terms of a trolley "problem" instead of trolley "cases," then the problem is normally formulated as follows: Why is "bystander" morally permissible while "footbridge" (to take what ought to count as the originals by Judy Thomson, 1976, 1985) is not morally permissible?

So, the problem is to explain the difference in ethical permissibility (or related moral difference, but it is normally a permissibility question) between two consequentialistically comparable cases. In a slogan: If there is no difference, then there is no problem either, just another funny case.

Do you see the connection between the trolley problem and COVID-19 now? Still not clicking? Ok, here we go: Herd immunity is obviously wrong, only those crazy Swedes from across the water could seriously contemplate it; lifting restrictions is a much more complex issue and everybody is doing it, so maybe wrong but not "obviously" wrong like pursuing herd immunity through contagion by 1% CFR. So lifting restrictions is bystander, basically, while herd immunity is "fat man" (sorry, "footbridge" is the correct denomination these days, I believe).

Before continuing, please consider the theoretical alternative according to which what is at play here is not the trolley problem but something closer to the action/omission (or doing/allowing) distinction: We will discuss this more in depth further below, but to begin with do notice that our "fat man" candidate is not the state of "herd immunity" but the *pursuit* of "herd immunity," which is an action or strategy, just as active as lifting restrictions in fact.

Does our analogy hold? That's the question that the rest of this chapter will try to answer. The classic way in which the trolley problem has been addressed – not Foot's own negative/positive duties approach (Foot 1967), which Thomson (1976, 1985) soon showed to be unsuccessful – is to say something along the following lines: There is a difference between the intuitively permissible cases and the consequentialistically parallel but intuitively impermissible cases. The difference, if we take bystander and footbridge, is that killing footbridge is a *means* to save the five while killing bystander is not a means but just a *side effect* of saving the five.

Does that sound familiar? Couldn't we argue that those excess deaths which will result from the pursuit of herd immunity are a means to achieve herd immunity while those excess deaths which will result from lifting lockdown restrictions are just a side effect of lifting restrictions?

Here we need to be careful, for the following reason: We need to distinguish between whether or not our new analogy works – namely, whether there really is a parallel between herd immunity and lifting restrictions, on the one hand, and the classic trolley cases, on the other hand – and whether or not this classic strategy for solving the trolley problem works.

The problem might be the analogy; or the problem might be the classic "solution" to the trolley problem (and the disjunction is inclusive, so there might also be a problem with both); but it's important to remember that our analogy and the classic solution are two different things, and to not confuse the possible success or failure of our new analogy with the possible success or failure of the classic "solution" to the trolley problem.

Let's identify the following four scenarios:

1) Analogy works & solution works
2) Analogy works & solution doesn't
3) Analogy doesn't work & solution does
4) Analogy doesn't work & neither does solution

Additionally, it is probably wise to distinguish between the claim that a classic "solution" to the trolley problem fails (as entailed in both 2 and 4 above) and the claim that the trolley problem is a genuine problem and not just another fancy case, both because an alternative solution (Kamm 2007) might be more suitable but also because maybe there wasn't anything to solve in the first place – and the solution's failure in 2 and 4 above doesn't need to depend on there not having been anything to solve in the first place.

This is where the relationship between the trolley problem and the *Doctrine of Double Effect* matters (Di Nucci 2014a, especially chapter 4).

12.3 Double pandemic?

Before proceeding, let us get the following uninteresting disanalogy out of the way first: While classic trolley cases are consequentialistically identical or at least comparable (fat chance, they are bloody thought-experiments, aren't they), herd immunity could be argued to be much more fatal than lifting restrictions. And that could be the reason why our analogy doesn't even begin to make sense, because we need effects that are much more comparable than the ones we selected from the COVID-19 pandemic.

Here I could play either the cheap philosophy card – it's an empirical issue, so beside the point – or the cheap epidemiology card – provisional data, jury still out – but let us be brave for a change and mention the obvious point that anybody denying the high mortality of lifting restrictions needs to confront the fact that basically every country which lifted restrictions in the middle of 2020 faced second – and even third – waves of infection between late 2020 and early 2021; and that in many such cases second and third waves caused more fatalities than so-called first waves.

That correlation isn't obviously by itself causation (even though we have plenty of preliminary evidence that the two are in fact causally related); neither it is quite the identity of negative effects that thought-experiments are meant to generate, but it is enough – I believe – to resist dismissing our analogy out of hand. The price of lifting restrictions is both real and steep; real enough that it is important to address its morality and also, in a further step, who ought to be held responsible.

Still, as I have argued in the past (Di Nucci 2014a, especially the last chapter), it would be a mistake to "treat" trolleys and the Doctrine as responsibility-issues; both are, historically and theoretically, permissibility-issues. So that responsibility questions, albeit relevant, must be handled in a separate further step.

Some basic translational work from "classic" trolleys to our "new" trolley turns up the following familiar options:

a) Both herd immunity pursuit and lifting lockdowns are morally wrong (translated from: there is no trolley problem because bystander isn't permissible either);
b) Neither herd immunity pursuit nor lifting lockdowns are morally wrong (translated from simple consequentialism: footbridge might be ugly, but it's just *necessary evil*, get on with it);
c) Herd immunity is monstrous but lifting lockdowns justifiable (translated from: the trolley problem as we know it, traditionally);
d) Lifting lockdowns is wrong but herd immunity isn't (I am not aware of anybody defending this particular combination on either side of the translation, but we are doing philosophy so we can't discount this particular corner of the logical space either).

If our analogy from classic trolley problems to our new trolley problem is to hold, then some version of (c) needs vindication. There is a genuine methodological question as to what would count as a vindication of (c) and – as elsewhere in this chapter – the question applies to both classic trolleys and our new trolley: Would it be enough of a vindication of (c) if there were to be different moral intuitions between the two otherwise comparable cases? Over the last two decades there has been a growing literature surveying moral intuitions, including trolley cases (Hauser 2006, Edmonds 2013, Di Nucci 2013a). Additionally, the way governments have dealt with the pandemic might also be taken to reflect different moral intuitions among voters, where herd immunity was beyond the pale but lifting restrictions wasn't.

We don't need to resolve this question but we need to at least point to the difference between thinking that different moral intuitions alone would amount to a vindication of (c) and thinking that a true vindication would need the successful application of some defensible moral principle. To be sure, as this methodological junction is found in both classic trolleys and our new trolley, what is at stake here is not the analogy but rather the truth of (c).

12.4 Why lifting lockdowns but not herd immunity?

The following is the central normative question that needs addressing: Why would it be morally permissible to lift lockdowns while herd immunity wouldn't be morally permissible, given that both can be foreseen to lead to increasing fatalities?

Here we need to do some pandemic ethics that is not directly relevant to the trolley problem before we can proceed: namely, it could be argued that the reason why "lifting lockdowns" might be (sometimes) ethically permissible while "herd immunity" won't be (under the empirical conditions described earlier and borrowed from the COVID-19 pandemic, to be sure), has nothing to do with the trolley problem because there are other considerations at stake, for example, the liberties of those upon which lockdowns have been imposed, or the well-being of groups particularly vulnerable to the restrictions in question (Lykkeskov & Di Nucci, forthcoming).

The two kinds of considerations above are very different from each other, but they have in common that they might offer normative reasons which are independent of the trolley problem, thereby ultimately collapsing our analogy while still vindicating (c). Are we sure, though, that such considerations would constitute a vindication of (c)? The question here is not whether such considerations would be enough to justify lifting restrictions and the foreseen fatalities that go along with such measure (that's a complex pandemic ethics question which is beyond the scope here); the question is whether such considerations are enough to draw a moral permissibility wedge between lockdown-lifting and herd-immunity.

Here the irony will not have escaped you: lifting-restrictions can be predicted to prolong the pandemic while herd-immunity (can be predicted to) shorten it; it is just that we commonly assume that the pandemic-prolonging plus foreseen fatalities equation that results from lifting lockdowns is defensible in a way in which the pandemic-shortening plus foreseen fatalities equation that results from herd immunity is not defensible.

I say this, again, not because I want to get into the complexities of pandemic ethics but only to point out that if you are worried about the liberty violation or the welfare of vulnerable groups during the lockdown (women, children, minorities), those worries might in fact end up supporting herd immunity pursuit more than they support lifting restrictions – so this strategy can't be the way to go for us because it doesn't vindicate (c), whatever one's position on the ethical and political plausibility of these further considerations is.

Let us take stock: We have looked at two alternative ways of vindicating (c) without appealing to something resembling trolleys:

I)   On the one hand, we have looked at the possibility that it is the difference in fatalities that might explain any difference in permissibility but have concluded that, quite apart from the fact that empirical data on fatalities in the middle of a pandemic (2020–2021) is inevitably premature and unreliable, second- and third-waves that have followed the lifting of restrictions around the world in 2021 speak against this option, because it isn't at all clear that lifting restrictions is clearly less fatal than pursuing herd immunity;

II) on the other hand, we have looked at the possibility that it is concern for civil liberties and the welfare of vulnerable groups that justifies lifting lockdowns but have concluded that – independently of the plausibility of these kinds of considerations – this would also speak in favor of pursuing herd immunity, given that the latter can actually be predicted to shorten the pandemic while lifting restrictions to prolong the pandemic.

Neither strategy (I) nor strategy (II) is, then, satisfactory for our purposes, because neither strategy can successfully distinguish between lifting lockdowns and pursuing herd immunity. So let us move on while obviously keeping in mind the possibility that the reason why those strategies both failed is simply that there is no ethical difference between lifting lockdowns and pursuing herd immunity.

The fact that the two strategies above fail doesn't obviously imply that the trolley problem is the only way to distinguish between the ethics of lifting restrictions and the evil of herd immunity, but it is at least a reason to try, which is what we now turn to doing.

Embracing the dialectic of the trolley problem, let us first of all assume that pursuing herd immunity is morally impermissible while lifting restrictions is not similarly morally impermissible (given some comparable background conditions, obviously). Having ruled out above two possible strategies that could have explained the difference in moral permissibility, what else could possibly do the trick?

Here is a further strategy that those of you familiar with trolley debates will recognize: when we lift restrictions, the extra fatalities that are the result of having lifted restrictions are not intended but merely foreseen; while when we pursue herd immunity, those extra fatalities are not only foreseen but also intended. Is this true, though?

In a standard interpretation (see, e.g., Bratman 1984 and 1987), this distinction does not result in a further distinction in which the herd immunity fatalities are intentional while lifting lockdown fatalities are not intentional; both are indeed intentional, but the former are also intended while the latter are unintended – this is obviously an important clarification when it comes to responsibility attributions, as there is no "unintentional" effect from which a lack of responsibility could potentially follow.

The above claim presupposes that the so-called Simple View of intentional action is false, as Bratman (1984, 1987) has famously argued (see also Di Nucci 2009, 2010, McCann 2010), so that there is logical space for intentional but unintended actions.

You might think this bit of action theory is itself unnecessary, but it helps us identify a further option that would indeed draw a distinction between the two cases but is arguably less plausible, namely, the idea that when we lift restrictions the fatalities that result from our policy change are not intentional; given that we lift restrictions fully aware of the relevant risks, that would not seem to be plausible. But again that is not what follows from the trolley strategy outlined above; the only implication is rather that those fatalities are not intended in the case of lifting the lockdown but are intended in the case of pursuing herd immunity.

Another way of basically making the same point that you will find in the trolley (and double effect) literature goes as follows: When we pursue herd immunity, we are not just aware that people will die as a result; we are actually intending for those people to die as a means to achieving herd immunity, so that those additional fatalities are an intended means to our goal of herd immunity.

When we lift restrictions, on the other hand, while we are again aware that people will die as a result – and let me remind the skeptical or Western-centric reader that I wrote this in April 2021, with the global pandemic achieving new all-time highs through the so-called Delta variant – we are not intending for anybody to die as a result of our lifting restrictions, so that those additional deaths are merely foreseen side effects of our policy change but not intended means to our goal of getting "normal" everyday life back.

Please take a deep breath and remind yourself of the following: We are neither trying to justify lifting lockdowns nor (god forbid) pursuing herd immunity early in a pandemic with 1% CFR; nor, in fact, are we trying to justify any moral difference between the two – we are only using those two recent and by now very well-known cases to discuss the trolley problem within healthcare. The argumentative consequence is the following: if you found the attempted distinction unpersuasive, what should you infer from that?

1) It could be that the distinction didn't convince you because the trolley strategy doesn't work; or
2) It could be that the distinction didn't convince you because there is no real analogy between genuine trolley cases and this "new" trolley case.

Only option (2) has further implications for pandemic ethics, which could lead us to for example question the widespread acceptability of lifting restrictions that we know will lead to more deaths as opposed to the taboo status of pursuing herd immunity, which we also know will lead to more deaths. And while these consequences for pandemic ethics are an interesting upshot of our discussion, they are not its primary focus.

We will now show that it is easy to distinguish in theory between options (1) and (2) as we just did, but that in practice (the practice of philosophy, so still theoretical practice, don't worry) things are a bit messy. Here's why.

One way of resisting the permissibility of lifting lockdowns against the impermissibility of pursuing herd immunity is to deny that when we pursue herd immunity, the additional deaths which result from our policy change are intended means to our end of achieving herd immunity. After all, we only intend for enough people to be infected (60%–80% of the population), we know that at least 1% of the infected will die, but we don't want or intend for them to die – only foresee their deaths.

What have we just done? This is classic trolley: We have borrowed the strategy utilized for the moral justification of lifting restrictions and applied it to herd immunity. Note this does not actually mean that herd immunity is justified, only that there is no difference between the two cases – so maybe the implication should rather be that lifting lockdowns wasn't justified to begin with either?

12.5 Super-remdesivir

Was this too fast? Let us take it one step at the time: what's behind this new idea that not even for the case of pursuing herd immunity can we argue that those additional deaths are intended means? One possible argument would have it that we only intend to infect but not for the infected to die, and this can be seen if we just suppose that, at the same early stage of the pandemic, we already have effective meds against the disease caused by the virus – say something like, or in fact hopefully better than, remdesivir against COVID-19, namely, a drug that does not prevent infection from the virus but does fight the disease caused by the virus effectively.

If we had super-remdesivir early in the pandemic, we could do the following: infect on purpose 60% to 80% of the relevant population but give them super-remdesivir before their infection leads to serious medical consequences. Remember, here the question is not whether this would be a viable epidemiological or indeed clinical strategy, the question is only whether our little thought-experiment can be used to show that even in the herd immunity case, we do not actually intend for anybody to die but only for them to be infected.

I know I am annoying, but I must caution you, dear reader, against making the following mistake: The relevant question is not whether in case we had super-remdesivir, then we wouldn't (need to) intend for anybody to die as a result of pursuing herd immunity. The relevant question is rather whether, given the super-remdesivir thought-experiment, even if we didn't have super-remdesivir (as we didn't early in the pandemic for the historical case of COVID-19), the very possibility is enough to show that those foreseen deaths which result from intended infection in the pursuit of herd immunity are actually unintended too, like with lifting lockdowns.

If the super-remdesivir thought experiment is successful, then we can argue that pursuing herd immunity does not imply an intention to kill anybody through intentional infection, but indeed only an intention to infect (but not necessarily to kill). This does not mean that there is no ethical difference between the pursuit of herd immunity and lifting lockdowns, but the success of the super-remdesivir thought-experiment would still have the following meaningful consequences:

- We cannot distinguish between the moral permissibility of lifting lockdowns and the moral impermissibility of pursuing herd immunity by the application of a classic trolley strategy that distinguishes between intended means and merely foreseen effects; additionally,
- The application of a classic trolley strategy that distinguishes between intended means and merely foreseen side effects risks legitimizing the pursuit of herd immunity early in a pandemic.

If you are a philosopher you probably care more about the former consequence; if you are an epidemiologist you probably don't care about the former but are concerned about the latter consequence. Have we made a travesty of pandemic ethics debates? Well, maybe – but that's trolley logics for you (or *trolleyology*). But speaking of presenting logical possibilities, I think the following two which result from our argument deserve particular attention:

- A possible conclusion that one might be tempted to draw from our argument isn't that it legitimizes herd immunity but rather that it shows what many epidemiologists and public health ethicists have been saying throughout, namely, that lifting lockdowns is irresponsible or, at the very least, the weaker version of that claim, namely, that it has fatal consequences that we must stand up and be counted for?
- The first consequence above is a pandemic ethics issue but, as we said all along, this chapter aims to contribute primarily to theoretical issues around the trolley problem actually, so here is the second consequence: If our argument is successful, you might worry that a certain double-effect-inspired classic strategy to deal with the trolley problem can justify just about anything, and that is why it should be rejected (on, *nota bene*, normative grounds rather than action-theoretical grounds), because it has implausible implications such as the legitimization of herd immunity.

This latter consequence doesn't need much further analysis not because it isn't significant (it is!) but because the literature already knows it as the so-called closeness problem (see, e.g., Di Nucci 2014a, Edmonds 2013, FitzPatrick 2006, Liao 2016, Nelkin & Rickless 2015, and Tadros 2015 as some representative discussions of a problem that goes all the way back to Foot's "original" paper, actually: Foot 1967).

The former consequence is one that you would certainly expect me to develop further as it would make an important contribution to pandemic ethics debates around COVID-19, but remember what this chapter's main task was. It would simply take us way too far into the ethics and politics of COVID-19 to properly deal with the former consequence, so I will just say that it should serve as an urgent reminder of the steep price of lifting restrictions that we are continuing to pay; it might be worth it – that is a different question; but arguing that those fatalities are unintended won't bring these people back (and, remember, unintended does not equal unintentional, so we are responsible for those fatalities as well).

12.6 Conclusion

I am not a big believer in conclusions: I have said what I wanted (and needed) to say; didn't take too long either, so no need for a summary, is there? Still, you might also be slightly disappointed that my argument stops just when things had started to get juicy. So let me offer a bonus track here instead of a needless conclusion: another way to try to apply trolleys to COVID-19, vaccines hesitancy.

My own country – Denmark – was the first in early 2021 to permanently stop the use of cheap and effective vaccines against COVID-19, AZ, and J&J. Why? Because there is some preliminary evidence that there might be a causal connection between said vaccine and very rare occurrences of sometimes fatal blood clots, which we will round to 0.001%.

The interesting thing about this policy decision for our purposes is the following: Given the difference between 0.001% and COVID-19 CFR of 1% – even a philosopher can do that much math, the latter is thousand times more fatal than the former! – there seems to some underlying non-consequentialistic assumption behind the Danish authorities' reasoning (what elsewhere I have called the "vicious circle of precaution," Di Nucci 2021).

Could it be the following? The 1% killed by COVID-19 isn't our killing – we are, at worst, letting them die – but the 0.001% killed by AZ and J&J would be our own intentional killing. But are we intending the latter deaths or only intentionally allowing them to happen as well so that the population can be vaccinated? OK, I believe you see where this is going, but it's for another day – let me just remind you that the same way in which we shouldn't confuse the "trolley problem" with the "doctrine of double effect," we should also distinguish between those two and the doing/allowing distinction (Quinn 1989a and 1989b are the classic dual-discussions of this difference in the literature).[3]

---

[3] Many thanks to Anne Lykkeskov, Isaac Wagner, and this volume's editor for valuable comments on an earlier draft of this chapter.

Bibliography

Abarbanell, L., & Hauser, M. D. 2010. "Mayan morality: An exploration of permissible harms" *Cognition* 115: 207–224.

Aghab Babaee, N. 2011. "Trolley dilemma and its implication in active and passive euthanasia" *Iranian Journal of Medical Ethics and History of Medicine* 4: 65–72.

Ahlenius, H., & Tännsjö, T. 2012. "Chinese and Westerners respond differently to the trolley dilemmas" *Journal of Cognition and Culture* 12: 195–201.

Alexander, J. 2013. "Getting Better," Workshop in honour of Philip Kitcher, Erasmus University, Rotterdam, November 7, 2013.

Alexander, J. 2019. "Is there an objective morality?" IAI TV 73, May 20, 2019, https://iai.tv/articles/is-there-an-objective-morality-auid-1237

Alexander, L., & Ferzan, K. K. (with S. Morse). 2009. *Crime and Culpability: A Theory of Criminal Law.* Cambridge: Cambridge University Press.

Andrade, G. 2019. "Medical ethics and the trolley problem" *Journal of Medical Ethics and History of Medicine* 12: 3.

Annas, J. 2011. *Intelligent Virtue.* Oxford: Oxford University Press.

Annas, J. 2015. "Virtue and duty: Negotiating between different ethical traditions" *The Journal of Value Inquiry* 49: 605–618.

Anscombe, G. E. M. 1958. "Modern moral philosophy" *Philosophy* 33: 1–19.

Anscombe, G. E. M. 1967. "Who is wronged? Philippa foot on double effect: One point" *Oxford Review* 5: 16–17.

Aquinas, T. Unknown/2006. *Summa Theologiae.* Cambridge: Cambridge University Press.

Aristotle. 2009. *The Nicomachean Ethics.* Translated by David Ross, revised by Lesley Brown. Oxford: Oxford University Press.

Arutyunova, K. R., Alexandrov, Y. I., & Hauser, M. D. 2016. "Sociocultural influences on moral judgments: East–west, male–female, and young–old" *Frontiers in Psychology* 7: 1334.

Avram, M., Hennig-Fast, K., Bao, Y., Pöppel, E., Reiser, M., Blautzik, J., . . . Gutyrchik, E. 2014. "Neural correlates of moral judgments in first-and third-person perspectives: Implications for neuroethics and beyond" *BMC Neuroscience* 15: 1–11.

Awad, E., Dsouza, S., Kim, R., Shulz, J., Henrich, J., Shariff, A., . . . Rahwan, I. 2018. "The moral machine experiment" *Nature* 563: 59–64.

Awad, E., Dsouza, S., Shariff, A., Rahwan, I., & Bonnefon, J. F. 2020. "Universals and variations in moral decisions made in 42 countries by 70,000 participants" *Proceedings of the National Academy of Sciences* 117: 2332–2337.

Axtell, G., & Olson, P. 2012. "Recent work in applied virtue ethics" *American Philosophical Quarterly* 49: 183–203.

Bago, B., Aczel, B., Kekecs, Z., Protzko, J., Kovacs, M., Nagy, T., . . . Gjoneska, B. Under review. "Moral thinking across the world: Exploring the influence of personal force and intention in moral dilemma judgments."

Bago, B., & De Neys, W. 2019. "The intuitive greater good: Testing the corrective dual process model of moral cognition" *Journal of Experimental Psychology: General* 148: 1782–1801. https://doi.org/10.1037/xge0000533

Bago, B., Kovacs, M., Protzko, J., Nagy, T., Kekecs, Z., Palfi, B., . . . Matibag, C. J. 2022. "Situational factors shape moral judgments in the trolley dilemma in Eastern, Southern, and Western countries in a culturally diverse sample" *Nature Human Behaviour* 6: 880–895.

Balleine, B. W., & O'Doherty, J. P. 2010. "Human and rodent homologies in action control: Corticostriatal determinants of goal-directed and habitual action" *Neuropsychopharmacology* 35: 48–69.

Banerjee, K., Huebner, B., & Hauser, M. 2010. "Intuitive moral judgments are robust across variation in gender, education, politics and religion: A large-scale web-based study" *Journal of Cognition and Culture* 10: 253–281.

Baron, J. 1994. "Nonconsequentialist decisions" *Behavioral and Brain Sciences* 17: 1–10.

Bartels, D. M., & Pizarro, D. A. 2011. "The mismeasure of morals: Antisocial personality traits predict utilitarian responses to moral dilemmas" *Cognition* 121: 154–161.

Bauman, C. W., McGraw, A. P., Bartels, D. M., & Warren, C. 2014. "Revisiting external validity: Concerns about trolley problems and other sacrificial dilemmas in moral psychology: External validity in moral psychology" *Social and Personality Psychology Compass* 8: 536–554. https://doi.org/10.1111/spc3.12131

Benjamin, D. J., Berger, J. O., Johannesson, M., Nosek, B. A., Wagenmakers, E. J., Berk, R., . . . Johnson, V. E. 2018. "Redefine statistical significance" *Nature Human Behaviour* 2: 6–10.

Bennett, J. 1980. *Morality and Consequences.* The Tanner Lectures on Human Values. *Online*: https://tannerlectures.utah.edu/_documents/a-to-z/b/bennett81.pdf

Bennett, J. 1995. *The Act Itself.* Oxford: Oxford University Press.

Berker, S. 2009. "The normative insignificance of neuroscience" *Philosophy and Public Affairs* 37: 293–329.

Bernhard, R. M., Chaponis, J., Siburian, R., Gallagher, P., Ransohoff, K., Wikler, D., . . . Greene, J. D. 2016. "Variation in the oxytocin receptor gene (OXTR) is associated with differences in moral judgment" *Social Cognitive and Affective Neuroscience* 11: 1872–1881.

Blair, R. J. R. 2007. "The amygdala and ventromedial prefrontal cortex in morality and psychopathy" *Trends in Cognitive Sciences* 11: 387–392.

Bonnefon, J.-F., Shariff, A., & Rahwan, I. 2015. "Autonomous vehicles need experimental ethics: Are we ready for utilitarian cars?" arXiv:1510.03346 [cs]. http://arxiv.org/abs/1510.03346

Bonnefon, J.-F., Sharrif, A., & Rahwan, I. 2016. "The social dilemma of autonomous vehicles" *Science* 352: 1573–1576.

Bostyn, D. H., & Roets, A. 2017. "Trust, trolleys and social dilemmas: A replication study" *Journal of Experimental Psychology: General* 146: e1–e7. https://doi.org/10.1037/xge0000295

Bostyn, D. H., Sevenhant, S., & Roets, A. 2018. "Of mice, men, and trolleys: Hypothetical judgment versus real-life behavior in trolley-style moral dilemmas" *Psychological Science* 29: 1084–1093. https://doi.org/10.1177/0956797617752640

Bostyn, D. H., Sevenhant, S., & Roets, A. 2019. "Beyond physical harm: How preference for consequentialism and primary psychopathy relate to decisions on a monetary trolley dilemma" *Thinking & Reasoning* 25: 192–206.

Bratman, M. 1984. "Two faces of intention" *Philosophical Review* 93: 375–405.

Bratman, M. 1987. *Intentions, Plans and Practical Reason.* Cambridge, MA: Harvard University Press.

Brown, M., & Sacco, D. F. 2017. "Is pulling the lever sexy? Deontology as a downstream cue to long-term mate quality" *Journal of Social and Personal Relationships.* 36 (3). https://doi.org/10.1177/0265407517749331

Business Insider. 2016. "Why Mercedes plans to let its self-driving cars kill pedestrians in dicey situations" www.businessinsider.nl/mercedes-benz-self-driving-cars-programmed-save-driver-2016-10/

Buss, S., & Westlund, A. 2018. "Personal autonomy" *The Stanford Encyclopedia of Philosophy* (Spring 2018 Edition), E. N. Zalta (Ed.), https://plato.stanford.edu/archives/spr2018/entries/personal-autonomy/

Byrd, N., & Conway, P. 2019. "Not all who ponder count costs: Arithmetic reflection predicts utilitarian tendencies, but logical reflection predicts both deontological and utilitarian tendencies" *Cognition* 192: 103995. https://doi.org/10.1016/j.cognition.2019.06.007

Campbell, R., & Kumar, V. 2012. "Moral reasoning on the ground" *Ethics* 122: 273–312.

Capraro, V., Everett, J. A. C., & Earp, B. D. 2020. "Priming intuition decreases instrumental harm but not impartial beneficence" *Journal of Experimental Social Psychology* 83: 142–149.

Carter, S. M. 2017. "Overdiagnosis, ethics, and trolley problems: Why factors other than outcomes matter" *BMJ* 358: j3872.

Caviola, L., Schubert, S., & Greene, J. D. 2021. "The psychology of (in)Effective altruism" *Trends in Cognitive Sciences*".

Caviola, L., Greene, J.D. 2021/under review. "Boosting the impact of human altruism".

Chaiken, S., & Trope, Y. (Eds.). 1999. *Dual-process Theories in Social Psychology* (Vol. xiii). New York: Guilford Press.

Chen, C., Decety, J., Huang, P. C., Chen, C. Y., & Cheng, Y. 2016. "Testosterone administration in females modulates moral judgment and patterns of brain activation and functional connectivity" *Human Brain Mapping*, 37: 3417–3430.

Chomsky, N. 1957. *Syntactic Structures* The Hague/Paris: Mouton.

Ciaramelli, E., Muccioli, M., Làdavas, E., & di Pellegrino, G. 2007. "Selective deficit in personal moral judgment following damage to ventromedial prefrontal cortex" *Social Cognitive and Affective Neuroscience* 2: 84–92.

Clarkson, E., & Jasper, J. D. 2022. "Individual differences in moral judgment predict attitudes towards mandatory vaccinations" *Personality and Individual Differences* 186: 111391.

Conway, P., & Gawronski, B. 2013. "Deontological and utilitarian inclinations in moral decision making: A process dissociation approach" *Journal of Personality and Social Psychology* 104: 216.

Conway, P., Goldstein-Greenwood, J., Polacek, D., & Greene, J. D. 2018. "Sacrificial utilitarian judgments do reflect concern for the greater good: Clarification via process dissociation and the judgments of philosophers" *Cognition* 179: 241–265. https://doi.org/10.1016/j.cognition.2018.04.018

Costa, A., Foucart, A., Hayakawa, S., Aparici, M., Apesteguia, J., Heafner, J., et al. 2014. "Your morals depend on language" *PLoS ONE* 9: e94842. /https://doi.org/10.1371/journal.pone.0094842

Cova, F., Strickland, B., Abatista, A., Allard, A., Andow, J., Attie, M., . . . Zhou, X. 2021. "Estimating the reproducibility of experimental philosophy" *Review of Philosophy and Psychology* 12: 9–44.

Craver, C. F., Keven, N., Kwan, D., Kurczek, J., Duff, M. C., & Rosenbaum, R. S. 2016. "Moral judgment in episodic amnesia" *Hippocampus* 26: 975–979.

Crockett, M. J. 2013. "Models of morality" *Trends in Cognitive Sciences* 17: 363–366. https://doi.org/10.1016/j.tics.2013.06.005

Crockett, M. J., Clark, L., Hauser, M. D., & Robbins, T. W. 2010. "Serotonin selectively influences moral judgment and behavior through effects on harm aversion" *Proceedings of the National Academy of Sciences* 107: 17433–17438.

Cunneen, M., Mullins, M., Murphy, F., Shannon, D. Furxhi, I., & Ryan, C. 2019. "Autonomous vehicles and avoiding the trolley (dilemma): Vehicle perception, classification, and the challenges of framing decision ethics" *Cybernetics and Systems* 51: 59–80.

Curtin, C. M., Barrett, H. C., Bolyanatz, A., Crittenden, A. N., Fessler, D. M., Fitzpatrick, S., . . . & Henrich, J. 2020. "Kinship intensity and the use of mental states in moral judgment across societies" *Evolution and Human Behavior* 41: 415–429.

Cushman, F. 2013. "Action, outcome, and value: A dual-system framework for morality" *Personality and Social Psychology Review* 17: 273–292.

Cushman, F., Gray, K., Gaffey, A., & Mendes, W. B. 2012. "Simulating murder: The aversion to harmful action" *Emotion* 12: 2–7. https://doi.org/10.1037/a0025071

Cushman, F., & Greene, J. D. 2012. "Finding faults: How moral dilemmas illuminate cognitive structure" *Social Neuroscience* 7: 269–279.

Cushman, F., Murray, D., Gordon-McKeon, S., Wharton, S., & Greene, J. D. 2012. "Judgment before principle: Engagement of the frontoparietal control network in condemning harms of omission" *Social Cognitive and Affective Neuroscience* 7: 888–895.

Cushman, F., Young, L., & Hauser, M. 2006. "The role of conscious reasoning and intuition in moral judgment: Testing three principles of harm" *Psychological Science* 17: 1082–1089.

Damasio, A. R. 1994. *Descartes' Error: Emotion, Reason, and the Human Brain*. New York: G.P. Putnam.

Dancy, J. 2004. *Ethics without Principles*. Oxford: Oxford University Press.

Darby, R. R., Horn, A., Cushman, F., & Fox, M. D. 2018. "Lesion network localization of criminal behavior" *Proceedings of the National Academy of Sciences* 115: 601–606.

Davnall, R. 2019. "Solving the single-vehicle self-driving car trolley problem using risk theory and vehicle dynamics" *Science and Engineering Ethics* 26: 431–449.

Daw, N. D., & Doya, K. 2006. "The computational neurobiology of learning and reward" *Current Opinion in Neurobiology* 16: 199–204.

Dewaele, J. M. 2004. "Blistering barnacles! What language do multilinguals swear in?" *Estudios de Sociolinguistica* 5: 83–105.

Dickinson, A., Balleine, B., Watt, A., Gonzalez, F., & Boakes, R. A. 1995. "Motivational control after extended instrumental training" *Animal Learning & Behavior* 23: 197–206.

Di Nucci, E. 2009. "Simply, false" *Analysis* 69: 69–78.

Di Nucci, E. 2010. "Rational constraints and the simple view" *Analysis* 70: 481–486.

Di Nucci, E. 2013a. "Self-sacrifice and the trolley problem" *Philosophical Psychology* 26: 662–672.

Di Nucci, E. 2013b. "Embryo loss and double effect" *Journal of Medical Ethics* 39: 537–540.

Di Nucci E. 2014a. *Ethics without Intention*. London: Bloomsbury.

Di Nucci, E. 2014b. "Contraception and double effect" *The American Journal of Bioethics* 14: 42–43.

Di Nucci, E. 2021. "The vicious circle of precaution" *JME Blog* https://blogs.bmj.com/medical-ethics/2021/03/18/the-vicious-circle-of-precaution

Doris, J. M., & Plakias, A. 2008. "How to argue about disagreement: Evaluative diversity and moral realism" In W. Sinnott-Armstrong (Ed.), *Moral Psychology, Vol. 2. The Cognitive Science of Morality: Intuition and Diversity*. 303–331. Cambridge, MA: MIT Press.

Edmonds, D. 2013. *Would You Kill the Fat Man? The Trolley Problem and What Your Answer Tells Us about Right and Wrong*. Princeton: Princeton University Press.

Evans, A. M. & Brandt, M. J. 2019. "Comparing the effects of hypothetical moral preferences on real-Life and hypothetical behavior: commentary on bostyn, sevenhant, and roets (2018)" *Psychological Science* 30: 1380–1382.

Everett, J. A. C., Colombatto, C., Awad, E., Boggio, P., Bos, B., Brady, W. J., . . . Crockett, M. J. 2021. "Moral dilemmas and trust in leaders during a global health crisis" *Nature Human Behaviour* 5: 1074–1088.

Everett, J. A. C., Faber, N. S., Savulescu, J., & Crockett, M. J. 2018. "The costs of being consequentialist: Social inference from instrumental harm and impartial beneficence" *Journal of Experimental Social Psychology* 79: 200–216. https://doi.org/10.1016/j.jesp.2018.07.004

Everett, J. A. C., & Kahane, G. 2020. "Switching tracks? Towards a multidimensional model of utilitarian psychology" *Trends in Cognitive Sciences* 24: 124–134. https://doi.org/10.1016/j.tics.2019.11.012

Everett, J. A. C., Pizarro, D. A., & Crockett, M. J. 2016. "Inference of trustworthiness from intuitive moral judgments" *Journal of Experimental Psychology: General* 145: 772–787. https://doi.org/10.1037/xge0000165

Feinberg, J. 1984. *Harm to Others: The Moral Limits of the Criminal Law*. Oxford: Oxford University Press.

Feinberg, M., Willer, R., Antonenko, O., & John, O. P. 2012. "Liberating reason from the passions: Overriding intuitionist moral judgments through emotion reappraisal" *Psychological Science* 23: 788–795.

Feltz, A., & May, J. 2017. "The means/side-effect distinction in moral cognition: A meta-analysis" *Cognition* 166: 314–327.

Finkelstein, C. 2003. "Is risk a harm?" *University of Pennsylvania Law Review* 151: 963–1001.

Fischer, J. M., & Ravizza, M. 1992. *Ethics: Problems and Principles*. Harcourt: Brace, Jovanovich.

Fitzpatrick, W. J. 2006. "The intend/foresee distinction and the problem of 'closeness'" *Philosophical Studies* 128: 585–617.

FitzPatrick, W. J. 2009. "Thomson's turnabout on the trolley" *Analysis* 69: 636–43.

Foot, P. 1967. "The problem of abortion and the doctrine of the double effect" *Oxford Review* 5: 5–15. Reprinted in P. Foot, *Virtues and Vices and Other Essays in Moral Philosophy*. 19–32. Oxford: Blackwell 1978. [Also Foot 1967/2002; 1967/2003]

Foot, P. 1967/2002a. "The problem of abortion and the doctrine of double effect" In P. Foot (Ed.), *Virtue and Vices and Other Essays in Moral Philosophy*. 19–32. Oxford: Oxford University Press. [Also Foot 1967; 1967/2003]

Foot, P. 1967/2003. "The problem of abortion and the doctrine of double effect" In P. Foot (Ed.) *Virtues and Vices and Other Essays in Moral Philosophy*. Berkeley and Los Angeles.: University of California Press. [Also Foot 1967; 1967/2002a]

Foot, P. 1977. "Euthanasia," *Philosophy & Public Affairs* 6: 85–112. Reprinted in P. Foot, *Virtues and Vices and Other Essays in Moral Philosophy* 33–61. Oxford: Blackwell, 1978.

Foot, P. 1978. *Virtues and Vices and Other Essays in Moral Philosophy*. Oxford: Blackwell.

Foot, P. 1984. "Killing and letting die" In J. Garfield (Ed.), *Abortion: Moral and Legal Perspectives*. 178–185. Amherst: University of Massachusetts Press. Reprinted in P. Foot, *Moral Dilemmas and Other Topics in Moral Philosophy*. 78–87. Oxford: Oxford University Press, 2002. [Also Foot 1994]

Foot, P. 1985a. "Utilitarianism and the virtues" *Mind* 94: 196–209.

Foot, P. 1985b. "Morality, action and outcome" In T. Honderich (Ed.), *Morality and Objectivity*. 23–38. London: Routledge and Kegan Paul. Reprinted in P. Foot, *Moral Dilemmas and Other Topics in Moral Philosophy*. 88–104. Oxford: Oxford University Press, 2002.

Foot, P. 1994. "Killing and letting die" In B. Steinbock and A. Norcross (Eds.), *Killing and Letting Die*, 2nd Edition. 280–89. New York: Fordham University Press. [Also Foot 1984]

Foot, P. 2001. *Natural Goodness*. Oxford: Oxford University Press.

Foot, P. 2002a, *Virtue and Vices and Other Essays in Moral Philosophy*. Oxford: Oxford University Press.

Foot, P. 2002b. *Moral Dilemmas and Other Topics in Moral Philosophy*. Oxford: Oxford University Press.

Fried, B. H. 2012a. "What *does* matter? The case for killing the trolley problem (or letting it die)" *The Philosophical Quarterly* 62: 1–25.

Fried, B. 2012b. "The limits of a nonconsequentialist approach to torts" *Legal Theory* 18: 231–262.

Friesdorf, R., Conway, P., & Gawronski, B. 2015. "Gender differences in responses to moral dilemmas: A process dissociation analysis" *Personality and Social Psychology Bulletin* 41: 696–713.

Frowe, H. 2015. *Defensive Killing*. Oxford: Oxford University Press.

Frowe, H. 2018. "Lesser-evil justifications for harming: Why we're required to turn the trolley" *The Philosophical Quarterly* 68: 460–480.

Fruge, C. 2019. "Possible intentions and the doctrine of double effect" *Ethics, Medicine and Public Health* 8:11–17.

Gawronski, B., Armstrong, J., Conway, P., Friesdorf, R., & Hütter, M. 2017. "Consequences, norms, and generalized inaction in moral dilemmas: The CNI model of moral decision-making" *Journal of Personality and Social Psychology* 113: 343–376. https://doi.org/10.1037/pspa0000086

Geipel, J., Hadjichristidis, C., & Surian, L. 2015. "How foreign language shapes moral judgment" *Journal of Experimental Social Psychology* 59: 8–17.

Gibbard, A. 2008. *Reconciling Our Aims*. Oxford: Oxford University Press.

Glenn, A. L., Raine, A., & Schug, R. A. 2009. "The neural correlates of moral decision-making in psychopathy" *Molecular Psychiatry* 14: 5–6.

Gogoll J.,& Müller J. F. 2017. "Autonomous cars: In favor of a mandatory ethics setting" *Science and Engineering Ethics* 23: 681–700.

Gold, N. Forthcoming. "Thought experiments in ethics" In Copp, D., Rosati, C., and Rulli, T. (Eds.), *Oxford Handbook of Normative Ethics*. Oxford: Oxford University Press.

Gold, N., Colman, A. M., & Pulford, B. D. 2014. "Cultural differences in responses to real-life and hypothetical trolley problems" *Judgment and Decision Making* 9: 65–76.

Goodall, N. 2016. "Away from trolley problems and toward risk management" *Applied Artificial Intelligence* 30: 810–821.

Graham, P. A. 2017. "Thomson's trolley problem" *Journal of Ethics and Social Philosophy* 12: 168–190.

Greene, J. D. 2007. "The secret joke of Kant's Soul" in Sinnott-Armstrong, W. (Ed.), *Moral Psychology Vol. 3: The Neuroscience of Morality: Emotion, Brain Disorders, and Development*. 35–79. Cambridge, MA: MIT Press.

Greene, J. D. 2013. *Moral Tribes: Emotion, Reason, and the Gap between Us and Them*. New York: Penguin Books.

Greene, J. D. 2014. "Beyond point-and-shoot morality: Why cognitive (neuro)science matters for ethics" *Ethics* 124: 695–726.

Greene, J. D. 2017. "The rat-a-gorical imperative: Moral intuition and the limits of affective learning" *Cognition* 167: 66–77.

Greene, J. D., Cushman, F. A., Stewart, L. E., Lowenberg, K., Nystrom, L. E., & Cohen, J. D. 2009. "Pushing moral buttons: The interaction between personal force and intention in moral judgment" *Cognition* 111: 364–371.

Greene, J. D., Huang, K., & Bazerman, M. 2022. "Redirecting Rawlsian Reasoning Toward the Greater Good" In M. Vargas & J. Doris (Eds.), *The Handbook of Moral Psychology*. 246–261. Oxford: Oxford University Press.

Greene, J. D., Morelli, S. A., Lowenberg, K., Nystrom, L. E., & Cohen, J. D. 2008. "Cognitive load selectively interferes with utilitarian moral judgment" *Cognition* 107: 1144–1154.

Greene, J. D., Nystrom, L. E., Engell, A. D., Darley, J. M., & Cohen, J. D. 2004. "The neural bases of cognitive conflict and control in moral judgment" *Neuron* 44: 389–400. https://doi.org/10.1016/j.neuron.2004.09.027

Greene, J. D., Sommerville, R. B., Nystrom, L. E., Darley, J. M., & Cohen, J. D. 2001. "An fMRI investigation of emotional engagement in moral judgment" *Science* 293: 2105–2108.

Greene, J. D., & Young, L. 2020. "The cognitive neuroscience of moral judgment and decision-making" in *The Cognitive Neurosciences*, Volume 6 (Ed. M.S. Gazzaniga). Cambridge, MA: MIT Press.

Gürçay, B., & Baron, J. 2017. "Challenges for the sequential two-system model of moral judgement" *Thinking & Reasoning* 23: 49–80. https://doi.org/10.1080/13546783.2016.1216011

Haidt, J. 2001. "The emotional dog and its rational tail: A social intuitionist approach to moral judgment" *Psychological Review* 108: 814–834.

Hájek, A. 2019. "Interpretations of probability" *The Stanford Encyclopedia of Philosophy* (Fall 2019 Edition), Edward N. Zalta (Ed.), URL = https://plato.stanford.edu/archives/fall2019/entries/probability-interpret/

Hannikainen, I. R., Machery, E., & Cushman, F. A. 2018. "Is utilitarian sacrifice becoming more morally permissible?" *Cognition* 170: 95–101.

Hanser, M. 1999. "Killing, letting die and preventing people from being saved" *Utilitas* 11: 277–295.

Hanser, M. 2019. "Understanding harm and its moral significance" *Ethical Theory and Moral Practice* 22: 853–870.

Hansson, S. O. 2012. "A Panorama of the philosophy of risk" In S. Roeser, R. Hillebrand, & M. Peterson (Eds.), *Handbook of Risk Theory*. 27–54. Dordrecht: Springer.

Hansson, S. O. 2013. *The Ethics of Risk: Ethical Analysis in an Uncertain World*. New York: Palgrave Macmillan.

Harris, J. 2020. "The immoral machine" *Cambridge Quarterly of Healthcare Ethics* 29: 71–79.

Harsanyi, J. C. 1955. "Cardinal welfare, individualistic ethics, and interpersonal comparisons of utility" *Journal of Political Economy* 63: 309–321.

Harsanyi, J. C. 1975. "Can the maximin principle serve as a basis for morality? A critique of John Rawls's theory" *American Political Science Review* 69: 594–606.

Hauser, M. 2006. *Moral Minds*. New York: HarperCollins.

Hauser, M., Cushman, F., Young, L., Kang-Xing Jin, R., & Mikhail, J. 2007. "A dissociation between moral judgments and justifications" *Mind & Language* 22: 1–21.

Hayakawa, S., Tannenbaum, D., Costa, A., Corey, J. D., & Keysar, B. 2017. "Thinking more or feeling less? Explaining the foreign-language effect on moral judgment" *Psychological Science* 28: 1387–1397.

Henrich, J., Boyd, R., Bowles, S., Camerer, C., Fehr, E., Gintis, H., … & Tracer, D. 2005. "'Economic man' in cross-cultural perspective: Behavioral experiments in 15 small-scale societies" *Behavioral and Brain Sciences* 28: 795–855.

Henrich, J., Heine, S. J., & Norenzayan, A. 2010. "The weirdest people in the world?" *Behavioral and Brain Sciences* 33: 61–83.

Himmelreich, J. 2018. "Never mind the trolley: The ethics of autonomous vehicles in mundane situations" *Science and Engineering Ethics* 21: 669–684.

Hofstede, G. H. 1984. *Culture's Consequences: International Differences in Work-related Values.* Vol. 5. London: Sage.

Hooker, B. 2002. *Ideal Code, Real World: A Rule-Consequentialist Theory of Morality.* Oxford: Oxford University Press.

Huang, K., Greene, J. D., & Bazerman, M. 2019. "Veil-of-ignorance reasoning favors the greater good" *Proceedings of the National Academy of Sciences* 116: 23989–23995.

Huang, K., Bernhard, R. M., Barak-Corren, N., Bazerman, M. H., & Greene, J. D. 2021. "Veil-of-ignorance reasoning mitigates self-serving bias in resource allocation during the COVID-19 crisis" *Judgment & Decision Making* 16: 1–19.

Hübner, D. & White, L. 2018. "Crash algorithms for autonomous cars: How the trolley problem can move us beyond harm minimization" *Ethical Theory and Moral Practice* 21: 685–698.

Hume, D., Selby-Bigge, L. A., & Nidditch, P. H. 1751/1975. *Enquiries Concerning Human Understanding and Concerning the Principles of Morals* 3rd Edition. Oxford: Clarendon Press.

Hurd, H. 1996. "The deontology of negligence," *Boston University Law Review* 76: 249–271.

Hurka, T. 2016. "Trolleys and permissible harm" In F. M. Kamm (Ed.), *The Trolley Problem Mysteries.* 135–150. Oxford: Oxford University Press.

Hursthouse, R. 1999. *On Virtue Ethics.* Oxford: Oxford University Press.

Hutcherson, C. A., Montaser-Kouhsari, L., Woodward, J., & Rangel, A. 2015. "Emotional and utilitarian appraisals of moral dilemmas are encoded in separate areas and integrated in ventromedial prefrontal cortex" *Journal of Neuroscience* 35: 12593–12605.

Jackson, F. 1991. "Decision-theoretic consequentialism and the nearest and dearest objection" *Ethics* 101: 461–482.

Jaeger, B., & van Vugt, M. 2021. "Psychological barriers to effective altruism: An evolutionary perspective" *Current Opinion in Psychology* 44: 130–134.

JafariNaimi, N. 2017. "Our bodies in the trolley's path, or why self-driving cars must *Not* be programmed to kill" *Science, Technology, & Human Values* 43: 302–323.

Kagan, S. 1989. *The Limits of Morality*. Oxford: Oxford University Press.

Kagan, S. 2016. "Solving the trolley problem" In F. M. Kamm (Ed.), *The Trolley Problem Mysteries*. 152–165. Oxford: Oxford University Press.

Kahane, G. 2012. "On the wrong track: Process and content in moral psychology" *Mind and Language* 25: 519–545.

Kahane, G. 2013. "The armchair and the trolley: An argument for experimental ethics" *Philosophical Studies* 162: 421–445. https://doi.org/10.1007/s110980119775-5

Kahane, G. 2014. "Intuitive and counterintuitive morality" In J. D'Arms and D. Jacobson (Eds.), *Moral Psychology and Human Agency: Philosophical Essays on the Science of Ethics*. 9–39. Oxford: Oxford University Press.

Kahane, G. 2015. "Sidetracked by trolleys: Why sacrificial moral dilemmas tell us little (or nothing) about utilitarian judgment" *Social Neuroscience* 10: 551–560.

Kahane, G., Everett, J. A. C., Earp, B. D., Farias, M., & Savulescu, J. 2015. "'Utilitarian' judgments in sacrificial moral dilemmas do not reflect impartial concern for the greater good" *Cognition* 134: 193–209. https://doi.org/10.1016/j.cognition.2014.10.005

Kahane, G., Everett, J. A. C., Earp, B. D., Caviola, L., Faber, N. S., Crockett, M. J., & Savulescu, J. 2018. "Beyond sacrificial harm: A two-dimensional model of utilitarian psychology" *Psychological Review* 125:131-164. https://doi.org/10.1037/rev0000093

Kahane, G., & Shackel, N. 2010. "Methodological issues in the neuroscience of moral judgement" *Mind & Language* 25: 561–582. https://doi.org/10.1111/j.14680017.2010.01401.x

Kahane, G., Wiech, K., Shackel, N., Farias, M., Savulescu, J., & Tracey, I. 2012. "The neural basis of intuitive and counterintuitive moral judgment" *Social Cognitive and Affective Neuroscience* 7: 393–402. https://doi.org/10.1093/scan/nsr005

Kahneman, D. 2003. "A perspective on judgment and choice: Mapping bounded rationality" *American Psychologist* 58: 697–720.

Kahneman, D. 2011. *Thinking, Fast and Slow*. New York, NY: Macmillan.

Kamm, F. M. 1985. "Supererogation and obligation" *The Journal of Philosophy* 82: 118–138.

Kamm, F. M. 1987. "The insanity defense, innocent threats, and limited alternatives" *Criminal Justice* 6: 61–76.

Kamm, F. M. 1989. "Harming some to save others" *Philosophical Studies* 57: 227–60.

Kamm, F. M. 1993. *Morality, Mortality, Vol. 1: Death and Whom to Save from It*. New York: Oxford University Press.

Kamm, F. 1996. *Morality, Mortality. Vol. 2: Rights, Duties and Status*. New York: New York University Press.

Kamm, F. M. 2000. "The doctrine of triple effect and why a rational agent need not intend the means to his end" *Proceedings of the Aristotelian Society, Supplementary Volume* 74: 21–39.

Kamm, F. M. 2007. *Intricate Ethics: Rights, Responsibilities, and Permissible Harm*. New York: Oxford University Press.

Kamm, F. M. 2009. "Neuroscience and moral reasoning: A note on recent research" *Philosophy & Public Affairs* 37: 330–345.

Kamm, F. M. 2012. *The Moral Target: Aiming at Right Conduct in War and Other Conflicts*. New York: Oxford University Press.

Kamm, F. M. 2013. *Bioethical Prescriptions: To Create, End, Choose and Improve Lives*. New York: Oxford University Press.

Kamm, F. M. 2013b. "The trolley problem" *International Encyclopedia of Ethics*. https://doi-org.ezproxy.lib.bbk.ac.uk/10.1002/9781444367072.wbiee252.pub2

Kamm, F. 2016. *The Trolley Problem Mysteries*. E. Rakowski (Ed.) Oxford: Oxford University Press.

Kamm, F. 2020a. "Use and abuse of the trolley problem: Self-driving cars, medical treatments, and the distribution of harm" In S. M. Liao (Ed.), *Ethics of Artificial Intelligence*. 79–108. New York: Oxford University Press.

Kamm, F.M. 2020b. "Parfit on the irrelevance of deontological distinctions" In M. Timmons (Ed.), *Oxford Studies in Normative Ethics*. 9–30. Oxford: Oxford University Press.

Kamm, F. M. 2021. "Duties that become supererogatory or forbidden?" In J. McMahan et al. (Eds.), *Principles and Persons: The Legacy of Derek Parfit*. 441–462. Oxford: Oxford University Press.

Kant, I. 1785/1994. *Groundwork of the Metaphysics of Morals*. Cambridge: Cambridge University Press.

Kant, I. 1785/1959. *Foundation of the Metaphysics of Morals*. Indianapolis: Bobbs-Merrill.

Kant, I. 2005. *The moral law: Groundwork of the metaphysic of morals* (2nd ed.). London, UK: Routledge.

Kauppinen, A. 2020. "Who should bear the risk when self-driving vehicles crash?" *Journal of Applied Philosophy* 38: 640–645. https://doi.org/10.1111/japp.12490

Keeling, G. 2019. "Why trolley problems matter for the ethics of automated vehicles" *Science and Engineering Ethics* 26: 293–307.

Keeling, G., Evans, K., Thornton, S., Mecacci, G., & Santoni de Sio, F. 2019. "Four perspectives on what matters for the ethics of automated vehicles" In G. Meyer & S. Beiker (Eds.), *Road Vehicle Automation*. 49–60. Berlin: Springer.

Kirkland, R. 2004. *Taoism: The Enduring Tradition*. London: Routledge.

Kitcher, P. 2011. *The Ethical Project*. Cambridge MA: Harvard University Press.

Kleingeld, P. 2020. "A Kantian solution to the trolley problem" *Oxford Studies in Normative Ethics* 10: 204–228.

Koenigs, M., Kruepke, M., Zeier, J., & Newman, J. P. 2012. "Utilitarian moral judgment in psychopathy" *Social Cognitive and Affective Neuroscience* 7: 708–714.

Koenigs, M., Young, L., Adolphs, R., Tranel, D., Cushman, F., Hauser, M., & Damasio, A. 2007. "Damage to the prefrontal cortex increases utilitarian moral judgments" *Nature* 446: 908–911. https://doi.org/10.1038/nature05631

Kohlberg, L. 1969. "Stage and sequence: The cognitive-developmental approach to socialization" In D.A. Goslin (Ed.), *Handbook of Socialization Theory and Research*. 347–480. Chicago: Rand McNally.

Kolber, A. 2009. "The organ conscription trolley problem" *The American Journal of Bioethics* 9: 13–14.

Korsgaard, C. M. 1996. *The Sources of Normativity*. Cambridge: Cambridge University Press.

Koven, N. S. 2011. "Specificity of meta-emotion effects on moral decision-making" *Emotion* 11: 1255–1261.

Kumar, R. 2015. "Risking and wronging" *Philosophy & Public Affairs* 43: 27–51.

Lafer-Sousa, R., & Conway, B. R. 2017. "#TheDress: Categorical perception of an ambiguous color image" *Journal of Vision* 17: 25–25.

LeBeau, P. 2016. "Google's self-driving car caused an accident, so what now?," *CNBC*, www.cnbc.com/2016/02/29/googles-self-driving- car-caused-an-accident-so-what-now.html

Lenman, J., & Shemmer, Y. 2012. "Introduction" In Lenman, J., & Shemmer, Y. (Eds.). *Constructivism in Practical Philosophy*. 1–17. Oxford: Oxford University Press.

Levin, S., & Wong, J. C. 2018. "Self-Driving Uber kills Arizona woman in first fatal crash involving pedestrian," *The Guardian*, www.theguardian.com/technology/2018/mar/19/uber-self-driving-car-kills-woman-arizona-tempe

Levine, E. E., Barasch, A., Rand, D., Berman, J. Z., & Small, D. A. 2018. "Signaling emotion and reason in cooperation" *Journal of Experimental Psychology: General* 147: 702–719. https://doi.org/10.1037/xge0000399

Li, Z., Xia, S., Wu, X., & Chen, Z. 2018. "Analytical thinking style leads to more utilitarian moral judgments: An exploration with a process-dissociation approach" *Personality and Individual Differences* 131: 180–184.

Liao, S. M. 2016. "The closeness problem and the doctrine of double effect: A way forward" *Criminal Law and Philosophy* 10: 849–863.

Lillehammer, H. 2004. "Moral error theory" *Proceedings of the Aristotelian Society* 104: 95–111.

Lin, P. 2015. "Why ethics matters for autonomous cars" In M. Maurer, J. Gerdes, B. Lenz, & H. Winner (Eds.), *Autonomous Driving: Technical, Legal and Social Aspects*. 69–85. Berlin: Springer.

Loh, E. 2018. "Medicine and the rise of the robots: A qualitative review of recent advances of artificial intelligence in health" *BMJ Leader* 2. https://bmjleader .bmj.com/content/2/2/59

Luetge, C. 2017. "The German ethics code for automated and connected driving" *Philosophy & Technology* 30: 547–558.

Lykkeskov, A., & Di Nucci, E. 2022. "COVID-19 and intergenerational justice: The case of Denmark" In G. Schweiger (Ed.), *Philosophical Perspectives on the Social Consequences of the COVID-19 Pandemic*. 51–63. Dordrecht: Springer.

MacAskill, W. 2015. *Doing Good Better: Effective Altruism and a Radical New Way to Make a Difference*. London: Guardian Faber Publishing.

Machery, E. 2009. *Doing without Concepts*. Oxford: Oxford University Press.

Machery, E. 2010. "Explaining why experimental behavior varies across cultures: A missing step in 'The weirdest people in the world?'" *Behavioral and Brain Sciences*, 33: 101.

MacIntyre, A. 1985. *After Virtue*, 2nd Edition. London: Duckworth.

Mackie, J. L. 1977. *Ethics: Inventing Right and Wrong*. Harmondsworth: Penguin Books.

Martins, A., Faisca, L., Esteves, F., Muresan, A., & Reis, A. 2012. "A typical moral judgements following traumatic brain injury" *Judgment and Decision Making* 7: 478–487.

McCann, H. 2010. "Di Nucci on the simple view" *Analysis* 70: 53–59.

McCarthy, D. 1997. "Rights, explanation, and risks" *Ethics* 107: 205–225.

McCormick, C., Rosenthal, C. R., Miller, T. D., & Maguire, E. A. 2016. "Hippocampal damage increases deontological responses during moral decision making" *Journal of Neuroscience* 36: 12157–12167.

McDowell, J. 1979, "Virtue and reason" *The Monist* 62: 331–350.

McKerlie, D. 1986. "Rights and risk" *Canadian Journal of Philosophy* 16: 239–251.

McMahan, J. 2005. "The basis of moral liability for defensive killing" *Philosophical Issues* 15: 386–405.

McMahan, J. 2009. *Killing in War*. Oxford: Oxford University Press.

McMahan, J. 2014. "Self-defense against justified threateners" In H. Frowe & G. Lang (Eds.), *How We Fight: Ethics in War*. 104–137. Oxford: Oxford University Press.

Mendez, M. F., Anderson, E., & Shapira, J. S. 2005. "An investigation of moral judgement in frontotemporal dementia" *Cognitive and Behavioral Neurology* 18: 193–197.

Michelin, C., Tallandini, M., Pellizzoni, S., & Siegal, M. 2010. "Should more be saved? Diversity in utilitarian moral judgment" *Journal of Cognition and Culture* 10: 153–169.

Mikhail, J. 2007. "Universal moral grammar: Theory, evidence and the future" *Trends in Cognitive Sciences* 11: 143–152.

Milgram, S. 1974. *Obedience to Authority: An Experimental View*. London: Tavistock Publications.

Mill, J. S., & Crisp, R. (Eds.) (1998). *Utilitarianism*. New York, NY: Oxford University Press.

Moore, A. B., Lee, N. L., Clark, B. A., & Conway, A. R. 2011. "In defense of the personal/impersonal distinction in moral psychology research: Cross-cultural validation of the dual process model of moral judgment" *Judgment and Decision Making* 6: 186–195.

Moretto, G., Làdavas, E., Mattioli, F., & Di Pellegrino, G. 2010. "A psychophysiological investigation of moral judgment after ventromedial prefrontal damage" *Journal of Cognitive Neuroscience* 22: 1888–1899.

Moser, E. I., Kropff, E., & Moser, M. B. 2008. "Place cells, grid cells, and the brain's spatial representation system" *Annual Review of Neuroscience* 31: 69–89.

Mounk, Y. 2020. "The extraordinary decisions facing Italian doctors" *The Atlantic*. March 11. www.theatlantic.com/ideas/archive/2020/03/who-gets-hospital-bed/607807/

Muda, R., Niszczota, P., Białek, M., & Conway, P. 2018. "Reading dilemmas in a foreign language reduces both deontological and utilitarian response tendencies" *Journal of Experimental Psychology: Learning, Memory, and Cognition* 44: 321–326.

Nadelhoffer, T., & Feltz, A. 2008. "The actor–observer bias and moral intuitions: Adding fuel to Sinnott-Armstrong's fire" *Neuroethics* 1: 133–144.

Nelkin, D. K., & Rickless, S. C. 2014. "Three cheers for double effect" *Philosophy and Phenomenological Research* 89: 125–158.

Nelkin, D. K., & Rickless, S. C. 2015. "So close, yet so far: Why solutions to the closeness problem for the doctrine of double effect fall short" *Noûs* 49: 376–409.

Nyholm, S., & Smids, J. 2016. "The ethics of accident-algorithms for self-driving cars: An applied trolley problem?" *Ethical Theory and Moral Practice* 19: 1275–1289.

Nyholm, S. 2018a. "The ethics of crashes with self-driving cars: A roadmap, I" *Philosophy Compass* 13: e12507.

Nyholm. S. 2018b. "The ethics of crashes with self-driving cars, A Roadmap, II" *Philosophy Compass* 13: e12506.

Nyholm, S. 2020. *Humans and Robots: Ethics, Agency, and Anthropomorphism.* London: Rowman & Littlefield International.

Oberdiek, J. 2017. *Imposing Risk: A Normative Framework.* Oxford: Oxford University Press.

Oftedal, G., Ravn, I. H., and Dahl, F. A. 2020. "Do we need empirical research on the use of trolley dilemmas in applied ethics? Reply to commentary by Heidi Matisonn" *Journal of Empirical Research on Human Research Ethics* 15: 300–301.

O'Neill, P., & Petrinovich, L. 1998. "A preliminary cross-cultural study of moral intuitions" *Evolution and Human Behavior* 19: 349–367.

Ord, T. 2020. *The Precipice: Existential Risk and the Future of Humanity.* New York: Hachette Books.

Orlove, R. 2016. "Now Mercedes says its driverless cars won't run over Pedestrians, That Would be Illegal" *Jalopnik.* https://jalopnik.com/now-mercedes-says-its-driverless-cars-wont-run-over-ped-1787890432

Parfit, D. 2011. *On What Matters.* Vol. 1 & 2. Oxford: Oxford University Press.

Parfit, D. 2017. *On What Matters.* Vol. 3. Oxford: Oxford University Press.

Patil, I., & Silani, G. 2014. "Reduced empathic concern leads to utilitarian moral judgments in trait alexithymia" *Frontiers in Psychology* 5: 501.

Patil, I., Zucchelli, M. M., Kool, W., Campbell, S., Fornasier, F., Calò, M., . . . Cushman, F. 2021. "Reasoning supports utilitarian resolutions to moral dilemmas across diverse measures" *Journal of Personality and Social Psychology* 120: 443–460. https://doi.org/10.1037/pspp0000281

Paxton, J. M., Ungar, L., & Greene, J. D. 2012. "Reflection and reasoning in moral judgment" *Cognitive Science* 36: 163–177.

Perkins, A. M., Leonard, A. M., Weaver, K., Dalton, J. A., Mehta, M. A., Kumari, V., . . . & Ettinger, U. 2013. "A dose of ruthlessness: Interpersonal moral judgment is hardened by the anti-anxiety drug lorazepam" *Journal of Experimental Psychology: General* 142: 612–620.

Perry, M. 2007. "Risk, harm, interests, and rights" In T. Lewens (Ed.), *Risk: Philosophical Perspectives.* 190–209. London: Routledge.

Petrinovich, L., & O'Neill, P. 1996. "Influence of wording and framing effects on moral intuitions" *Ethology and Sociobiology* 17: 145–171. https://doi.org/10.1016/0162-3095(96)00041-6

Petrinovich, L., O'Neill, P., & Jorgensen, M. 1993. "An empirical study of moral intuitions: Toward an evolutionary ethics" *Journal of Personality and Social Psychology* 64: 467–478. https://doi.org/10.1037/0022-3514.64.3.467

Phelps, E. A. 2006. "Emotion and cognition: Insights from studies of the human amygdala" *Annual Review of Psychology* 57: 27–53.

Plunkett, D., & Greene, J. D. 2019. "Overlooked evidence and a misunderstanding of what trolley dilemmas do best: Commentary on Bostyn, Sevenhant, and Roets (2018)" *Psychological Science* 30: 1389–1391.

Prinz, J. 2007. *The Emotional Construction of Morals.* Oxford: Oxford University Press.

Purves, D., Jenkins R., & Strawser B. J. 2015 "Autonomous machines, moral judgment, and acting for the right reasons" *Ethical Theory and Moral Practice* 18: 851–872.

Quinn, W. S. 1989a. "Actions, intentions, and consequences: The doctrine of doing and allowing" *Philosophical Review* 98: 287–312.

Quinn, W. 1989b. "Actions, intentions, and consequences: The doctrine of double effect" *Philosophy and Public Affairs* 18: 334–351.

Quinn, W. (1989a). "Actions, intentions, and consequences: The doctrine of doing and allowing" In Foot, P. (Ed.), *Morality and Action.* 149–174. Cambridge: Cambridge University Press.

Railton, P. 1985. "Locke, stock, and peril: Natural property rights, pollution, and risk" In M. Gibson (Ed.), *To Breathe Freely.* 89–123. Totowa, NJ: Rowman and Littlefield. Reprinted in Peter Railton. 2003. *Facts, Values, and Norms: Essays toward a Morality of Consequence.* 187–225. Cambridge University Press.

Rakowski, E. 1993. "Taking and saving lives" *Columbia Law Review* 93: 1063–1156. Reprinted in J. Harris (Ed.) 2001. *Bioethics.* 205–299. Oxford: Oxford University Press.

Rawls, J. 1971. *A Theory of Justice.* Cambridge, MA: Harvard University Press.

Rawls, J. 1993. *Political Liberalism.* New York: Columbia University Press.

Raz, J. 1986. *The Morality of Freedom.* Oxford: Oxford University Press.

Rehman, S., & Dzionek-Kozłowska, J. 2020. "The Chinese and American students and the trolley problem: A cross-cultural study" *Journal of Intercultural Communication* 20: 31–41.

Rehren, P., & Zisman, V. 2022. "Testing the intuitive retributivism dual process model" *Zeitschrift Für Psychologie* 230:152–163.

Reynolds, C. J., & Conway, P. 2018. "Not just bad actions: Affective concern for bad outcomes contributes to moral condemnation of harm in moral dilemmas" *Emotion* 18: 1009–1023. https://doi.org/10.1037/emo0000413

Rhim, J., Lee, G. B., & Lee, J. H. 2020. "Human moral reasoning types in autonomous vehicle moral dilemma: A cross-cultural comparison of Korea and Canada" *Computers in Human Behavior* 102: 39–56.

Rickless, S. C. 1997. "The doctrine of doing and allowing" *Philosophical Review* 106: 555–575.

Rickless, S. C. 2011. "The moral status of enabling harm" *Pacific Philosophical Quarterly* 92: 66–86.

Robotics Business Review. 2019. "Trolley dilemmas shouldn't influence self-driving policies, experts argue" www.roboticsbusinessreview.com/unmanned/trolley-dilemmas-should-not-formulate-self-driving-policies/

Rodríguez-Alcázar, J., Bermejo-Luque L., & Molina-Pérez, A. 2020. "Do automated vehicles face moral dilemmas? A plea for a political approach" *Philosophy & Technology*. doi: 10.1007/s13347-020-00432-5.

Rom, S. C., Weiss, A., & Conway, P. 2017. "Judging those who judge: Perceivers infer the roles of affect and cognition underpinning others' moral dilemma responses" *Journal of Experimental Social Psychology* 69: 44–58. https://doi.org/10.1016/j.jesp.2016.09.007

Ross, W. D. 1930. *The Right and the Good*. Oxford: Oxford University Press.

Royzman, E. B., & Baron, J. 2002. "The preference for indirect harm" *Social Justice Research* 15: 165–184.

Ryazanov, A. A., Knutzen, J., Rickless, S. C., Christenfeld, N. J.S., & Nelkin, D. K. 2018. "Intuitive probabilities and the limitation of moral imagination" *Cognitive Science* 42: 38–68.

Ryazanov, A. A., Wang, S. T., Rickless, S. C., McKenzie, C. R.M., & Nelkin, D. K. 2021. "Sensitivity to shifts in probability of harm and benefit in moral dilemmas" *Cognition* 209: 104548.

Sacco, D. F., Brown, M., Lustgraaf, C. J. N., & Hugenberg, K. 2017. "The adaptive utility of deontology: Deontological moral decision-making fosters perceptions of trust and likeability" *Evolutionary Psychological Science* 3: 125–132. https://doi.org/10.1007/s40806-016-0080-6

Santoni de Sio, F. 2017. "Killing by autonomous vehicles and the legal doctrine of necessity" *Ethical Theory and Moral Practice* 20: 411–429.

Scanlon, T. M. 1998. *What We Owe to Each Other*. Cambridge, MA: Harvard University Press.

Scanlon, T. M. 2008. *Moral Dimensions*. Cambridge MA: Harvard University Press.

Shenhav, A., & Greene, J. D. 2010. "Moral judgments recruit domain-general valuation mechanisms to integrate representations of probability and magnitude" *Neuron* 67: 667–677.

Shenhav, A., & Greene, J. D. 2014. "Integrative moral judgment: Dissociating the roles of the amygdala and ventromedial prefrontal cortex" *Journal of Neuroscience* 34: 4741–4749.

Shenhav, A., Rand, D. G., & Greene, J. D. 2012. "Divine intuition: Cognitive style influences belief in God" *Journal of Experimental Psychology: General* 141: 423.

Schoettle, B., & Sivak, M. 2015. *A Preliminary Analysis of Real-world Crashes Involving Self-driving Vehicles*. Ann Arbor: The University of Michigan Transportation Research Institute.

Sheskin, M., Chevallier, C., Adachi, K., Berniūnas, R., Castelain, T., Hulín, M., … & Baumard, N. 2018. "The needs of the many do not outweigh the needs of the few: The limits of individual sacrifice across diverse cultures" *Journal of Cognition and Culture* 18: 205–223.

Shweder, R. A., Much, N. C., Mahapatra, M., & Park, L. 1997. "The 'big three' of morality (autonomy, community, divinity) and the 'big three' explanations of suffering" in Brandt, A. M., & Rozin, P. (Eds.), *Morality and Health*. 119–169. New York: Routledge.

Singer, P. 1972. "Famine, affluence, and morality" *Philosophy & Public Affairs* 1: 229–243.

Singer, P. 1975. *Animal Liberation: A New Ethics for Our Treatment of Animals*. New York: HarperCollins.

Singer, P. 1981. *The Expanding Circle: Ethics and Sociobiology*. Oxford: Oxford University Press.

Singer, P. 2005. "Ethics and intuitions" *The Journal of Ethics* 9: 331–352. https://doi .org/10.1007/s10892–005-3508-y

Singer, P. 2010. *The Life You Can Save: How to Do Your Part to End World Poverty*. New York: Random House.

Singer, P. 2015. *The Most Good You Can Do: How Effective Altruism is Changing Ideas about Living Ethically*. Melbourne: Text Publishing.

Smart, J. J. C., & Williams, B. 1973. *Utilitarianism: For and Against*. Cambridge: Cambridge University Press.

Smith, K., & Hatemi, P. K. 2020. "Are moral intuitions heritable?" *Human Nature* 31: 406–420.

Sorokowski, P., Marczak, M., Misiak, M., & Białek, M. 2020. "Trolley dilemma in Papua. Yali horticulturalists refuse to pull the lever" *Psychonomic Bulletin & Review* 27: 398–403.

Spranca, M., Minsk, E., & Baron, J. 1991. "Omission and commission in judgment and choice" *Journal of Experimental Social Psychology* 27: 76–105.

Stevens, M. 2017. "The greater good" *Mind Field*. Season 2. Episode 1 (December 6, 2017). Retrieved May 20, 2021.

Street, S. 2012. "Coming to terms with contingency: Humean constructivism about practical reason" In J. Lenman & Y. Shemmer (Eds.), *Constructivism in Practical Philosophy*. 40–59. Oxford: Oxford University Press.

Street, S. 2010. "What is constructivism in ethics and metaethics?" *Philosophy Compass* 5: 363–384.

Street, S. 2008. "Constructivism about reasons." *Oxford Studies in Metaethics*, 3: 207–245.

Sugden, R. 2004. *The Economics of Rights, Co-operation and Welfare*. Basingstoke: Palgrave Macmillan.

Suter, R. S., & Hertwig, R. 2011. "Time and moral judgment" *Cognition* 119: 454–458.

Sutton, R. S., & Barto, A. G. 2018. *Reinforcement learning: An introduction*. Cambridge, MA: MIT Press.

Sütfeld, L.R. et al. 2017. "Using virtual reality to assess ethical decisions in road traffic scenarios: Applicability of value-of-life-based models and influences of time pressure" *Frontiers in Behavioral Neuroscience* 11: 122.

Swann Jr, W. B., Gómez, Á., Dovidio, J. F., Hart, S., & Jetten, J. 2010. "Dying and killing for one's group: Identity fusion moderates responses to intergroup versions of the trolley problem" *Psychological Science* 21: 1176–1183.

Swanton, C. 2003. *Virtue Ethics: A Pluralistic View*. Oxford: Oxford University Press.

Tadros, V. 2015. "Wrongful intentions without closeness" *Philosophy & Public Affairs* 43: 52–74.

Tassy, S., Oullier, O., Mancini, J., & Wicker, B. 2013. "Discrepancies between judgment and choice of action in moral dilemmas" *Frontiers in Psychology* 4: 250.

Taurek, J. 1977. "Should the numbers count?" *Philosophy & Public Affairs* 6: 293–316.

Taylor, M. 2016. "Self-driving Mercedes-Benzes will prioritize occupant safety over pedestrians", *Car and Driver*. www.caranddriver.com/news/a15344706/self-driving-mercedes-will-prioritize-occupant-safety-over-pedestrians/

Technology Review. 2018. "Should a self-driving car kill the baby or the grandma? Depends on where you're from" www.technologyreview.com/2018/10/24/139313/a-global-ethics-study-aims-to-help-ai-solve-the-self-driving-trolley-problem/

The Tesla Team. 2016. "A tragic loss" Tesla Blog, www.tesla.com/ blog/tragic-loss

Terbeck, S., Kahane, G., McTavish, S., Savulescu, J., Levy, N., Hewstone, M., & Cowen, P. J. 2013. "beta Adrenergic blockade reduces utilitarian judgement" *Biological Psychology* 92: 323–328.

Thomas, B. C., Croft, K. E., & Tranel, D. 2011. "Harming kin to save strangers: Further evidence for abnormally utilitarian moral judgments after ventromedial prefrontal damage" *Journal of Cognitive Neuroscience* 23: 2186–2196.

Thomson, J. J. 1971. "A defense of abortion" *Philosophy and Public Affairs* 1: 47–66.

Thomson, J. J. 1976. "Killing, letting die, and the trolley problem" *The Monist* 59: 204–217.

Thomson, J. J. 1977. *Acts and Other Events*. New York: Cornell University Press.

Thomson, J. J. 1985. "The trolley problem" *Yale Law Journal* 94: 1395–1415. Reprinted in J. J. Thomson. *Rights, Restitution and Risk*. W. Parent (Ed.) 94–116. Cambridge MA: Harvard University Press.

Thomson, J. J. 1986a. "Self-defense and rights," in Thomson 1986f, 33–48.

Thomson, J. J. 1986b. "Some ruminations on rights," in Thomson 1986f, 49–65.

Thomson, J. J. 1986c. "Rights and compensation," in Thomson 1986f, 66–77.

Thomson, J. J. 1986d. "Some questions about government regulation of behavior," in Thomson 1986f, 154–172.

Thomson, J. J. 1986e. "The trolley problem," in Thomson 1986f, 94–116.

Thomson, J. J. 1986f. *Rights, Restitution and Risk*. W. Parent (Ed.) Cambridge MA: Harvard University Press.

Thomson, J. J. 1990. *The Realm of Rights*. Cambridge MA: Harvard University Press.

Thomson, J. J. 1991. "Self defense" *Philosophy & Public Affairs* 20: 283–310.

Thomson, J. J. 2008. "Turning the trolley" *Philosophy & Public Affairs* 36: 359–374.

Thomson, J. J. 2016. "Kamm on the trolley problems" In F. M. Kamm (Ed.), *The Trolley Problem Mysteries*. 113–134. Oxford: Oxford University Press.

Tinghög, G., Andersson, D., Bonn, C., Johannesson, M., Kirchler, M., Koppel, L., & Västfjäll, D. 2016. "Intuition and moral decision-making – the effect of time pressure and cognitive load on moral judgment and altruistic behavior" *PloS ONE* 11: e0164012.

Tolman, E. C. 1948. "Cognitive maps in rats and men" *Psychological Review* 55: 189–208.

Trémolière, B., De Neys, W., & Bonnefon, J. F. 2012. "Mortality salience and morality: Thinking about death makes people less utilitarian" *Cognition* 124: 379–384.

Trémolière, B., & Bonnefon, J.-F. 2014. "Efficient kill–save ratios ease up the cognitive demands on counterintuitive moral utilitarianism" *Personality and Social Psychology Bulletin* 40: 923–930. https://doi.org/10.1177/0146167214530436

Uhlmann, E. L., Zhu, L. (Lei), & Tannenbaum, D. 2013. "When it takes a bad person to do the right thing" *Cognition* 126: 326–334. https://doi.org/10.1016/j .cognition.2012.10.005

Uman, L. S. 2011. "Systematic reviews and meta-analyses" *Journal of the Canadian Academy of Child and Adolescent Psychiatry* 20: 57.

Unger, P. 1995. *Living High and Letting Die: Our Illusion of Innocence.* Oxford: Oxford University Press.

Van Zyl, L. 2018. *Virtue Ethics: A Contemporary Introduction.* New York: Routledge.

Van Zyl, L. 2020. "Virtuous and right action: A relaxed view" In C. Halbig, & F. U. Timmermann (Eds.), *Handbuch Tugend und Tugendethik.* 49–63. Wiesbaden: Springer.

Venture Beat. 2018. "MIT study explores the 'Trolley Problem' and self-driving cars" https://venturebeat.com/2018/10/24/mit-study-explores-the-trolley-problem-and-self-driving-cars/

Verfaellie, M., Hunsberger, R., & Keane, M. M. 2021. "Episodic processes in moral decisions: Evidence from medial temporal lobe amnesia" *Hippocampus* 31: 569–579.

Voorhoeve, A. 2009. *Conversations on Ethics.* Oxford: Oxford University Press.

Wakabayashi, D., & Conger, K. 2018. "Uber's self-driving cars are set to return in a downsized test" *New York Times,* www.nytimes.com/2018/12/05/technology/ uber-self-driving-cars.html

Wallach, W., & Allen, C. 2009. *Moral Machines: Teaching Robots Right from Wrong.* Oxford: Oxford University Press.

Wallisch, P. 2017. "Illumination assumptions account for individual differences in the perceptual interpretation of a profoundly ambiguous stimulus in the color domain: 'he dress'" *Journal of Vision* 17: 5.

Washington Post. 2015. "Driverless cars are colliding with the creepy trolley problem" www.washingtonpost.com/news/innovations/wp/2015/12/29/will-self-driving-cars-ever-solve-the-famous-and-creepy-trolley-problem/

Washington Post. 2016. "Google's chief of self-driving cars downplays 'The Trolley Problem'" www.washingtonpost.com/news/innovations/wp/2015/12/01/googles-leader-on-self-driving-cars-downplays-the-trolley-problem/

Wiech, K., Kahane, G., Shackel, N., Farias, M., Savulescu, J., & Tracey, I. 2013. "Cold or calculating? Reduced activity in the subgenual cingulate cortex reflects decreased emotional aversion to harming in counterintuitive utilitarian judgment" *Cognition* 126: 364–372.

Williams, B. 1993. "Moral incapacity" *Proceedings of the Aristotelian Society* 93: 59–70.

Winking, J., & Koster, J. 2021. "Small-scale utilitarianism: High acceptance of utilitarian solutions to trolley problems among a horticultural population in Nicaragua" *PLos ONE*, 16: e0249345.

Winskel, H., & Bhatt, D. 2020". The role of culture and language in moral decision-making" *Culture and Brain* 8: 207–225.

Wolkenstein, A. 2018. "What has the trolley dilemma ever done for us (and what will it do in the future)? On some recent debates about the ethics of self-driving cars" *Ethics and Information Technology* 20: 163-173.

Wood, A. 2011. "Treating humanity as an end in itself" In D. Parfit (Ed.), *On What Matters*, Vol. 2. 58–82. Oxford: Oxford University Press. https://doi.org/10.1093/acprof:osobl/9780199572816.003.0003

Woodcock, S. 2017. "When will a consequentialist push you in front of a trolley?" *Australasian Journal of Philosophy* 95: 299–316. https://doi.org/10.1080/00048402.2016.1212909

Woollard, F. 2015. *Doing and Allowing Harm*. Oxford: Oxford University Press.

Woollard, F. 2017. "Double effect, doing and allowing, and the relaxed nonconsequentialist" *Philosophical Explorations* 20: 142–158.

Wong, D. B. 2009. *Natural Moralities: A Defense of Pluralistic Relativism*. Oxford: Oxford University Press.

Xiang, X. 2014. *Would the Buddha Push the Man Off the Footbridge? Systematic Variations in the Moral Judgment and Punishment Tendencies of Han Chinese, Tibetans and Americans* (Doctoral dissertation, Harvard University).

Yamamoto, S. & Yuki, M. 2019. "What causes cross-cultural difference in reactions to the trolley problem? A cross-cultural study on the roles of relational mobility and reputation expectation" *Research in Social Psychology* 35: 61–71.

Index

For EU product safety concerns, contact us at Calle de José Abascal, 56–1°,
28003 Madrid, Spain or eugpsr@cambridge.org.

www.ingramcontent.com/pod-product-compliance
Ingram Content Group UK Ltd.
Pitfield, Milton Keynes, MK11 3LW, UK
UKHW030900150625
459647UK00021B/2713